Geo-economic Perspectives in the Global Environment

The Covid-19 pandemic brought about significant changes in the world order. It not only reshaped the global geopolitical architecture but also created newer challenges and opportunities for international trade and businesses. This book deliberates on these new global realities through a multidisciplinary perspective. It delves into various key issues pertaining to finance, infrastructure, policy, geostrategy, and entrepreneurship in the Indian context. The volume discusses themes such as geostrategic shifts and their impact on the Indo-Pacific region, the effects of Covid-19 on international and economic security, India–China bilateral ties, FDI spill over on domestic firms, entrepreneurship education in India, and the Thai Canal project.

Rich in insights on various geo-economic perspectives that continue to shape the global business environment, the book will be useful for students and scholars of sociology, business management, business economics, international trade, geopolitics, international relations, political sociology, and political studies. It will serve as a useful reference for academics, researchers, think tanks, industry professionals, and policymakers.

Faisal Ahmed is Professor in the International Business Area teaching trade and geopolitics at FORE School of Management, New Delhi, India. His research and consulting interests include Indo-Pacific region, China's trade and geopolitics, trade agreements, and SDGs. He has been consultant to the United Nations Economic and Social Commission for Western Asia and other organisations. He has also worked on projects supported by the Ministry of Commerce and Industry, Government of India. He holds doctorate and master's degrees from India. He also holds an executive certification in geopolitical analysis from Geneva. He has published papers in refereed national and international journals. His books include *The Belt and Road Initiative: Geopolitical and Geoeconomic Aspects* and *Business Environment: Indian and Global Perspective*. He has also published two edited books on India–ASEAN engagements, and India's foreign policy in the WANA region. Additionally, he has published three monographs on the grassroots reach-out of India's foreign trade policy; India's experiences in trade agreements; and EEZ and the United Nations Convention on Law of the Sea. He is frequently invited as an expert and panellist by institutions and think tanks in India and abroad. Moreover, his articles have appeared in leading newspapers and he is frequently interviewed as an expert by national and international media.

Arbuda Sharma is Assistant Professor in the International Business Area at FORE School of Management, New Delhi, India. She is a Fellow in Management (FPM) from XLRI Jamshedpur and holds a master's degree in international business (MIB) from Bharathiar University. She has over 12 years of experience in leading academic and research institutions, and has worked in various domains like pharmaceutical, fashion, foreign trade, and real estate, among others. Her research interests include trade policy, WTO issues, multinational corporations, and global brand adaptions. She has published papers in reputed national and international journals. Her teaching interests include global business environment, international economic organizations and international business.

Geo-economic Perspectives in the Global Environment

Edited by Faisal Ahmed and
Arbuda Sharma

Routledge
Taylor & Francis Group
LONDON AND NEW YORK

First published 2023
by Routledge
4 Park Square, Milton Park, Abingdon, Oxon OX14 4RN

and by Routledge
605 Third Avenue, New York, NY 10158

Routledge is an imprint of the Taylor & Francis Group, an informa business

British Library Cataloguing-in-Publication Data
A catalogue record for this book is available from the British Library

Library of Congress Cataloging-in-Publication Data
Names: Ahmed, Faisal, editor. | Sharma, Arbuda, editor.
Title: Geo-economic perspectives in the global environment / edited by Faisal Ahmed and Arbuda Sharma.
Description: 1 Edition. | New York, NY : Routledge, 2023. | Includes bibliographical references and index.
Identifiers: LCCN 2022031634 | ISBN 9781032309026 (hardback) | ISBN 9781032407791 (paperback)
Subjects: LCSH: India--Foreign economic relations--China. | China--Foreign economic relations--India. | United States--Foreign economic relations--China. | China--Foreign economic relations--United States. | COVID--19 (Disease)--India. | Finance--India.
Classification: LCC HF1590.I5 C44 2023 | DDC 337.54051--dc23/eng/20220919
LC record available at https://lccn.loc.gov/2022031634

ISBN: 978-1-032-30902-6 (hbk)
ISBN: 978-1-032-40779-1 (pbk)
ISBN: 978-1-003-35470-3 (ebk)

DOI: 10.4324/9781003354703

Typeset in Sabon
by SPi Technologies India Pvt Ltd (Straive)

Contents

Figures

Tables

Contributors

Alexandre Lambert, Academic Director, GIGS, Geneva, Switzerland.

B.B. Mishra, Professor, Department of Business Administration, Utkal University, Bhubaneswar, Odisha, India.

Dimple Vyas, Research Scholar, Department of Economics, Janardan Rai Nagar Rajasthan Vidyapeeth (Deemed-to-be University), Udaipur (Rajasthan), India.

Fikret Birdişli, Associate Professor, Department of International Relations, Inonu University, and Director of Center for Strategic Researches (INUSAM), Turkey.

Hediye Gamze Türkmen, Senior Lecturer, Işık University, Istanbul, Turkey.

Hitesh Bhatia, Associate Professor, Navrachana University, Vadodara, India.

Ipsita Padhi, Research Scholar, Department of Business Administration, Utkal University, Bhubaneswar, Odisha, India.

Kunwar Milind Singh, Associate Professor, Economics and International Business Area, Lal Bahadur Shastri Institute of Management, New Delhi, India.

Md. Absar Alam, Assistant Professor, M.K.S. College, LNMU, Darbhanga, Bihar, India.

Md. Shahnawaz Abdin, Assistant Professor, Department of Management, SMBS, Jamia Hamdard, New Delhi, India.

Mitrajit Biswas, Research Scholar, O.P. Jindal Global University, Kolkata, India.

Mohd. Faheem, Lecturer & Head, Indian Studies Program, Pridi Banomyong International College, Tha Prachan Campus, Thammasat University, Bangkok, Thailand.

Mukesh Kumar, Assistant Professor, M.K.S. College, LNMU, Darbhanga, Bihar, India.

Neha Taneja Chawla, Assistant Professor, Navrachana University, Vadodara, India.

Rahul Kumar, Research Scholar, Department of Management, SMBS, Jamia Hamdard, Delhi, India.

Rajiv Sood, Research Scholar, School of Management Studies, Punjabi University, Patiala, India.

Shweta, Research Scholar, Department of Management, SMBS, Jamia Hamdard, Delhi and Assistant Professor, College of Vocational Studies, University of Delhi, Delhi, India.

Suman Pamecha, Principal, M. V. Shramjeevi College, Janardan Rai Nagar Rajasthan Vidyapeeth (Deemed-to-be University), Udaipur (Rajasthan), India.

Vikas Singla, Assistant Professor, School of Management Studies, Punjabi University, Patiala, India.

Vishal Singh Bhadauriya, Research Scholar, Department of History, Banaras Hindu University, Varanasi, India.

Preface

The Covid-19 pandemic brought about significant changes in the world order. It not only reshaped the global geopolitical architecture but also created newer challenges and opportunities for international trade and businesses. In the evolving context, firms have looked forward to developing more innovative and technologically induced business models for their sustenance. Whether it is the multinational enterprises (MNEs) or the small and medium enterprises (SMEs), they have all been compelled to revisit their business models, strategic orientations and internationalisation pursuits. There has been a massive disruption in the global supply chains as well as the global value chains. The new global realities have also casted a significant impact not only on the country-level variables but on the firm-level factors as well. The management functions of the firms too have witnessed a paradigm shift.

In November 2020, FORE School of Management, New Delhi, organised a two-day FORE International Business Conference (FIBC) to deliberate on the Future of Business in the New Global Realities. FIBC 2020 brought together eminent scholars, academics, corporate professionals and diplomats to deliberate on the new global realities and the future roadmap. The aim was to engage in a pragmatic dialogue relevant to global business and policy-making efforts. It involved deliberations on several multidisciplinary issues pertaining to understanding the global business environment. The present edited volume contains some selected and revised papers presented therein.

The present book titled *Geo-economic Perspectives in the Global Environment* is divided into three sections, each representing a unique sub-theme.

The first section of the book pertains to the geo-strategic and policy perspectives. This section comprises four chapters. The first one is on geostrategic shifts and their impact on the Indo-Pacific region. It reflects on China's rise and the associated geopolitical and geo-economic transformations. The next chapter studies the effect of Covid-19 on the security issues at the economic, political, and ontological levels. Another chapter delves deep into understanding the nuances of public diplomacy, nation branding and soft power with reference to India. Finally, the last chapter in this section examines the evolution of India–China bilateral ties.

The second section of the book contains the chapters that examine the financial and infrastructural perspectives. It begins with the chapter that carries out a systematic literature review on FDI spillover on domestic firms in developing economies, and suggests a future research agenda. Another chapter develops a case study on covid-19 and the financial crisis of 2008 and examines the market efficiency in the Indian stock market. Also, this section contains a chapter on the Thai Canal project and assesses it from a regional geo-economic perspective. Finally, this section contains a chapter on smart cities from an Indian perspective.

The third section of the book examines the business and sociological perspectives. It begins with a chapter on entrepreneurship education in the Indian context. This is followed by another one on assessing the growth of store brands in uncertain markets. Another chapter presents a rural marketing case of consumer durables in India. Also, there is a chapter that carries out an analytical study on consumer perception and purchase intention for green consumer durable products. Further, this section also contains a chapter that focuses on the determinants of quality perception of students in online learning. Finally, the last chapter pertains to the newspaper industry and examines the role of prices in readership trends.

This book carries useful insights on various geo-economic perspectives that continue to shape up the global business environment. It will serve as a useful reference for academics, researchers, think tanks, industry professionals and policymakers.

Acknowledgements

We express our sincere gratitude to Dr B.B.L. Madhukar, Chairman, FORE School of Management, New Delhi, and Professor Vinayshil Gautam, Vice Chairman, FORE School of Management, New Delhi, for their kind support and encouragement.

We are also grateful to Dr Jitendra K. Das, Director, FORE School of Management for his unfathomable support and continuous guidance.

Also, the financial and infrastructural support provided by the FORE School of Management is gratefully acknowledged.

Last but not the least, we express our heartfelt thanks to the contributing authors and the reviewers for their great efforts in making this edited volume possible.

Part I

Geo-strategic and Policy Perspectives

1 Geostrategic Shifts and Their Impact on the Indo-Pacific Region

Alexandre Lambert

Introduction: Towards 'Neo-Cold War' Containment?

Geostrategic considerations related to the Indo-Pacific Region (IPR) typically cluster around the triangular relationship between the 'big three' – China, India, and the US. While Western powers, latest since the British Empire, have always been largely focussing on (control over) China and India in their geostrategic calculus over Asia, the contemporary approach of the US seems to considerably amplify the 'Indian factor', however, only since the second term of President George Bush Junior (2005–2009).[1] This has to do with the sharp rise of China since the turn of the 21st century and, thus, its transformative role in becoming Asia's dominant regional power and its current potential to quickly advance towards global superpower status. Consequently, this shift in US foreign policy from a prioritized partnership with China, mainly due to commercial reasons, towards a nascent geostrategic alignment with India to eventually *contain* China would then crystallize with the Obama Administration's 'Asia Pivot' a few years later, and its *global rebalancing strategy*, namely, to shift its geostrategic focus from Europe and the Middle East to the Asia-Pacific, with initial focus on the South China Sea (SCS) and now broadly the Indo-Pacific area, with the Indian Ocean Region (IOR) becoming increasingly relevant in geostrategic analysis. In this context, India plays a key role in the geostrategic redistribution of power. In fact, according to Mohan, India has morphed 'from being largely irrelevant to Sino-US relations ... [and is] ... now emerging as a major factor'.[2]

Thus, at first view, US–China–India relations are basically conceived according to what could be called, e.g., within US national security strategy, a 'triangularization'.[3] From a realist theoretical point of view, such a strategic concept conventionally elaborates on a perceived 'balance of power' with America on one side and Asia's two giants on the other side, while the exclusive superpower status of the US would simultaneously assure an *asymmetrical* power correlation in its favour. Looking more closely, however, and since geostrategic discourses keep being framed by de facto 'neo-colonial' perspectives on Asia, the two main geostrategic scenarios brought up coincide with either China or India aligning with the US to

DOI: 10.4324/9781003354703-2

balance each other inside Asia. In contrast, and with the typical framing of Western perspectives on Asia in mind, the third scenario of a potentially anti-US, and thus, implicitly, anti-imperial, *China-India-alignment* is conventionally portrayed as significantly less likely.[4]

This also resonates with the geostrategic thinking prevalent in the *post–Cold War era* that took shape in the context of an *acute global power vacuum* left with the collapse of the Soviet Union in 1991 that would lead to America remaining the only superpower in the world. This would in turn result in a shift from bipolarity to *unipolarity* during the 1990s, and while post-Soviet Russia kept focusing on domestic challenges and transition. This has, however, changed with the Russian Federation's *geostrategic reassertion* as a leading continental power in Eurasia under Vladimir Putin, let alone with the strategic rapprochement of Moscow and Beijing hitherto. At the same time, and to the extent that the US and Russia would still cooperate in the international fight against terrorism in the aftermath of 9/11 and Russia kept being associated by Western geostrategic circles via the G8 or even the NATO–Russia council, a *US strategic encirclement of China* was technically feasible, including in post-Soviet Central Asia and given the US military presence in Afghanistan. However, with China rolling out the *Belt and Road Initiative (BRI)* in 2013 and given the conflict escalations in both Ukraine and Syria a year later that led to a clear-cut geostrategic alienation of Russia and the West, Eurasia's chessboard is completely reset, as the West's historical sanctions on Russia post its annexation of Crimea have essentially led to an ever deeper and more comprehensive *Sino-Russian strategic partnership*[5] across the past two decades.

With regard to the Indo-Pacific region, it is precisely against this background that the new rapprochement between New Delhi and Washington, D.C., is to be understood. Given the one-time continental power bloc emerging in Eurasia with strategically coinciding epicentres in Moscow and Beijing, the only option for a rump 'Western bloc' to contain this new 'Sino-Eurasian' *continental* colossus is to strategically integrate India in its *maritime* global hegemony. Yet, the main 'steppingstone' within such a US calculus appears to be the very circumstance that India, unlike Japan, has all geopolitical parameters at hand, let alone in a prospective, to openly *compete* (vs. cooperate) with America, not only in a medium term over dominance in the IOR but even as a global power in a longer prospective. Delhi might also opt for more cooperation (vs. regional power competition) with Beijing. Either ways, as pointed out by Lawandi, the risks associated with potentially unrealistic expectations put on either side of an Indo-American strategic partnership or even military alliance, let alone one that would read anti-Chinese, risks intoxicating that very same partnership.[6] While the US shows a considerable degree of economic interdependence with China, the latter has also become India's main trading partner. Moreover, since 2017, the Middle Kingdom took over the US as the largest economy in the world. That year, China's GDP measured in terms of Purchase Power Parity (PPP) was \$19.617 trillion, compared to \$19.519

trillion in the case of the US.[7] Consequently, in geo-economic terms, the above-mentioned asymmetry within the US–China–India triangular relationship is eventually shifting from the US to China. In other terms, two decades into the 21st century, unipolarity is being replaced by more global balance of power, and more precisely, a more *multipolar international order* is in the making. Still, ever since the Anglo-American invasions of Afghanistan and Iraq post 9/11, some neo-conservative circles in Washington, D.C., have been explicitly projecting a 'New American Century' ('Project for a New American Century', PNAC),[8] with the objective to eventually maintaining a US-centric unipolar world system. However, Charles Krauthammer, who reportedly created the term and notion of the 'unipolar moment', would refer to it not only to caution but to 'exhort' the American government in its attempt to 'democratise' the Middle East, calling such an undertaking as 'enormous, ambitious and arrogant'.[9]

What seems clear is that in contrast to the situation after WWII, the West, including the US itself, is not anymore strong enough today, neither *economically* nor *technologically*, to 'over-power' a new adversary bloc from within the 'Global South', nurtured by 'emerging markets' along 'returning (continental) powers' like Russia, with Russia and China sitting at its military-strategic core, and with the BRICS[10] serving as the geostrategic structuring vehicle. Projected on the Indo-Pacific relations, India's evolving strategic paradox is that while it might indeed wish to align with the US to balance China, e.g., militarily, it is likely to collaborate more with China economically, and even to prospectively challenge the US – just like any other power, including China – over strategic leadership in the Indian Ocean,[11] which is India's vital maritime neighbourhood after all. However, a strategic dilemma might in turn emerge in South Asia, to the extent that Washington, D.C., may choose Delhi over Islamabad as the privileged military partner in South Asia,[12] a strategic positioning of the US that might fuel another regional arms race between India and Pakistan. At the same time, America's contemporary 'allies' may no more count on (real or perceived) US 'military primacy',[13] to the extent they could do during the Cold War. According to a war simulation exercise carried out in 2019 by the Pentagon and RAND Corporation, America's armed forces, including their main international military alliance, NATO, would lose a direct military confrontation against both Russia and China, e.g., over Ukraine in Eastern Europe or even Taiwan in the West Pacific.[14]

Yet, elaborating on strategic concepts developed during geostrategic context of the Cold War, the predominant geostrategic thinking at the White House and the Pentagon keeps suggesting a *de facto 'Neo-Cold War' containment*, this time of *both* Russia *and* China. As pointed out by Dmitri Trenin, with such a simultaneous two-front containment strategy against Eurasia's two continental giants, connected with each other by a 4,000+ km long joint border, Washington is taking a considerable risk. In contrast, Moscow keeps a more careful and more balanced strategic course towards Beijing and Washington, in that it pursues a 'equilibrium, though not equidistance' with China and the US.[15] Given also that already now, the US alone spends almost half of the entire world's defence budget, the associated risks for US foreign policy might fuel an 'imperial overstretch' syndrome on behalf of Uncle Sam. And even if both Japan and India, Asia's two geo-economic powers next to China, would join the balancing effort, the West's calculation may still underestimate that post-Soviet Russia learnt vital lessons from the past, e.g., to avoid direct confrontation with the West,[16] and given that a *Moscow-Beijing axis* may turn out to be 'un-containable' anyhow, especially if Berlin might join the axis, e.g., along the BRI.

Therefore, arguably, with the BREXIT on one end (Eastern Europe) and both a relaunched Quad and the new, exclusively Anglo-Saxon AUKUS deal on the other end with Australia (Indo-Pacific), the Anglo-American Hegemony's calculation might be – precisely so – to fuel *WWIII*, again from Europe, and accordingly, to launch a now Germany-top-heavy EU, but via a de facto NATO command, against Russia (a historical *déjà vu*!), or to at least force another regime change at Moscow, in order to re-take control of *Eurasia's heartland*, which would be the prize to be paid to sustainably contain China. However crazy this may sound, Banerjee and Ling in turn brilliantly explain that the associated geostrategic culture prevalent in the West not only denies crucial historical accounts, e.g., of Sino-Indian millennial past, but also inappropriately channels strategic thinking towards a neo-Cold War '*hypermasculine*' war game attitude.[17] Be it as it may, at the present historical trajectory, the world, here and there, is constrained to take a vital choice: either endorse China's suggestion to reinvigorate the 'Silk Roads' that once inter-connected the world and therewith appeased and help sustain its prosperity or the world leaders choose an arguably outdated and toxic logic of 'perptualized warfare', whose very rationale may only result in a 'nuclear Armageddon'.

Decline of Western Leadership and Global Re-balancing to Asia

Since the turn of the 21st century, world affairs are shaped by a comparative decline of the 'old superpower', i.e., the US, and the rise of China as a 'new superpower' that is increasingly capable of challenging America as the dominant hegemony, not just in Asia but also in other parts of the world. This 'rejuvenation of the Middle Kingdom' in the early 21st century is accompanied by a lasting *transformation of the world's political geography*, transferring the centre of global power from the *Euro-Atlantic* area, where it has been residing for the past two hundred years, (back) to Asia and the *Indo-Pacific* area, where it was lying for most of humanity's historical past and ever since the dawn of civilization. And this global power shift is likely to accelerate with the enduring novel coronavirus (Covid-19) global pandemic.

Conventionally, geostrategic analysis tends to put much of its attention on comparative *military power* de-emphasizing considerations elaborating more on *economic power*, although there seems to be a misunderstanding, including when it comes to how the (old) 'containment' strategy during the Cold War would have been conceived. As I have recently outlined in a historical review, the architect of the US containment policy over the Soviet Union, George Kennan, would design containment ways more in economic than in military terms.[18] Thus, in a world increasingly shaped by economic interdependence, and in a geostrategic context in which military conflict escalation among great powers could quickly result in a global nuclear war, *geo-economics* is gaining in relevance, as governments may opt to turn more to *economic statecraft* rather than military build-up in defence and pursuit of national interests. In other terms, contemporary *geostrategic positioning* elaborates on factors like infrastructures, diplomacy, technology and economics.[19] For instance, as illustrated by the BRI, and given that *inter-regional connectivity* projects lay at the heart of China's grand strategy, the Asian space is being literally 're-engineered' to become a new geo-strategic pole within a *nascent Sino-Asian world order*. That's why in one of my recent contributions, I eventually conjectured that world affairs are currently experiencing a prominent 'return of (political) geography' along a potential reset of humanity's historical clock.[20]

Almost exactly two decades ago, in 2001, China was accepted as a new member State at the World Trade Organization (WTO), an event that caught a great amount of attention not just in China but across the developing world. Meanwhile, Western liberal societies have been struggling with three interrelated traumatic experiences hitherto shaking the geopolitical and geo-economic foundations of their global power base and dominance, the combination of which increasingly undermines Western leadership, credibility and reliability towards strategic partners, if not formal military allies.

Legacies of 20 Years of Counterterrorism and Delusions about 'Liberal Democracy'

Upon the turn of the 21st century, the West's first traumatic experience was triggered by the terrorist attacks by Al Qaeda on American soil on September 11, 2001 ('9/11') and a few years later also in Europe. Given the deep psychological shock that especially the events of 9/11 would provoke and be felt almost like an 'existential threat' especially on America's shores of the North-Atlantic, the Western world would hitherto focus on national security prerogatives at the detriment of both economic freedoms and civil liberties. With military interventions in Afghanistan (2002) and Iraq (2003) after 9/11, Western leadership across the North Atlantic embarked on what the George Bush Junior Administration arrogantly called a 'Global War on Terror' (GWOT), explicating that this would be a 'war with no foreseeable end'. Twenty years on, with the colossal collateral damage that the GWOT has brought about and especially with the Middle East suffering a literate 'regional world war' shock, many may have forgotten that the GWOT took shape in the midst of an intra-Western leadership crisis with the US and Britain on one side and Germany and France on the other side – the hard core of the European Union (EU), and in the terms of political geography, Western Europe's main (continental; e.g., from Britain's view) powers.

Thus, NATO's strategic core of the two Atlantic Sea powers (the US and Britain), and with the tacit agreement of Israel, would hitherto embark on a 'perpetual warfare' strategic course against a biased shortlist of states and regimes, especially in the Middle East and West Asia, blamed for 'sponsoring terrorism'. This would not only tend to put upside-down the United Nations Charter, which is the core of international law and multilateral diplomacy; it would deliberately undermine the normative concept of 'perpetual peace', which has been lying at the ideological heart of the West's global leadership after WWII. It arguably coincides with the eventual subversion of the 'American Dream', nurturing the perception that there might have been a 'neo-Orwellian turn'[21] at Washington, D.C. In fact, there is a rather anti-democratic tendency affecting Western leadership and subsequent US Administrations at the White House. For instance, the GWOT was designed on the de facto neo-conservative *Bush Doctrine* of pre-emptive or even preventive warfare.[22] As neither the Obama nor the Trump Administrations were able to halt the war-waging political machinery run by an ever more powerful military-industrial complex, Biden himself just approved a historical national 'defence budget' of $700+ billion while paying only lip service to the very meaning of democracy at his 'Summit of Democracies'.[23]

Since the GWOT was pursued with an adjacent agenda coinciding with a de facto 'war on Islam', this would transcend the territorial and cultural boundaries of the mostly Arabic Middle East, as it would deeply impact security and stability in the Indo-Pacific region along the 'Islamic arc' which holds a significant share of the world's Muslim populations. Meanwhile, the West's two-decade-long 'military adventurism' has come at a heavy prize. According to the Harvard's Belfer Centre, the GWOT has hitherto cost the American taxpayer well over $5 trillion, as the US alone would lose some 15,000 soldiers,[24] even more that it was driven by 'political lies', if not fatal strategic miscalculation.[25] After all, the case of Iraq effectively demonstrated that democracy can't be 'enforced' militarily, let alone exported to other countries, as if it was a commercial commodity to be traded; to work properly, democracy must be home-grown.[26] Yet, subsequent Administrations at the White House have continued playing with fire, despite massive evidence collected across the past two decades that 'regime change policies' are not only 'dangerous and destructive' but condemned to fail.[27]

Global Financial Crisis and the Geo-Economic Return of Asia

The second traumatic experience that had a lasting implication for Western global leadership, including from a moral point of view, has been the collapse and financial meltdown at Wall Street in 2008. Fuelled by a literate culture of 'casino capitalism', Martin Jacques has argued that this 'financial crisis' would be symptomatic for the decline of America and the rise of China.[28] Meanwhile, Joseph Stiglitz (Noble Prize laureate for Economics) and Linda J. Bilmes had estimated the cost of the war in Iraq at $3 trillion, arguing that $4–5 trillion would probably be a more reasonable number,[29] herewith anticipating early on what the Belfer Center now confirms. Moreover, they illustrated that Western leadership would effectively suffer from some moral flaw. For instance, while the US would spend $12 billion per month on the war in Iraq alone, the White House would veto a bill passed by Congress to provide insurance to poor American children, arguing that the country may not afford it – the amount equalling just a few days of fighting in Iraq. Most importantly, they saw a direct correlation between the way the GWOT was conducted and what they would call the (many) 'weaknesses' of the US economy.[30] While the financial crisis would not only further weaken the US dollar, already suffering from inflation, but also spread soon over the Atlantic, severely affecting European economies and the Euro, Asia in turn seems to have better resisted, thanks to lessons learned from the Asian Financial Crisis of the late 1990s.

Comparative Retraction of Western Economies and the Rise of Emerging Markets

According to Standard Chartered,[31] by 2030, among the top-ten economies of the world, China will be clearly no. 1, as even India (no. 2) will have surpassed the US (currently the largest economy). Among the top-ten world economies, in a decade from now, the majority will represent *emerging economies*. Inside the Indo-Pacific, the *Indian Ocean* may become increasingly important in comparison to the West Pacific, a trend reflected not only by average comparative growth rates but also by the strong demographic patterns along fast urbanization and infrastructure-induced industrialization in South Asia and Sub-Saharan Africa (SSA). In fact, the lion's share of the world's prospective population growth will occur in both SSA and South Asia. According to the United Nations Population Fund, especially SSA's population is about to explode, with estimates reaching from 2.5 billion (conservative) to 4.0 billion (optimistic) by 2100.

After SSA, the second fastest growing world region demographically is and will remain South Asia, with India alone growing to up to 1.8 billion by the end of this century. Already at present, South Asia encompasses 43% of Asia's and almost a quarter of the world's population.[32] Moreover, with a comparatively small territorial extent of 5 million square kilometres, and as its population will further grow from currently 1.9 billion to 2.23 billion by 2050,[33] South Asia will remain the most densely populated region while becoming the most important prospective consumer market in the world. And like SSA, this trend is nurtured by both infrastructure-induced industrialization and sustained urbanization patterns. Since South Asia's urban population already grew by +130 million in the first decade of the 21st Century (2001–2011), this represents an increase of more than the entire population of Japan within a decade, and as it is forecasted to grow further by +250 million until 2030.[34] To compare, this is slightly less than the entire US population and four times the German population.

Geo-economic Transformation of the Indo-Pacific Region (IPR)

Thus, major geostrategic shifts as described above happen in direct correspondence with the transformation of the political geography of the Indo-Pacific area itself, reflected by at least three tidal events that have shaped this particular world region across the past decade, as further described in this section.

Belt and Road Initiative (BRI) Reformatting Asia's Spatial Order

Launched by China's new leadership under Xi Jinping in 2013, the BRI was a direct response to the Obama Administration's pivot to Asia and the above-mentioned global rebalancing strategy that occurred one decade ago (2011) and herewith came shortly after the outfall of the financial crisis springing from Wall Street back in 2008. With this strategic pivot to Asia, President Obama decided to relocate 60% of the US Navy to the Pacific in direct response to China's strategic assertion in the SCS. As a co-initiative, the Obama Administration launched negotiations on the Trans-Pacific Partnership (TPP),[35] a project to set up a vast free trade area with the aim of isolating China commercially. Nick-named 'anybody but China', this phenomenon has also been referred to as the 'Obama doctrine', reflecting that China had effectively become America's new 'international enemy image'.[36] However, while the US did withdraw from the TPP under the Trump Administration, even during his predecessor, the Congress had failed to ratify it. And while neither the Obama nor the Trump Administrations were able to push back China's steady advancement in the Indo-Pacific region, President Biden hasn't managed to re-stimulate the TPP, while his new 'Build Back Better World' (B3W), potentially considered as a counter-weight or alternative to China's BRI – just like has been the case with the TPP itself – turns out to be geopolitically motivated, though geoeconomically flawed.[37] Meanwhile, Japan and India jointly tried to offer alternative, 'quality'- infrastructure connectivity projects to counter the BRI. However, compared to China's BRI benefitting from an all-of-government and all-of-economy support, co-funding from China's main state banks and state-owned enterprises, as well as the new 'Silk Road Fund' (SRF), connectivity projects proposed by other regional players suffer from comparative under-funding and receive much less political backing, neither by economic elites nor via economic statecraft.

The BRI's facts are speaking for themselves. Involving some 120 countries around the global, including more than a critical mass of countries across the Indo-Pacific, covering more than one third of global GDP and spanning almost two thirds of the world population, the BRI has quickly emerged as a key geostrategic 'hot-topic' of the early 21st century. Its implications for the Indo-Pacific region are huge, since it occupies the BRI's maritime epicentre. In fact, the combination of BRI's *six continental economic corridors ('One Belt')* and the *21st Century Maritime Silk Road ('One Road')* effectively reinvigorates the *Ancient Silk Roads (ASR)* and their two-track (continental and maritime) connectivity grids that once linked Han China with the Roman Empire. With its economic corridors and spatial industrial zones set to fuel industrialization along the BRI, and with both 'soft' and 'smart' infrastructure complementing the 'hard' infrastructure grid at land, sea, outer-space and via cyber-space, the BRI is effectively re-engineering the spatial realities of international relations with implications well beyond Asia, likely to result in a new, Sino-Asian world order.

In the context of the Indo-Pacific area, the BRI has triggered national insecurity concerns especially in India, perceiving it as *strategic encirclement* by China, a phenomenon also referred to as the 'string of pearls'. As pointed out by Gurpreet Khurana, China's investments in strategic sea ports in the Indian Ocean such as in Pakistan (Gwadar), Sri Lanka (Hambantota) and Bangladesh (Chittagong), although not explicitly expressed by Beijing, could be used as potential military facilities.[38]

Asian Infrastructure Investment Bank Reframing the Regional Development Architecture

Next to the BRI, the second tidal event affecting the Indo-Pacific occurred when Xi Jinping inaugurated the Asian Infrastructure Investment Bank (AIIB) in Beijing in 2015. Also, by 2014, the BRICS had established their New Development Bank (NDB), nick-named the 'BRICS Bank'. Notably, the AIIB and NDB are considered as potential alternatives to the US-led post-WWII Bretton Woods System, namely the International Financial Institutions (IFIs) composed of the World Bank and the International Monetary Fund (IMF). Meanwhile, the new China-led AIIB fills a vital gap in the regional promotion of critical infrastructure in Asia and herewith serves as another key funding institution of the BRI. According to the Asian Development Bank (ADB), Asia alone will require some $20 trillion of infrastructure investments over the coming decades. And in contrast to the situation with the BRI, India hasn't only been in favour from the beginning but is co-leading the AIIB with China.

To illustrate the potential by which the AIIB is affecting the global redistribution of geo-economic power, it suffices to note that while neither the US nor Japan has yet joined the China-led development bank, all of the remaining principle allies of the US were participating at the inaugural meeting at Beijing to become founding members, including Australia, Canada, Germany, Israel, South Korea, and the United Kingdom. And especially in the case of London's decision, it eventually echoed as a major blow at Washington, D.C.

Regional Comprehensive Economic Partnership Redefining Free Trade in Asia

The third geostrategic tsunami affecting the Indo-Pacific region has been the successful negotiation and conclusion of the Regional Comprehensive Economic Partnership (RCEP) in 2020, which herewith represents the currently largest regional trade bloc in the world. Initiated from within the Association of Southeast Asian Nations (ASEAN), interestingly, beyond the ten member states of ASEAN, the RCEP includes China along with America's main allies in the Western Pacific, including the most important economies in this region viz. Australia, Japan, South Korea, and New Zealand. Arguably, this represents another blow to US foreign commercial policy in the Asia-Pacific, since it also contrasts with the failure of the TPP and given that the US is not part of the RCEP. Moreover, Japan, the most important strategic ally of the US and a potential bulwark against China in East Asia, has been promoting another major regional free trade project, the Comprehensive and Progressive Agreement for Trans–Pacific Partnership (CPTPP).

On the one hand, with the CTPP, Japan seeks to put in place and lead a regional trade architecture as a counter-weight to an increasingly assertive and dominant China and especially as it has become the dominant economy within the RCEP. On the other hand, however, Tokyo does in turn keep the door open for an eventual accession to the CPTPP by the Middle Kingdom. Notably, this contrasts with what the US would have pursued via its TPP initiative, namely to *ex ante* exclude China from it. Moreover, while the US, again, appears absent from the CPTPP, and while China is in turn considering joining, the UK's recent accession request to the CPTPP[39] appears interesting, since it coincides with the BREXIT and the circumstance that the EU, just like the US, appears largely absent from any of the new regional trade blocs. And in contrast to the US absence from or failure to shape new regional free trade areas, its Northern American neighbours may take a different stance. For instance, according to the Asia-Pacific Foundation of Canada, the scenario of 'Canada joining the historic agreement (RCEP) would be a clear sign of Canada's commitment to a "diverse and inclusive" Asia Pacific grounded in an emboldened spirit of global multilateralism'.[40]

From 'EURasia' towards 'eurASIA'

Next to the maritime dimension of the Indo-Pacific and Asia's adjacent *rimland* accordingly, it is important to look also inside Eurasia's *heartland*, where the geo-economic epicentre has been pivoting from Europe to Asia. The factors contributing to this geostrategic shift with lasting effects on the Indo-Pacific region are described in this sub-chapter.

Russia Pivot to Asia and Boost of the Comprehensive Sino-Russian Strategic Partnership

In a brilliant essay published in 2014 in *Foreign Affairs*, John Mearsheimer found that it was the West that triggered the crisis in Ukraine and especially the US that pushed Kiev to join NATO, hereby crossing a geopolitical hard-line from a Russian national security perspective.[41] To paraphrase the US attempt to draw countries in Russia's vital neighbourhood, like Ukraine or even Georgia, into NATO, Mearsheimer righty compared it to a scenario by which China would forge an impressive military alliance, e.g., across the Pacific, and would invite Canada and Mexico into it. And what appears symptomatic about the shape of Western leadership when further looking at the September–October issue of *Foreign Affairs* – coinciding with the peak of the conflict escalation between Russia, the US and the EU, which brought the world to the brink of a Third World War – is that it's cover page eventually titled, 'See America: Land of Decay and Dysfunction', shows a virtual picture of a demolished Congress building. The geostrategic consequences of the geopolitical and geoeconomics contention with Russia over Ukraine would have severe ramifications not only for European economies. Since the US and EU jointly imposed draconian economic and political sanctions on Russia post its annexation of Crimea, as the West also threw the Russians out of the G8, Russia had no other choice than to pivot to Asia and turn away from Europe accordingly. As a matter of fact, Russia has been Europe's main energy provider. With heightened pressure by Washington on Berlin to freeze Nord Stream II, it is projected that especially the German economy could suffer most of the negative consequences. In any event, in contrast to the US anti-China Asia pivot described earlier, Russia pivot to Asia reads pro-Chinese. The present section elaborates on three major geostrategic implications for the Indo-Pacific region.

Moscow's decision to strategically pivot away from Europe and turn instead to Asia implied that Russia and China would further deepen their already existing Comprehensive Strategic Partnership (CSP), while the very same process enhanced the strategic role of the Shanghai Cooperation Organisation (SCO) in Asia. In fact, almost exactly twenty years ago, after having sorted out their old intra-Eastern bloc leadership rivalries of the Cold War period, and having resolved also some remaining border disputes, Beijing and Moscow, under the new Putin Administration, already back in 2001, had established the first CSP and would also launch the SCO the same year. While the ever more deepening Sino-Russian CSP is shifting the geopolitical gravitation centre in Eurasia from Europe to Asia, the joint accession of both India and Pakistan to the Sino-Russian-led SCO in 2017 entails that a colossal continental power bloc has emerged in Eurasia, with Beijing and Moscow jointly leading it. Meanwhile, with Russia initiating the *Eurasian Economic Union (EEU)* as a Eurasian counterpart to the EU, Eurasia's geo-economic architecture further pivots from the Atlantic to

Asia. At the same time, the EEU could prospectively serve as a territorial and administrative link facilitating the further integration of Eurasia along the BRI.

Last but not least, with South Asia's two demographic powerhouses, India and Pakistan, now on board, the total population of the SCO jumped from originally a quarter to currently 40% of the world population, making it by far the largest regional organization in the world, including in terms of its prospective economic potential, let alone its stabilizing role for Asia and the Indo-Pacific area. Also, Iran finally joining the SCO in 2021[42] significantly enhances opportunities for multilateral diplomacy, conflict prevention and regional confidence-building in Asia, including in West Asia.

The Polar Silk Roads and the New Strategic Significance of the Northern Pacific

With the new Sino-Russian strategic collaboration, and in combination with new climatic patterns in the northern arctic region, a *new geo-spatial corridor* is opened in the form of a 'North-Western passage' around Eurasia. Stimulated also by China's recent strategic initiatives such as the BRI, Russia is not only investing heavily in developing the necessary naval infrastructure grid along the new *Northern Silk Route (NSR)*, leading mostly along its northern shelf of Siberia, but Moscow and Beijing have also agreed on *'Power of Siberia' (PoS)*, a monumental, $400 billion energy grid project that will transport natural gas via continental pipelines from the Yamal natural gas fields across Siberia to East Asia.

Next to Korea, not only Japan but also India seems be interested in the NSR, as reflected in their participation at the 5th Eastern Economic Forum held in Vladivostok on 4–6 September 2019, and it appears as if herewith, all key Asian economies are implicitly benefiting from the new strategic collaboration between Moscow and Beijing:

> The importance of India and Japan's participation in the 5th Eastern Economic Forum ... can only be appreciated by recognizing this cooperative strategy between Russia and China. Both nations have recently transformed the ambitious development plans of Russia's Far East and Arctic region into a Polar Silk Road – bringing the BRI into Russia's Arctic.[43]

Moreover, there is the *Bering Strait Tunnel* project that, if realized, could play a supplemental role in boosting overseas investments in the Northern Pacific littoral, something that could bring China and the US way closer to each other.[44] This giga-project also represents a strategic amendment to the BRI, in that it would literally create a 'World-Land-Bridge' connecting the World Island (Eurasia plus Africa) with the Americas. And if both Canada and the US could agree to complete the last mile of such an integrated Northern-Hemispheric connectivity grid, then people will once be able to step into a train in London and travel Eastward way through the Northern Hemisphere and get off from the train at New York City.

Regarding Trans-Pacific relations, there are even two more giga-infrastructure projects on either side of the earth's largest ocean that could permanently transform this particular part of the world with significant implications also for the IPR. The first one is the planned inter-oceanic 'Kra Canal' in Thailand that would connect the Kra Isthmus with the Bay of Bengal and herewith offer an alternative and faster transport root from the Pacific to the Indian Ocean in comparison to the Strait of Malacca in Malaysia and Singapore, and as it would considerably boost Thailand's geostrategic position as an interface in the IPR. And like the above-mentioned Bering Strait Crossing, the Kra Canal project is not new, as both projects' histories reach back a century. The second giga-infrastructure project, on the other side of the Pacific, is the 'Grand Nicaragua Canal', a new trans-oceanic canal connecting the Atlantic with the Pacific which would compensate for the Panama Canal's limited capacity. Both canal projects receive support from China; however, the US position remains ambiguous, since both projects would strengthen China's comparative geostrategic position, and despite the fact that China would be willing also to invest so that the Panama Canal's capacity could be enhanced.

While the US is not willing to invest significant financial capital into alternative connectivity projects, let alone in the IPR, that could seriously compete with China's ones, America does in turn try to create new military alliances with the obvious aim to contain China. Accordingly, the US has relaunched the *Quadrennial Security Dialogue (QSD; Quad)* with Australia, India and Japan, once referred to as an 'Asian Arc of Democracy' by former Japanese Prime Minister Shinzo Abe. Furthermore, the US seeks to fortify the trilateral strategic collaboration with Australia and the UK ('AUKUS'), that even from the perspective of peer Western powers appears like an increasingly 'exclusive Anglo-Saxon alliance'. In fact, Australia's recent decision to favour both the US and Britain over France to procure nuclear submarines might lead to new frictions in Euro-Atlantic community, including inside NATO. At the same time, it could favour multipolarity in the IPR since it could lead to intra-Western competition over strategic naval bases between France and Britain/US. It might also lead to more multipolarity and diversified balance of power schemes at the global stage. On the one hand, Australia could soon send its AUKUS-run nuclear submarines way up to the Northern Pacific and even into the polar region. On the other hand, with Britain's strategic choice, along the BREXIT, to opt for closer strategic cooperation with the US and Australia in the IPR, a move that is likely to further weaken the EU's common foreign and defence policy, France could re-balance power in Europe by means of a rapprochement with Russia to help shape a pan-European security architecture and herewith transcend the new East–West divide imposed by NATO, as Paris could turn to Delhi to collaborate in the field of strategic submarine development.[45]

New Geo-Economic Game in West Asia and the Arab Sea

According to a political map drawn by India's defence establishment, demarcating Asia's main sub-regions, interestingly, Delhi's representation of South Asia includes Iran,[46] a country that could otherwise also be considered as part of West Asia. Anyway, while India is drawing increasing attention also to Afghanistan since the recent withdrawal of US troops, the Persian Gulf and especially Iran may indeed re-emerge as an important strategic partner to help connect India with the Eurasian heartland. Moreover, ever since the Achaemenid Empire, Persia's core territories across and North of the *Persian Gulf* would always link South Asia with Europe across the Mediterranean and herewith anticipate not only the ASR but also serve like a rotating platform for the redistribution of power in world history.

Moreover, Indo-Iranian relations may also become more strategic due to at least two major connectivity projects to link West Asia with South Asia. First, India and Iran have been collaborating on the *Iran-Pakistan-India (IPI) natural gas pipeline*, which is however objected by the US, who in turn supports the *Turkmenistan-Afghanistan-Pakistan-India (TAPI)* natural gas pipeline. Furthermore, as a counterweight to the BRI's *China-Pakistan-Economic Corridor (CPEC)* and the strategically important port of *Gwadar*, Delhi has been in talks with Teheran to deliver the *International North-South Transport Corridor (INSTC)* and develop the port of *Chabahar*, an alternative North–South strategic corridor to connect Mumbai with St. Petersburg across strategic minerals–rich Central Asia and the Caspian basin regions. While the delivery of the INSTC has been slowed down due to US economic sanctions on Iran, India could use the AIIB to assure strategic funding and also turn to the SCO, with Iran now on board, as a multilateral platform to facilitate regional conflict prevention mechanisms and confidence-building measures, including, and with Pakistan, for the benefit of security, stability and prosperity in South Asia.

Conclusion: The Indo-Pacific Is the Geo-Strategic Shift

While the geo-economic strength of both America and Europe, including the US dollar and euro, appears increasingly weakened since the turn to the 21st century, not just China but the whole of Asia has been moving back into the focus of world affairs, let alone world business. In fact, China's 'rejuvenation' as a global power is going hand in hand with its reinvigoration of the once legendary *ASR*, and along the rise of other (re-)emerging economies in Asia and beyond. With Parag Khanna, the (joint) leaders of the Global South occasionally call this syndrome as the 'Rise of the Rest'.[47] This implies that there is also a significant return of 'Asian values', as Khanna further explicates that 'Afghan and Pakistani societies find Chinese infrastructural rehabilitation superior to both Soviet suppression and US manipulation'.[48]

The notion of a 'Free-and-Open Indo-Pacific' area as promulgated by the Quad members not only suffers from potentially contingent geostrategic priorities set at Washington, Tokyo, Melbourne and Delhi; for instance, while Japan and India may legitimately claim to be 'major Asian democracies',[49] India and China are in turn Asia's major developing countries and emerging economies. Thus, there is no way Tokyo and Delhi might forge an 'entente' in Asia to balance China, just like France and Russia would have done in Europe to balance Germany. It also suffers from strategic flaws, including a badly defined notion of 'democracy' and the fact that the leader within the group, the US, is increasingly losing the geoeconomics race against China in setting the new regional trade standards in Asia. After all, as both Washington and Brussels increasingly project so-called 'value'-based rhetoric about international cooperation and norms in midst of economic and financial crisis, their geostrategic advisors seem to ignore basic lessons of *geography* and spatial realities. For instance, as an illustration of the high acceptance, if not popularity that the BRI is enjoying, e.g., in South-East Asia, William Jones, former White House correspondent for Executive Intelligence Review, postulates that 'geography can teach even the most dull-witted in which direction a prosperous future for ASEAN lies'.[50] Also exemplified in the case of Gulf Cooperation Council (GCC) member states who all have significant BRI-related agreements with China, Beijing's rapid expansion of its strategic influence in West Asia could lead to a scenario 'eclipsing India's position in the region',[51] and to the extent that India is not catching up with China in its intention to master alternative regional connectivity projects. Even in the context of South Asia, portrayed as caught in a 'New Great Game' as exemplified by geopolitical contestations over the CPEC, Hussein and Jamali insist that 'geography plays the ultimate role in the making of strategies and policies'.[52]

In conclusion, while major geostrategic shifts are affecting the IPR, it is precisely the tidal changes occurring in this specific part of the world that ultimately nurture those geostrategic shifts. To move forward, it would be beneficial to revisit strategic culture and transcend arguably out-dated and military-top-heavy geopolitical concepts that may have made sense in the context of the Cold War, but which tend to become redundant, if not irrelevant, in the context of world affairs today, in the context of which geoeconomics will play an increasingly dominant role. Worse, in harsh contrast to Western and (in the context of the IPR) overseas powers' de facto neo-colonial claims and rhetoric of creating a regional alliance of liberal democracies modelled along a 'globalized' NATO, the reality on the ground has been that 'Western powers seem to have largely lost institutional brakes on waging war'.[53] Also, while international news outlets have portrayed recent events occurring in Kazakhstan exactly the same way as they did with Ukraine, Syria, Burma or even Venezuela, namely that one single country in the world may dictate who is 'democratic' and who is not, the reality is that South Korea, Japan, India, China and Kazakhstan jointly attended and brough high-level delegations to the most recent Eastern Economic Forum 2021 in Vladivostok, attended by 4,000 participants and 59 national delegations, concluding no less than 380 agreements and envisaging a 'Greater

Eurasian Partnership'.[54] While Washington tries to shape 'mental connectivity' schemes among co-called 'like-minded' nations and using perceived democracy-deficit as a 'casu belli', Beijing prefers to keep track with diplomatic protocol of international and multilateral cooperation, while building 'physical infrastructure' on the ground to shape the next generation of regional and global leadership.

In fact, the world faces an interesting historical analogy to the creation of NATO in Europe during the Cold War, to militarily contain the Soviet Union. According to NATO's first secretary general, Sir Hastings Ismay, the geopolitical rationale for the establishment of the North-Atlantic Alliance was to 'keep America in, the Russian out from, and Germany down' in Western Europe. In strange similarity, some contemporary strategic thinkers may wish to frame the formation of a global alliance of democracies to (implicitly) contain China as follows: 'keep the US in, *lift India up*, and keep China out' of the Indian Ocean.[55] For all those who have been studying European history, this has precisely been the scenario in Europe's hell-like road into WWII, since it was precisely Nazi Germany who was eventually 'lifted up' militarily and technologically, e.g., by Anglo-American money flowing from New York and the London City, to then launch it against the Soviet Union.[56] At this point, it is much less likely that India, currently being 'lifted-up' militarily by the US, would launch itself into a destructive war against China. What seems to be more of concern is the extent to which contemporary strategic thinkers tend to forget the basic algebra of even geography itself. For instance, regarding geographic location of major power, it is posited: 'in the global context, the Pacific- and the Indian oceans are poised to acquire greater strategic salience for the major powers of the 21st century, three among them – ... China, India and the US – are located in Asia'.[57] Obviously, if America, as stated, was really 'located in Asia', then Indonesia could be 'located in South America', just like Australia could be 'located in Africa'!

Of course, as the Anglo-American Empire still claims world hegemonic leadership, and therewith needs to forge new military alliances in the Indo-Pacific to contain China's quasi un-haltable rise, it will progressively rely on strategic collaboration with India. As Russia already pivoted to Asia in a China-friendly fashion, the ultimate nightmare and de facto checkmate for the Western Empire would be a Sino-Indian alignment. That's why America is making everything to frame India–China relations as if it was shaped by an 'adversarial character', let alone with border disputes, e.g., in the Himalaya, being the main lines of contention between Delhi and Beijing.[58] The problem with this is that such an assessment is based on Asia's geopolitical realities of just the past hundred years, referred to in China as the 'century of humiliation' by Western colonial powers. It does therewith neglect Asia's historical realities of the preliminary centuries, and accordingly, long-cycle historical analysis. Ironically, about by the same time when British colonial rule would impose the 'McMahon Line' (1911–1945) in an attempt to eventually 'fix' Tibet as a 'buffer state' in-between British India and China,[59] in Central Asia, British explorer Aurel Stein, who created the term and notion of 'Serindia' in a seminal archaeological work, demonstrated how Buddhism once migrated along the ASR from India to China over one thousand years ago and herewith nurtured one of the richest inter-cultural and trans-border commercial exchanges in human history. Notably, Stein would compose the term 'Serindia' of India and China, since the ancient term 'seres' would refer to the 'people of silk', thus the Chinese.[60]

Acknowledgments

The author would like to thank the three anonymous reviewers for their precious feedbacks, comments and suggestions.

Notes

1 Mohan, 1.
2 Ibid, 3.
3 Banerjee and Ling, 2.
4 Ibid, with reference to John Graver's seminal article: "The China-India-US Triangle: Strategic Relations in the Post-Cold War Era", NBR Analysis 2002.
5 Huaxia.
6 Lalwandi.
7 Frankel.
8 Source Watch. Reportedly, the PNAC has been a neo-conservative think tank, operating from 1997 to 2006, with 'strong ties' to the American Enterprise Institute (AEI) – a (right-leaning) private non-profit American institution of research founded in 1943 by American industrialist Lewis H. Brown. Furthermore, William Kristol and Robert Kagan, PNAC founding members, seem to have relaunched the so-called 'PNAC 2.0' in the framework of The Foreign Policy Initiative (FPI). It appears as if the FPI, operating from 2009 to 2017, would have constituted of a 'loose coalition of individuals' with the aim of influencing American foreign policy in a way to potentially benefit Israel. "Foreign Policy Initiative" (Wikipedia).
9 Porter.
10 Brazil, Russia, India, China, South Africa.
11 Ahmed and Lambert, "Amid geopolitical shifts, who will rule the Indian Ocean?"
12 With the US increasingly turning to Delhi for strategic and military cooperation, while China is receiving more support by China.
13 Brands and Hal.
14 Vankin.
15 Trenin.
16 Zagorsky. In 2008, the government of the Russian Federation, under the Administration of President Medvedev, proposed a Pan-European Security Treaty at the Organization for Security and Cooperation in Europe (OSCE), a proposal which was however rejected be the US and several NATO countries.
17 Banerjee and Ling.
18 Lambert, Post-Cold War NATO Enlargement. 2022.
19 Reginold.
20 Lambert, Geopolitics of China's Belt- and Road Initiative. 2021.
21 Ghébali, 132.
22 "The Bush Doctrine". As pointed out in the report of the Carnegie Endowment for Peace, Bush Doctrine has been a constitutive part of the GWOT, affirming the 'legitimacy of an American preventive strike' (initially in the case of the US

military invasion of Afghanistan in 2001, then of Iraq two years later), while emphasizing (including to its allies) the notion that 'If you are not with us, you are against us'. Consequently, with the Bush Doctrine, US foreign policy went beyond the Truman Doctrine of 'containment', or even the Reagan Doctrine of 'supporting freedom fighters'; its effect was 'shedding multilateralism' and pursuing a 'more active, unilateral approach'. Ibid.
23 Zayas.
24 Nazanin, 1.
25 Baud.
26 Lambert, "Democracy by Force".
27 Larison.
28 Jacques.
29 Stiglitz.
30 Ibid.
31 "World's top 10 economies by 2030", Source: Dejardin.
32 South Asia, Wikipedia.
33 Ibid.
34 World Bank.
35 See also the later section of this chapter on Regional Comprehensive Economic Partnership Redefining Free Trade in Asia.
36 Engdahl. Full Spectrum Dominane.
37 Ahmed and Lambert, China's – not US – plan offers big deal for SMEs.
38 Khurana, 4.
39 Comprehensive and Progressive Agreement for Trans-Pacific Partnership (CPTPP).
40 Gold.
41 Mearsheimer.
42 Motamedi.
43 Ehret.
44 Bering Strait crossing.
45 Thomann.
46 Singh.
47 Khanna.
48 Khanna, 117.
49 Cannon, 195.
50 Jones.
51 Upadhyaya, 14.
52 Hussain and Jamali, 304.
53 Cunningham.
54 Outcomes of the Eastern Economic Forum 2021.
55 Khurana, 7.
56 Cunningham.
57 Khurana, The Indo-Pacific Region, 9.
58 Khurana, China's String of Pearls, 5.
59 Gupta.
60 Ahmed and Lambert, Belt and Road Initiative, 24.

References

Ahmed, Faisal and Lambert, Alexandre, "Amid geopolitical shifts, who will rule the Indian Ocean?", *The Hindu Business Line*, 15 June 2020. https://www.thehindubusinessline.com/opinion/amid-geopolitical-shifts-who-will-rule-the-indian-ocean/article31832780.ece

Ahmed, Faisal and Lambert, Alexandre, *Belt and Road Initiative: Geopolitical and Geoeconomic Aspects*, Routledge, Oxon/New York, 2021.
Ahmed, Faisal and Lambert, Alexandre, "China's – not US's – plan offers big deal for SMEs", *The Korea Times*, 14 February 2022. https://www.koreatimes.co.kr/www/opinion/2021/12/137_313385.html
Ashraf, Eram, "Map of the international North–South transport corridor", *Research Gate*, 2020. https://www.researchgate.net/figure/Map-of-International-North-South-Transport-Corridor-INSTC_fig3_343796661
Banerjee, Payal and Ling. L.H.M., "Hypermasculine war games: Triangulating US–India–China", The New School, International Affairs, Working Paper, no. 12, August 2006.
Baud, Jacques, "Terrorisme: Mensonges politiques et stratégies fatales de l'Occident", Rocher, Monaco, 2016.
Brands, Hal and Edelman, Eric, "The crisis of American military primacy and the search for strategic solvency", *The US Army War College Quarterly: Parameters* 46, no. 4, Winter 2016, 27–42. https://press.armywarcollege.edu/parameters/vol46/iss4/5
Cannon, Brendon, "Grand strategies in contested zones: Japan's Indo-Pacific, China's BRI and Eastern Africa",*Rising Powers Quarterly* 3, no. 2, 2018, 195–221.
"Comprehensive and Progressive Agreement for Trans-Pacific Partnership (CPTPP): United Kingdom Formal Accession Request to the Comprehensive and Progressive Agreement for Trans-Pacific Partnership (CPTPP)", n.d. https://www.dfat.gov.au/trade/agreements/in-force/cptpp/comprehensive-and-progressive-agreement-for-trans-pacific-partnership
Cunningham, Finian, "Why Russia is ready to check-mate the U.S. and its western empire", *Strategic Culture*, 11 January 2022. https://www.strategic-culture.org/news/2022/01/11/why-russia-ready-check-mate-us-and-western-empire
De Soyres, François, Mulabdic, Alen, Murray, Siobhan, Rocha, Nadia and Ruta, Michele, "How the belt and road initiative could reduce trade costs", *Vox EU*, 27 November 2018. https://voxeu.org/article/how-belt-and-road-initiative-could-reduce-trade-costs
Desjardins, Jeff, "Chart: The world's largest 10 economies in 2030", *Visual Capitalist*, 11 January 2019. https://www.visualcapitalist.com/worlds-largest-10-economies-2030.
Ehret, Matthew, "India joins the polar silk road", *Rising Tide Foundation*, 17 October 2019. https://risingtidefoundation.net/2019/10/17/india-and-other-asian-nations-join-the-polar-silk-road.
Engdahl, William, *Full Spectrum Dominance: Totalitarian Democracy and the New World Order*, Third Millennium Press, Chippenham, 2009.
Engdahl, William, "De–dollarization of the BRICS", *Modern Diplomacy*, 4, April 2016. https://moderndiplomacy.eu/2016/04/04/de-dollarization-of-the-brics
Farooq, Abbad, "Marketing China–Pakistan economic corridor: Promoting Pakistani perspective", *The Geopolitics*, 15 January 2020. https://thegeopolitics.com/marketing-china-pakistan-economic-corridor-promoting-pakistani-perspectived
FFQO (Freight Forward Quote Online), "Kra Isthmus canal Thailand international shipping mega-canal", 30 November 2018. https://www.freightforwarderquoteonline.com/news/international-shipping-transformed-three-mega-canals/attachment/kra-isthmus-canal-thailand-international-shipping-mega-canal

Frankel, Jeffrey, "Is China overtaking the US as a financial and economic power?", *The Guardian*, 29 May 2020. https://www.theguardian.com/business/2020/may/29/is-china-overtaking-the-us-as-a-financial-and-economic-power
Frankopan, Peter, *The Silk Roads: A New History of the World*, Bloombury, London and New York, 2015.
Ghébali, Victor-Yves, "Les Droits de l'Homme Dans la Région de l'OSCE: Le Bilan Problématique des Démocraties Occidentales", *Relations Internationales* 132, 2007, 23–31.
Gold Rian, "Multilateralism makes a comeback: The RCEP, Canada, and China", *Asia-Pacific Foundation of Canada*, 18 January 2021. https://www.asiapacific.ca/publication/multilateralism-makes-comeback-rcep-canada-and-china
Gosh, Imam, "These countries will have the largest populations – By the end of the century", *World Economic Forum/Visual Capitalist*, 8 September 2020. https://www.weforum.org/agenda/2020/09/the-world-population-in-2100-by-country
Gupta, Karunakar, "The McMahon line 1911–1945: The British legacy", *The China Quarterly* 47, September 1971, 521–545.
Wikipedia, "Quadrennial security dialogue", n.d. https://en.wikipedia.org/wiki/Quadrilateral_Security_Dialogue
Huaxia (ed.), "Xi's high expectations for closer, stronger China-Russia partnership", *Xinhua Net*, 16 December 2021. http://www.news.cn/english/2021-12/16/c_1310376802.htm
Hussain, Mehmood and Jamali, Ahmed Bux, "Geo-political dynamics of the China–Pakistan economic corridor: A new great game in South Asia", *Chinese Political Science Review* 4, 2019, 303–326.
Jacques, Martin, *When China Rules the World: The Rise of the Middle Kingdom and the End of the Western World*, Penguin, London, 2009.
Jones, William, "Blinken's foray into Southeast Asia cut short by Covid-19", *CGTN News*, 16 December 2021. https://news.cgtn.com/news/2021-12-16/Blinken-s-foray-into-Southeast-Asia-cut-short-by-COVID-19-162Ephb7vgc/index.html
Khanna, Parag, *The Future is Asian: Global Order in the Twenty-First Century*, Hachette UK, London, 2019.
Khurana, Gurpreet, "China's 'String of Pearls' in the Indian Ocean and its security implications", *Strategic Analysis* 32, no. 1, January 2008, 1–39.
Khurana, Gurpreet, *The Indo–Pacific Region: The Emerging Geopolitical and Security Environment*, Dictus Publishing, 2018, Academia. https://www.academia.edu/35884449/THE_INDO_PACIFIC_REGION_The_Emerging_Geopolitical_and_Security_Environment_2018
Lalwandi, Sameer, "Great expectations: Asking too much of the US–India strategic partnership", *The Washington Quarterly* 452, no. 3, Fall 2019, 41–64.
Lambert, Alexandre, "Democracy by force", In: Wilson, Isaiah and Forest, James (eds.), *Handbook of Defence Politics: International and Comparative Perspectives*, Chapter 4 (46–63), Routledge, London/New York, 2009.
Lambert, Alexandre, *Geopolitics of China's New Silk Road: Return of Geography and Reset of the Historical Clock*, Aracne, Rome, 2021.
Lambert, Alexandre, "Post-Cold war NATO enlargement and the geopolitical instrumentalization of 'Liberal Peace': Lessons from George Kennan", In: Criekemans, David (ed.), *Geopolitics and International Relations: Grounding World Politics Anew*, Chapter 6 (221–243), Brill/Nijhoff, Leiden/Boston, 2022.
Larison, Daniel, "No way around it, all regime change policies are bound to crash and burn: A new book finds that failure is baked in the cake yet the US insists on

playing with the fire again and again", *Responsible Statecraft*, 29 November 2021. https://responsiblestatecraft.org

Longbottom, Wil, "Return to London please, via Moscow: Kremlin paves way for East to West rail link after approving $99bn Bering Strait tunnel", *Mail Online*, 22 August 2011. https://www.dailymail.co.uk/news/article-2028854/99bn-Bering-Strait-tunnel-approved-Kremlin-paves-way-East-West-rail-link.html

Mearsheimer, John, "Why the Ukrine crisis is the fault of the west", *Foreign Affairs* 93, no. 5, September/October 2014, 77–84.

Meltdown in Tibet, "Map of the major rivers sourced in Tibet", n.d. https://www.meltdownintibet.com/f_maps.htm

Michler, Andrew, "Russia green lights $65 Billion Siberia–Alaska rail and tunnel to bridge the Bering Strait!", *Inhabitat*, 23 August 2011. https://inhabitat.com/russia-green-lights-65-billion-siberia-alaska-rail-and-tunnel-to-bridge-the-bering-strait

Mohan, C. Raja, "India, China and the United States: Asia's emerging strategic triangle", MacArthur Foundation & Lowy Institute for International Policy, *Strategic Snapshots*, February 2011.

Motamedi, Maziar, "What Iran's membership of Shanghai cooperation organization means", *Aljazeera*, 19 September 2021. https://www.aljazeera.com/news/2021/9/19/iran-shanghai-cooperation-organisation

Nazanin, Azizian, "Easier to Get into War Than to Get Out: The Case of Afghanistan", Harvard Kennedy School: Belfer Center for Science and International Affairs, Paper, July 2021.

"Outcomes of the Eastern Economic Forum 2021", *Roscongress News*, 6 September 2021. https://roscongress.org/en/news/itogi-vostochnogo-ekonomicheskogo-foruma-2021

P&GL (Pipeline and Gaz Journal), "Gazprom begins preparation for power of Siberia-2", 18 May 2020. https://pgjonline.com/news/2020/05-may/gazprom-begins-preparation-for-power-of-siberia-2

Pocress, Michael, "The Asian century just arrived. Now get ready", *Cornell University, SC Johnson College of Business*, 4 September 2020. https://business.cornell.edu/hub/2020/09/04/asian-century-just-arrived

Porter, Patrick, "Unipolar America: Another imperial delusion ends", *Engelberg Ideas*. https://engelsbergideas.com/essays/unipolar-america-another-imperial-delusion-ends

Reginold, Remo, "China's Machtpolitik anders lesen", *Stiftung Lilienberg Unternehmerforum*, August 2019. https://www.lilienberg.ch/publikationen/chinas-machtpolitik-anders-lesen-beispiel-seidenstrassen-projekt-1

Rusila, Ari, "Russia's strategic shift to the East continues: Now India", *Global Review News Network*, 23 January 2015. https://globrev.wordpress.com/2015/01/23/russias-strategic-shift-to-east-continues-now-india

Sen, Amiti, "India speeding up FTA talks with Switzerland, Norway, Iceland", *The Hindu Business Line*, 31 December 2019. https://www.thehindubusinessline.com/economy/india-speeding-up-fta-talks-with-switzerland-norway-iceland/article30445025.ece

Singh, Harjeet, "Extended South Asian region", *Indian Defence Review* 22, no. 2, April–June 2007, date of issue: 01 October 2011. http://www.indiandefencereview.com/spotlights/extended-south-asian-region-i

Source Watch, "Project for a new American century", n.d. https://www.sourcewatch.org/index.php/Project_for_the_New_American_Century

South Asia, n.d. https://en.wikipedia.org/wiki/South_Asia
Stiglitz, Joseph, "The Three Trillion Dollar War", public speech (24 April 2008), hosted by: The Levy Economics Institute, the Bard Economics Program, and the Economics Club, edited transcript. https://www8.gsb.columbia.edu
Takenaka, Kiyoshi and Park, Ju–min, "Japan aims to expand CPTPP trade pact as UK, China eye membership", *Reuters Business News*, 20 November 2020. https://www.reuters.com/article/us-apec-summit-japan/japan-aims-to-expand-cptpp-trade-pact-as-uk-china-eye-membership-idUKKBN2800AF
Thomann, Pierre-Emmanuel, "La nouvella alliance AUKUS dans l'Indo-Pacifique: Quelles leçons pour la géopolitique de la France?", *Revue Défense Nationale*, 10 November 2021. https://www.defnat.com/e-RDN/vue-tribune.php?ctribune=1439
Trenin, Dmitri, "The impact of Sino-American Rivalry on Russia's relations with China", *Charnegie Moscow Center, Foreign and Security Policy, Pax Sinica*, 10 October 2021. https://carnegiemoscow.org/commentary/85580
Upadhyaya, Cdr Shishir, "India's maritime security relations with the gulf cooperation council countries – Prospects amid rising Chinese influence", *Maritime Affairs: Journal of the National Maritime Foundation of India, Academia*, 2019. https://www.academia.edu/39472837/Indias_maritime_security_relations_with_the_gulf_cooperation_council_countries_Prospects_amid_rising_Chinese_influence_View_Crossmark_data
Vankin, Jonathan, "Russia, China will crush U.S. In world war III, Pentagon-Backed war simulations show massive American defeats", *Inquisitr*, 12 March 2019. https://www.inquisitr.com/5338482/russia-china-u-s-world-war-iii-simulations
Wikipedia, "Berting Strait Crossing", n.d.-a https://en.wikipedia.org/wiki/Bering_Strait_crossing
Wikipedia, "Foreign Policy Initiative", n.d.-b https://en.wikipedia.org/wiki/Foreign_Policy_Initiative
World Bank, "Leveraging urbanization in South Asia", n.d. https://www.worldbank.org/en/region/sar/publication/urbanization-south-asia-cities
Your Free Template, 'Shanghai cooperation organization templates', n.d. https://yourfreetemplates.com/shanghai-cooperation-organization-templates
Zagorski, Andrei, "The Russian proposal for a treaty on European security: From the medvedev initiative to the corfu process", In: IFSH (ed.), *OSCE Yearbook 2009*, (43–59), Baden-Baden, Moscow, 2010.

2 The Effect of Covid-19 on the Security Issues at the Economic, Political, and Ontological Level

Fikret Birdişli

Introduction

Security has a broad context because it's a multidimensional concept. Therefore, it has been used and associated with many subjects from politics to the other fields of experimental science.

In political science, security has paramount value for existence of state and its responsibilities and functionality by all its variety forms (Schmidt, 2016, pp. 206-212). So the meaning of security is not only the desired condition for phenomena but also stimulation for durable stability and legality. Hence, the breaking of the relevance of security is perceived as a threat. Economic power occupies the first place of this relation in terms of the sovereignty of the state and the power hierarchy in the international system.

However, the relationship between security and the economy had been behind strategic and military matters for many years until a new framework for security studies was drawn after the Cold War. According to Buzan and colleagues, widening the concept of security has been met with hesitation at the beginning because it may endanger the intellectual coherence of security. Probably, they were in fear that allowing non-military issues to achieve security status would have undesirable and counterproductive effects on the entire fabric of social and international relations (Buzan et al., 1998, p. 2).

Nevertheless, elapsed time proved the tight relationship between economic and security matters. But this relationality has two dimensions at the macro and micro levels which is in overlap with the systemic and systematic levels. Macro/systemic levels are related to international economy politics and micro/systematic levels are related to domestic economies. But both of them are intersected by supply chains and globalization of production. In other words, both international and local economies are negatively affected by the disruption of the supply chain, as if perceived the problem as a security issue. Therefore, over time, it has been realized that the meaning of economic security is more than general stability against global shock because production and flows of the commodity are dependent on the relational trust of both internal and international actors and their transactions continuously. Until this point in history, the problems that would

DOI: 10.4324/9781003354703-3

fundamentally affect this relationality were overlooked. The global pandemic, however, has revealed this relationality now.

The traditional approach to international security tends to ignore societal and economic relations unless problems with military matters are directly at stake. Therefore, usually, some epidemics, such as HIV/AIDS, have been evaluated as local or domestic problems despite the large number of deaths that have been documented (Elbe, 2002, pp. 159–77).

But, the economic matters have been put forward more from other secondary dynamics in security studies, especially after the 1973 Middle East crisis which affected the international economy badly. This brought up the question of whether Third World supplier cartels could disrupt the Western economy by raising prices or restricting supply, whereas consideration of deterrence logics outside the superpower framework was rare.

This time, the concern on global health also has been one of the prominent anxieties for both politicians and academicians in security matters. As the pandemic has affected the global economy. Therefore, it is a reality that the lives and livelihood of the overwhelming majority of people on this planet are at greater risk from the pandemic than from wars, terrorism, or any other form of violence (McInnes, 2008, p. 275).

So, this chapter evaluates the effect of the pandemic on the security frame with a focus on the variety of results in the economic and political areas. Besides, the chapter also explores how the pandemic has triggered ontological security concerns related to economic and political matters because of rationality and deterministic results.

Security, Economy, and the Pandemic

Humankind has faced many diseases throughout its long history. The oldest one is the plague of Galen in ancient times around AD 165. It was probably a kind of smallpox or measles that affected Anatolia, Egypt, Greece, and Italy. It was assumed that this disease was carried by Roma soldiers returning from Mesopotamia and caused the killing of over five million people.

The plague of Justinian seen around AD 541 was another outbreak that spread through the Byzantine Empire and Mediterranean port cities and caused the killing of up to 25 million people.

But, the Black Death was the most famous outbreak and it badly affected Europe, Africa, and Asia, with an estimated death toll of between 75 and 200 million people. This disaster was assumed that come up in Asia and was carried by fleas living on the rats usually on merchant ships to the other parts of the world. The cholera pandemic spread twice in history, around the 19th and 20th centuries, both of which caused over 1.5 million deaths. And flu pandemics occurred around 1890, 1918, 1956, and 1968. HIV/AIDS has proven itself as a global pandemic, killing more than 36 million people since 1981. Now, the latest pandemic appeared in December 2019 in China and was named Covid-19. This new virus spreads incredibly quickly harming people because no one has immunity. Besides, the remarkable point of this pandemic, both the national and global economies are badly affected because of globalization and its negative reflection on the supply chain (MPH Online, 2020). As it has been understood, all diseases faced by humans in the historical period shook up social life on multidimensional sides. But usually, the cost of the disasters has been regarded according to the effect on the population and national economy. But recently, the multidimensional effect of the pandemic on human life has begun to be considered a security problem due to its increasing load on society.

According to experts, two factors bring together the subject of health and security issues. The first one is the growing acceptance of the broadening of the security agenda in the non-defense areas (Ripsman and Paul, 2016, p. 201). The second one is the specific interests and endeavors of some individuals to the problem.

First, globalization has caused the broadening of the national security agenda in non-defense areas such as trade, ecology, and health. So, perceived threats increasingly cover economic, environmental, and societal dimensions which include disease-related problems too.

Second, some prominent leaders used their bureaucratic and political positions and powers to focus the attention of the global community on the health issues in the world security agenda (McInnes, 2008, p. 277).

In this context, especially two leading people deserve notice. One of them is the Norwegian politician Gro Harlem Brundtland, who was the director-general of the World Health Organization from 1998 to 2003. She is also known for having chaired the Brundtland Commission which presented the Brundtland Report on sustainable development.

The other person is Richard Holbrooke, the UN Ambassador of the United States. Holbrooke was a prominent figure in the securitization of HIV/AIDS.

When he visited Africa in 1999, Holdbrook realized not only the scale of the HIV/AIDS pandemic but also that the existing aid-based approaches were failing to deal with the crisis. Moreover, the potential of the social consequences of the pandemic was beginning to become apparent, including in state stability. Therefore, he strived to place pandemics on the Security Council's agenda (McInnes, 2008, p. 277).

From that time, new infectious diseases such a SARS and H5N1 have occupied the world's agenda as not only economic and social issues but also security matters.

Besides, these diseases have been perceived as a product of the increased movement and interaction of goods and people in wider geographical areas.

Some others see that the main reason for the perceived direct threat of such disasters to security is related to the increasing spread of these problems to the Western states. For example, the Avian Flu transmitted from human to human affected 25–30% of people living in the West and caused too many deaths.

For this reason, the cost of pandemics to Western countries has caused the development of multinational effort and extraordinary alliance, and both affected and unaffected countries have made effort to accurately identify and report cases in a timely manner.

The second effect of pandemics in the context of security concerns is related to the economic cost of the disasters to the world. For example, the most immediate and dramatic economic effects of SARS firstly occurred in Asia, but later, every market in the global economy was at some point impacted directly or indirectly by the epidemic. So, the cost of SARS more accurately estimated based on near-term expenditures and losses in key sectors such as medical expenses, travel and related services, consumer confidence, and investment. According to some calculations it has been estimated that the short-term global cost of lost economic activity due to SARS was approximately $80 billion (Lee and McKibbin, 2004).

Despite this considerable number, sometimes, researches on the economic consequences of infectious diseases such as malaria and HIV/AIDS have limited themselves to the cost and burden to the health system. In this situation, the economic burden of the epidemic has been estimated on the private and non-private medical costs associated with the disease, such as expenditures on diagnosing and treating the disease.

For example, according to UNAIDS (the Joint United Nations Programme on HIV/AIDS), 42 million people globally are living with HIV/AIDS. And the medical costs of various treatments of HIV patients, including highly active antiretroviral therapies (HAARTs), are estimated to be more than $2,000 per patient per year. So, all economic estimates and calculations for this disease have remained related to the local economic burden and have not included the general economic system of the world.

All these developments show that pandemics should be handled on a global scale rather than local, and the seriousness of the economic and social effects force us to take it as a global security issue. Because it is crystal clear that the economic domino effect of the pandemic and its heavy burden on local economies due to the expansion of the supply chain on a global scale shows that the effect of the pandemic is bigger and in varied dimensions than expected. Despite all these multidimensional approaches, especially one of the neglected things about the costs of pandemics is the societal dimension of disaster.

Recent events prove that pandemics may have the capacity to cause social disruption and threaten the stability of a state by a crisis of confidence. For example, the confidence in the state may reduce because of failure to provide a basic level of protection against all kinds of effects of a disease. This distrust often manifested itself as anti-vaccination against the state's campaign.

Besides, the negative economic repercussion of the pandemic may cause the triggering of social inequality and public disorder because the privilege of some people to obtain access to better treatment or drugs potentially leads to discontent at the vast communal level.

Also, large-scale epidemics may also drive economic decline by forcing the government to increase spending on health in the percentage of GDP and to cause reducing productivity due to the drop of many employees from production because of health problems.

The reduction of internal and external investments due to the lack of business confidence and the raising of the insurance cost for health provision may create another negative effect on the economy and cause massive decline (McInnes, 2008, p. 279)

Some concern about the epidemic is related to a more specialized area. For example, a high rate of HIV infection among security forces and skilled persons such as teachers and health workers created social and political unrest around the 2000s also.

Some Defense Health Agency reports showed that the spreading of Covid-19 in the US Military is highly dramatic (Kasper et al., 2020, p. 2417).

An outbreak of Covid-2019 occurred on the USS *Theodore Roosevelt*, a nuclear-powered aircraft carrier with a crew of 4,779 personnel. This ship is very strategic for the US Army and a part of the fleet of the biggest ships the Navy has ever built (Farley, 2021).

Official records show that the highest prevalence of HIV disease in sub-Saharan African states, but its triggers point to the spreading of this disease by military persons. Because in sub-Saharan Africa, HIV infection rates among the military have been determined often higher than that among civilians (Azuonwu and Erhabor, 2012). This was a real concern for Western countries because of peacekeeping forces and personnel in service (CRS, 2019; Elflein, 2020). This is because soldiers are a high-risk group by risky behavior such as contact, injuries, incidents of sexual violence, etc. So they may carry infection by returning to their post and community. A high infection rate may drive high-security risk by fall out of many soldiers and security personnel from their service (McInnes, 2008, p. 281).

These records show that the security anxiety and risk about pandemics has high prevalence. So all of these probabilities about the crucial effects of any pandemic or widespread health problem on the societal and political order in the context of security shouldn't be exempted in macro and microeconomic calculations.

Multidimentional Effect of Covid-19 Pandemic

It's crystal clear that the world is passing through a very impressive time and is witnessing important days of history because of the Covid-19 pandemic. Hence, we may say that these days touch on the ontological security feeling of humans.

It is widely accepted that security is a core value for both individuals and the community and it's also evolving in parallel to everything in the world.

Therefore, security is a feeling, a demand, a situation, a politics, and a vision that bears on in our lifetime. Hence, it is not surprising to realize that security is a dynamic process according to the context also. For this reason, Barry Buzan (2009) has called motivations of this evolutionary dynamic process of security as "driving forces".

The others are great power politics, technology, key events, the internal dynamics of academic debates, and institutionalization. These five factors shape the concept of security as a relational externality.

According to Busan's typology, the category of technological developments and important events are remarkable in terms of the pandemic that we are facing today as Buzan considers technological developments as having the potential to prevent or eliminate the effects of diseases and environmental problems; he gives the example of HIV/AIDS.

According to Buzan (2009), diseases and environmental problems are events with non-permanent effects that can be eliminated by the effect of technology.

But the pandemic we are facing today may affect every corner of social and economic life, even our personal lives. So it seems that the Covid-19 pandemic may have perpetual effects on many things if it takes longer to be eliminated. The following lines summarize this reality in the main category of ontological, political, and economical levels.

a) **Ontological Level:** Ontological security has been used as a term by Antony Giddens (1991) to describe the contradiction of the modern world and the psychological dilemmas of modern life on the individual.

   But, this term is used in the "insecurity literature", to present catastrophic events such as climate disasters, terror attacks such as September 11, or wars.

   In the critical approach, the feeling of insecurity has been investigated in the context of peace and conflict studies. Therefore, the situation of uncertainty has been accepted as the source of ontological insecurity.

   So, the broadening of the concept of security and the unit of analysis debate continues in much recent work on ontological security also. Therefore, a focus on ontological security has become increasingly convenient for conceptualizing responses to challenges in the uncertain world order in which conflict, terror, disasters, migration, and discourses of all insecurity issues prevail (Kinnvall and Jennifer, 2018).

   Security is a fundamental feeling and at the top of the hierarchy of needs of humans. And the condition of insecurity is a kind of urgency that it should be rid of immediately by any proper tools.

   In the case of the pandemic, despite all the technological capacity and weapon assets, people's inability to face this virus triggers the feeling of ontological insecurity. Because for the first time, many feel this helpless in a long time.

   Observations and surveys show that the increased mortality rate every day around affects the subconscious of people. So the threats toward the fundamental experience of "being" shouldn't be omitted by political planers and academicians.

Indeed, people are strengthened by solidarity with their fellow men. But this pandemic separates humans from their relatives and forces them to stand alone against disease. Therefore, the corona pandemic leaves a deep effect and feeling on human psychology and may divert their priorities. These may affect their socio-political loyalties and economic behaviors also.

There is plenty of report about the implications of Covid-19 on mental health and substance use. According to the findings, the Covid-19 pandemic and the resulting economic recession have negatively affected many people's mental health and created new barriers for people already suffering from mental illness and substance use disorders. For example, during the pandemic, about 4 in 10 adults have reported to have had symptoms of anxiety or depressive disorder in the United States (Panchal et al., 2021).

A survey conducted among 130 countries in six regions has evaluated how the provision of mental, neurological, and substance use services has changed due to Covid-19 and the types of services that have been disrupted. And it has tried to understand how countries are adapting to overcome these challenges. According to the report, over 60% reported disruptions to mental health services for vulnerable people, including children and adolescents (72%), older adults (70%), and women requiring antenatal or postnatal services (61%). Around three-quarters reported at least partial disruptions to school (%78) and workplace (75%) mental health services (WHO, 2020).

Besides, the feeling of being secure is related to the feeling of belonging to a particular place or community. As both individual and social desperation in the face of the pandemic negatively affects the feeling of "being at home", it triggers the feeling of ontological insecurity. The isolation caused by the corona affect and damage ontological security feeling and increases the risks of the healing process.

b) **Political Level:** In the Westphalian system, the state has been perceived as the best guardian of human security (Belamy, 2008, p. 422). Therefore, when a state failed to protect its citizens from genocide, mass killing, ethnic cleansing, and other disasters emerged and pathological insecurity feeling triggers a mentality of questioning the legality of state or authority.

Surely, a pandemic causes serious pressure on the government's economies and households. Therefore, if citizens suffer a shortage of food, jobs or medical supplies, the governments may be perceived as insufficient to respond to these challenges. This would drive civil unrest and cause a legality crisis for the government and even states.

The other problem is the probability of the emergence of instability or a political vacuum because of the infection of political leaders themselves in fragile countries. Especially leader-centered authoritarian regimes are vulnerable because of the lack of durable democracy in organizations.

lNevertheless, even in developed countries that currently manage outbreak, long-term civil unrest may cause some manifest, regime changes, and period of social disorder.

In this process, some public discussions revolve around the question of which type of political system – authoritarian or democratic – has been better able to manage the extraordinary circumstances brought about by the pandemic.

Nevertheless, the situation that emerges has a nature that goes beyond the regime types because reactions to the pandemic have largely depended on certain features of national cultures, such as individuals' compliance with collective habits, sense of civic duty, public trust, and respect for government decisions, regardless of any big "civilizational" divide.

This is observed in large differences in collective reactions between, for instance, the more obedient South Korea, Taiwan, and Israel, on the one hand, and the southern states of the US, Russia, and France, known for their entrenched defiance of state decisions, on the other.

According to Laruelle (2021), reactions have also varied by social group. The resistance expressed by some citizens to the lockdown in the name of freedom – and the need to continue working – has revealed socioeconomic lines of friction rarely exposed in pre-pandemic times.

Besides, domestic demands and requirements may trigger the nationalist movement also. The nationalist governments tend to control the national economy by some restrictions or interference to foreign investment or confiscation of assets in new regulations which are controversial to the global economy. So, the pandemic and its results could amplify the current wave of anti-globalism. This time, suppressed and controlled economic activities may be more open to the next economic shocks and even the government may default on payments and salaries. In stronger economies, national economy budgets that are forced to provide economic stimulus or rescue packages may regulate again their payment priorities in international finance and trade.

In Covid-19 pandemic, new regulations aimed at tackling down the pandemic are increasing at the expense of our freedoms. Therefore, the rise of illiberal democracy that we have been witnessing for a while could increase even more. Therefore, it is a serious human security risk that some limitations slyly become permanent while struggling with the pandemic. But after a while, populist policies and discourses may become unusable by not attracting attention, as the economic and social problems faced by society cannot be easily eliminated.

In this situation, as we approach the end of the pandemic, we may witness a rising demand for rational policies and populism losing ground.

At the global level, the pandemic of Covid-19 may increase the feeling of humanism instead of xenophobia as common disasters are getting humans close to each other and fostering feelings of altruism. According to some surveys, six potential sources of stress have been identified during the pandemic (Barzilay et al., 2020):

a) Contracting the virus
b) Dying from the virus
c) Currently having the virus
d) Having a family member contract the virus
e) Unknowingly infecting others
f) Experiencing a significant financial burden

Based on this study, it appears that people are more worried about others than themselves when reporting their Covid-19-related concerns.

The other controversial issue and critics were about international organizations. The problem was related to, firstly, the World Health Organization, and then great organizations such as the United Nations and NATO also have been criticized because of their functionality.

From the beginning of the pandemic, the World Health Organization has been at the center of criticism. The WHO has been criticized about the governance of global health and because of its inability to question China's handling of the outbreak in Wuhan. According to these critiques, organizations could better prepare the world for a dangerous disease, but the the WHO failed to act decisively (Fidler, 2020). These critics arise from high expectations about IGOs and are coming from the lack of real information about their structure because the criticism raises questions about the WHO's authority to challenge states during serious outbreaks for the good of global health. But international organizations are not independent actors of international areas. Their responsibility and activities have been restricted by the consent of states by restricted subjects and their authority in the context of conventions.

So it should be realized that international organizations that especially have global responsibilities need more support, authority, and functional ability to regulate the anarchical nature of the international area.

c) **Economic Level:** Obviously, the most salient effect of the Covid-19 pandemic in the short term has been on the economic security issue. The increasing attention to economic security as a special area in security studies is related to the broadening concept of security after the end of the Cold War.

While there is no consensus on the definition of economic security, it has been defined to include having adequate income level and assets, access to benefits such as paid leave and health insurance, and some control over job content and the opportunity to build a career.

Another definition includes "individual and collective rights (such as worker rights protected by law and the right to be represented by trade unions), the opportunity for income-earning activities, protection of income-earning work, working conditions that are safe and promote well-being, and the opportunity to gain and retain skills". So the common area of economic security is related to individuals and their well-being and the macro- and micro-level economy (Pana-Cran et al., 2020). The objective of economic security concerns the securing of the key supply chains involving foreign sources. The other one is market-access security.

Economic security includes both the micro-level and macro-level. It's crystal clear that the Covid-19 pandemic has affected all of them. According to Rosecrance and Thompson (2003, p. 377), economic relationships between countries affect their security links, but how important they are is uncertain. Widely accepting reality is based on the liberal approach that trade might forge a closer security relationship, reducing the likelihood of military conflict.

Generally, less developed countries are dependent on more developed nations, and it has been assumed that they try to cut ties with advanced countries for independence. But economic crises that emerged on pandemics prove that the world economy is more fragile and connected because of multidimensional dependency.

The macro-level economy is related to the global working of a liberal economy and its economic agents such as trade, foreign direct investment, and international finance and foreign aid policies.

According to the World Trade Organization, world trade will continue to face strong challenges in 2019 and 2020 after growing more slowly than expected in 2018 due to rising trade tensions and increased economic uncertainty (UNCTAD, 2020).

Foreign Direct Investment (FDI) flows are expected to fall by more than 30% in 2020 even under the most optimistic scenario for the success of the public health and economic support policy measures taken by governments related to the Covid-19 pandemic and the resulting recession (Nugroho, 2006).

Foreign aid statistics have been affected badly by pandemics also, but the movement of some specific material related to health and pandemic increased. Besides the number of people pushed into poverty due to Covid-19 also increased. The Covid-19 pandemic is adversely affecting worker well-being in many ways, including through decreased economic security. The economic aspects of overall health and well-being, along with physical, psychological, and social aspects, are a fundamental focus of the problem.

Another remarkable thing is the effect of Covid-19 on the trade. The trade of developed countries has been restricted while many developing or underdeveloped countries have been liberated. In general, the most recent estimates in the OECD Economic Outlook suggest an unprecedented collapse in the first half of 2020, an almost 13% decline in global GDP (UNCTAD, 2020).

All of these may drive to systemic crises because of the disturbing of the integrity of the international economic system. Therefore, the effect of the corona virus pandemic on the economy is a matter of international security.

It should be remembered that international security aims to protect or secure the international system and community as a whole. This umbrella includes societal harmony, political equilibrium, and economic stability. In other words, the meaning of international security is systemic security which depends on the integrity of the international economic system. But it seems to be that the corona pandemic threatens all of them. Therefore, even if vaccination is successful, this pandemic will have lasting effects on society, the economy, and politics.

Conclusion

The Covid-19 pandemic has badly affected most of the world nations in many dimensions. After the first reported case, the virus spread to other countries very fast because of human movement and economic activities. The main reason for this speed and the heavy effect was no one has immunity to this virus and it has badly affected social and economic life because of globalization and the supply chain. These experiences show us the importance of services in the economy besides production sectors. The effect of economic crises on the micro-level fed ontological insecurity feeling which harms the legitimacy of political authority.

This ontological insecurity feeling is triggered by political, economic, and societal problems related to pandemics. Besides, it drew persons to anxiety and some psychological problems because of feelings of loneliness.

The feeling of being secure is related to the feeling of belonging to a particular place or community. So, this feeling may wear out by negatively effect of the loss of 'feeling at home" after any disaster.

In the Westphalian system, the state has been perceived as the best guardian of human security. Hence, when a state failed to protect its citizens from widespread disasters such a genocide, mass killing, ethnic cleansing, and pandemic this feeling of pathological insecurity triggers the questioning of the legality of the state or authority.

In Covid-19 pandemic, new regulations aimed at tackling down the pandemic are increasing at the expense of our freedoms. Therefore, the rise of illiberal democracy that has been witnessed for a while could increase even more. Therefore, it is a great human security risk that some limitations become permanent slyly while struggling with the pandemic.

Despite this negative effect, at the global level, the Covid-19 pandemic may increase the feeling of humanism instead of xenophobia as common disasters are getting humans close to each other and fostering feelings of altruism.

The other negative effects of the pandemic have been on international organizations. The World Health Organization has been at the center of criticism during the pandemic. Actually, some of these criticisms are related to high expectations about efficiency of the IGO owing to insufficient knowledge about the functionality of such as organizations.

Throughout the pandemic, there has been a widespread expectation that the World Health Organization should intervene directly and effectively to solve the problem.

In this regard the performance of the World Health Organization has been questioned and the organization is often found to be insufficient.

This criticism and expectation is not quite right because international organizations are not independent actors of the international area. Their authority, responsibility and mobility have been restricted by the consent of states according to treaties about their functionality. Based on these criticisms and the need, it may be said that the pandemic shows the necessity to change the classical approach to international organizations and improve their structural and functional roles.

The most salient effect of the Covid-19 pandemic in the short term has been on the economic security issue. The increasing attention to economic security as a special area in security studies is related to the broadening concept of security after the end of the Cold War.

While there is no consensus on the definition of economic security, it has been defined to include having adequate income level and assets, access to benefits such as paid leave and health insurance, and some control over job content and the opportunity to build a career.

Another definition includes "individual and collective rights (such as worker rights protected by law and the right to be represented by trade unions), the opportunity for income-earning activities, protection of income-earning work, working conditions that are safe and promote well-being, and the opportunity to gain and retain skills". So, the common area of economic security is related to individuals and their well-being and the macro- and micro-level economy.

In this frame, the most remarkable effect of pandemics on the economy has been related on the trade of developed countries because of the supply chain. In developing or underdeveloped countries, the economy and its reflection on the population has been limited relatively because of the relationship between the government and the people. Besides, refusing to be vaccinated in the context of rights and liberty causes more problems in the relationship between the state and its people in developed countries.

Obviously, in general, local and global economies have been negatively affected on the multidimensional side by the pandemic. Besides, it seems that the Covid-19 pandemic caused the security and economic issues to become more intertwined than ever before. And probably the effect of corona might create more permanent results on individuals and at the societal, state, and global level as never seen before. These events coincided with the beginning of a period when the world started to undergo a radical change globally ontologically. Probably, the result will be much more different than ever before.

References

Azuonwu, Obire and Erhabor, O. 2012, "HIV among military personnel in the Niger delta of Nigeria". *Journal of Community Health* Feb; 37(1), 25–31.

Barzilay, R., Moore, T.M., Greenberg, D.M. et al. 2020, "Resilience, COVID-19-related stress, anxiety and depression during the pandemic in a large population enriched for healthcare providers". *Translational Psychiatry* 10, 291.

Belamy, Alex J. 2008, *The Responsibilty to Protect, Security Studies: An Introduction*, (ed. Paul D. Williams), London: Routledge.

Buzan, Barry 2009, *The Evolution of International Security Studies*, Cambridge: Cambridge University Press.

Buzan, Barry, Waever, Ole and de Wille, Jaab 1998, *Security, A new Framework for Analysis*, Boulder, CO: Lynne Rienner Publishers.

CRS (Congressional Researche Services). 2019, "HIV/AIDS in the military", https://www.everycrsreport.com/files/2019-05-31_IF11238_0792b1f24de35529d62758322bceeb20fac93e9c.pdf, reached at 25.11.2021.

Elbe, Stefan 2002, "HIV/AIDS and the changing landscape of war in Africa." *International Security* 27(2), 159–77.

Elflein, John 2020, "Countries with the highest prevalence of HIV in 2000 and 2020", https://www.statista.com/statistics/270209/countries-with-the-highest-global-hiv-prevalence/, reached at 25.11.2021.

Farley, Josh 2021, "USS Theodore Roosevelt arrives in Bremerton for overhaul at the Puget sound naval shipyard", *Kitsap Sun*. https://www.kitsapsun.com/story/news/2021/07/22/uss-theodore-roosevelt-arrives-bremerton-overhaul-shipyard/8065615002/

Fidler, David P. 2020, "The World health organization and pandemic politics", *Think Global Health*.

Giddens, Antony 1991, *Modernity and Self-Identity*, Chambrige UK: Blackwel Publication.

Kasper, Matthew R., Geibe, Jesse R. et al. 2020, "An outbreak of Covid-19 on an aircraft carrier", *The New England Journal of Medicine* 17, 2417–26.

Kinnvall, Caterina and Jennifer, Mitzen 2018, "Ontological security and conflict: The dynamics of crisis and the constitution of community", *Journal of International Relations and Development*, 21(3). https://doi.org/10.1057/s41268-018-0161-1

Laruelle, Marlene 2021, "What the Covid-19 pandemic tells us about illiberalism", *Italian Institute for International Politics*. https://www.ispionline.it/en/pubblicazione/what-covid-19-pandemic-tells-us-about-illiberalism-31076

Lee, Jong-Wha and McKibbin, Warwick 2004, *Estimating the Global Economic Costs of SARS*. National Academy Press. https://www.ncbi.nlm.nih.gov/books/NBK92473/

McInnes, Colin 2008, *"Health", Security Studies: An Introduction*, (ed. Paul D. Williams), London: Routledge.

Nugroho, Ganjar. 2006, "Constructivism and International Relations", Global & Strategies, Th. II, No. 1, Abingdon/UK.

Pana-Cran, Rene, Ray, Tapas, Bushnell, Tim and Quay, Brian 2020, "Economic Security during the COVID-19 pandemic: A healthy work design and well-being perspective", https://blogs.cdc.gov/niosh-science-blog/2020/06/22/economic-security-covid-19/, reached at 28.11.2021.

Panchal, Nirmita, Kamal, Rabah and et al. 2021, "The implications of COVID-19 for mental health and substance use", https://www.kff.org/coronavirus-covid-19/issue-brief/the-implications-of-covid-19-for-mental-health-and-substance-use/, reached at 28.11.2021.

Ran, Barzilay, Moore, Tyler M., Greenberg, David M., DiDomenico, Grace E., Brown, Lily A., White, Lauren K., Gur, Ruben C., Gur, Raquel E. 2020, "Study finds signs of altruism in people's COVID-19", *Translational Psychiatry* 10(1). DOI: 10.1038/s41398-020-00982-4

Rosecrance, Richard and Thompson, Peter. 2003, "Trade, foreign investment and security", *Annual Review Political Science*, www.arjournnals.annualreviwe.org, reached at 16.01.2007.

Schmidt, Brian C. (2016), "The Primicy of National Security", Foreign Policy, (ed. Steve Smith, Amelia Hadfield, Tim Dune), Oxford University Press.

UNCTAD, 2020, "Impact of the COVID-19 pandemic on trade and development: Transitioning to a new normal", https://unctad.org/system/files/official-document/osg2020d1_en.pdf, reached at 26.11.2021.

WHO (World Health Organizations), 2020, " COVID-19 disrupting mental health services in most countries, WHO survey", https://www.who.int/news/item/05-10-2020-covid-19-disrupting-mental-health-services-in-most-countries-who-survey, reached at 23.11.2021.

3 Public Diplomacy, Nation Branding and Soft Power for Global Outreach

India in the 21st Century

Mitrajit Biswas

Introduction

The modern world is a world of information and counter-information. The importance of building up a brand or reputation for a country has taken a new way in the world of the 21st century. Expansion in the world from the perspective of history has happened through mercantilism, which were nothing but private ventures. They established themselves by advertising their intentions to the established kingdoms of parts of Asia and Africa and even Latin America. Once they were established through their public relations executives like Sir Thomas Roe in India and many others in different parts of the world, they began the next step of political expansion. History has taught us the importance of public outreach and this is what drives the public outreach initiatives even today. "The system of African countries as for example define the concept of how many tribes came together to form a country that has defined borders although debatable amidst the fragile citizenship notion" (Adejumobi, 2001). However, even in the modern times the idea of public relations is still very much there. This is where the world of today has moved into. The corporate entities and the colonial entities apart from the royalties that had dominated the public relations of human history have now evolved into a new system of political connections from the public relations angle. The chapter started on the note that it is a world of social media or new media. Information can be created and manipulated, and most importantly, communication can be powerful. It is a very important phase of modern human evolution. In the world of today the fight for public relations has moved global. The Covid-19 crisis was born amid the already crumbling, if not completely shattered, times of globalization.[1]

In the age of the emergence of a new world order and surely in the post-Covid-19 crisis, the emergence of a new world order and post-covid-19-crisis is no more a buzzword. The world dynamics have been shifting and so has the concept of public relations. First and foremost, public relations are sometimes demeaned as a propaganda tool. Well, that is a very ignorant term used, as public relations definitely has an aspect of sending out the message across but the important factor is outreach. Every country and especially their leadership have an important role in the world of today related to public outreach.

DOI: 10.4324/9781003354703-4

> Therefore, the world of today where the political vibrancy and also in the garb of that separatist movements have picked up necessitates a call that the supposed commonality is also not a perfect answer for the creation of the uniform nation which the European system tied to create as the very first project from statehoods.
>
> (Mouzelis, 1999)

This is where the modern public relations have also been evolving through the development of social media. The concept of soft power and the public outreach of countries has evolved through access of social media to a large and once marginalized section of communities, which also includes common citizens. The world today exists for the influence and the power grab that have always been there for the centuries of human history and its evolution. The idea of the modern information outreach is now more organized and led by the head of a state or the top directives as it used to be in earlier times with monarchies. Today, the political connections are more frequent and on the go. The advent of the digital media has created a society of information access all the time. It could be an overwhelming information epidemic, but these are the present times.

Focus of the Chapter

The world of the 21st century today definitely has polarizations, but there is also an equal subset of equations that need to be understood too. The public relations build-up of countries today is about the way the countries and their leadership progress in matters of how the countries should put out their structures of culture as well as political views. "However, the key to the solving of the immigration crisis lies in tracing the routes of the migrants and most importantly the source of trafficking" (Anderson, 2013). The advent of new media and its various uses have been slowly evolving over a period of time. Today, the use of Twitter is no longer limited to personal communication but has become an important tool – a tool which is used to send out hashtags, create global trends and most importantly, as related to the theme of the chapter, for public relations and political networking. The idea of the world of today is that every person irrespective of his or her personal stature can play a role in the way the world comes together. Public relations, as the word signifies, is the personal equation aspect of an individual and the way that personal equation can impact or influence. This is the way that the world of today is evolving over the idea of personal equations and how social media can influence them.

> However as mentioned the process of the battle to provide for the containment of new forms of illegal immigration in an increasing disparate world since 1990 the end of cold war has been the biggest development in human civilization.
>
> (Segal et al., 2010)

The next phase of building relationships and political networking today is about those personal equations. Apart from this, social media has also created a level playing field. Every country has an equally fair chance.

Today, social media and its accessibility is the most important aspect of how the public relations aspects of all countries tend to be. Most of the countries, apart from their foreign affairs departments, are now maintaining a separate social media channel. This includes the public diplomacy as well as the cultural channels. Having a social media channel is important for the world leaders and their country's foreign ministry as well as the information departments encompassing all the ministries. Tourism, public diplomacy and the cultural departments all play an important role in the world of social media and how the public outreach happens today. This is where the personal equation can help to build the brand of a country also through personal leadership and their charismatic influence. The following of some of the world's top social media actors and their public outreach cannot be denied. There may be critics of social media and the leaders or the ministries who are using it. "The use of digital medium is done to promote aid, charity and constructive development is done by nations" (Kunczik, M. 1997). However, social media has a huge outreach. Personal equations between leaders have been a key holing point for public outreach and political networking, which brings us to the context of the slow and steady increase in the use of social media by the Indian leadership. However, before that, the notion of the world's best diplomatic practices and soft power efforts also needs to be looked at from new social media. Today, the world dynamics have changed because of the new media dynamics.

Research Questions

The research questions here are not specifically based on hypothesis formulation.

1) Did nation brand change during the pandemic in terms of aid and welfare?
2) Is the idea of nation branding competitive and important in today's world?
3) What are the areas to look at for nation brand enhancement apart from conventional areas such as tourism?
4) Why is this an important time for the nation brand to be rebooted?

Conceptual Framework of Nation Branding in Terms of Marketing Theory

The goal of the research is to find out how important the use of digital media is for public diplomacy and marketing of "soft power". Soft power is a concept developed by Joseph Nye, Jr., which involves the use of resources which would compel the thought process to change in favour of the nation.

In the 21st century, the idea of the use of digital media is very important for the successful projection of a country's image and selling (Transformation of Diplomacy, 2010). In the sphere of the digital world, the information and the discourse in media, articles and newsletters would be a critical component for the country (Place branding and Public Diplomacy, 2008). There have been various components to measuring soft power as the concept is very malleable (Europe-Asia Studies, 2014). However, the most important component for this research work is the idea of digital media. There are already a lot of talks about the impact of public diplomacy and soft power projection. The understanding of the current attempt is to find out the ways in which the element of "strategy of digital content" is important for assumed positive nation branding via use of digital media. The work would involve an understanding of how important the application of digital media is in the context of soft power usage via foreign policy for branding of a nation. The whole idea revolved around constructing the image of a nation. However, the main objective would be to understand what would be the implications of media projection in the application of soft power strategy for nation branding. Soft power index, which is published on an annual basis, includes the component of culture and economics as two major sub-indices. The use of the concepts of digital media constructs needs to be deciphered. There the concept of digital media and its deciphered value would be important. Making the research more interactive and moving it away from the already done and dusted concepts of power projection with international relations context is new. The idea, however, is now to expand the work from the already constructed works. It is very surprising to find that work on soft power and foreign policy place too much focus on the policy aspect and at the level of how the government pushes it forward through strategic endeavours, investments and collaboration. This is where this research project which looks into the digital sphere and the promotion of public diplomacy through the digital sphere is important. "The gamut of tweets, videos, blogs and articles either through the government sources and non-government sources is an important aspect of the current foreign policy making of many countries" (Fan Y., 2007). Modern diplomacy and power projection is more towards softer aspects. "The digital sphere is the new front for message dissemination influencing people's opinion and perception" (SCHMIDT, 2008).

How the Chapter Can Contribute to the Gap of Literature

There is already a digital diplomacy index which talks about the impact of the digital sphere and the propagation of the message of various governments through public diplomacy discourse. However, the objective of the present research is to find out the ways in which the element of "strategy of digital content" is important in application of the soft power for nation branding through digital media. The research would involve the working of the digital media for assumed "positive influence". The areas of the application of soft power through public diplomacy implementation and practice should come with the course of the research work in the form of digital media discourse. "Soft power" is a malleable term and its exact use for diplomatic practice is still very much understudied, with most of the discourse focusing on the US, Canada, EU, etc. The present research looks to understand if digital media reinforces soft power or negates it by studying a sample of countries, the details of which are mentioned subsequently. Now the main purpose of any research work is to build on a theory or come up with a model which can back up the theory. Here for the research idea is more on the building up of a broad idea already floated by Professor Joseph Nye Jr. and find new measures through digital media. There have also been models and reports which have mentioned the measurement metrics. However, the motivation of the research is to look beyond the measurement and success of its applications. It is to find out how much the implementation of the tool is being looked at from the context of nation branding through global diplomacy affairs and where the importance of strategic use of digital media lies.

Leadership Required for Projection of Power

The idea of the world of social media is to break the barriers of communication. India's very early leadership started with Nehru, who was no doubt seen as a charming political leader. However, there was no social media and the political outreach of Nehru in India was based on personal contacts and the multilateral forums that were evolving over that time period. "The continent of Asia has had a rich history and had been at the forefront of the global cultural and political narratives for a very long time" (Bogardus, 1927). At time of decolonization, the way India made its steps forward was based on Nehru's choices. His personal choices were the ones that drove India's political networking and also its public outreach. Especially, the way India made its first steps towards the world through the nonaligned movement was definitely a method of outreach. It is in the same way that the personal equation of Nehru with Gamel Abdel Nasser and Marshal Tito, apart from Indonesia's Sukarno, formed the first vestiges of India's political networking. It was on India's first steps that her personal equations were built upon. This would have a ramification in the context of India itself, not to mention the world and its personal charismatic leaders who had always heralded the idea of new political networking. India got a newly appointed leader due to their sheer popularity in the public sphere.

The next phase of Indian outreach and the political networking era started under Nehru's daughter Indira Gandhi. She was the closest authoritarian leadership that India could get during the post-independence period. The demise of Nehru and the unfortunate yet mysterious death of Nehru's successor, Lal Bahadur Shastri, was definitely a blow to the nascent Indian nation. However, the tough time called for a tough leader and there came Indira Gandhi. The time just after the wars with Pakistan and China in the decade of the 60s had not only drained India out but was also a time of vulnerability. India was also in the midst of the cold war and the US support extended to Pakistan in terms of weapons and political support was also a major issue to India. Moreover, India also did not have the self-sufficiency in terms of the economic and financial output needed. This was the time when the idea of strong leadership and change of India's stance was needed. It was the time for the emergence of Indira Gandhi, who brought India glory by assertively defeating Pakistan and creating a new nation in the form of Bangladesh. The success of the first industrialization efforts as well as the strong personality of Indira Gandhi brought India a new form of public outreach. Her political networking impact was different but nevertheless a fresh breath of rejuvenation that India needed at that moment. India's new regional position was established thereafter.

Aspect of India's Power Projection

Next in line would be Atal Behari Vajpayee, a man who was more grounded in his ideas for India and his cultural notions. He had survived the pressures of the political instability that had surrounded Indian politics for a long time, especially in the 90s. At the onset of the new millennia Vajpayee was a man who had strong ideas and wanted India to take advantage of the new millennia. India's discrete nuclear test and the murky times India got embroiled in after that were determinedly and strongly handled by the leadership of Atal Behari Vajpayee. His outreach was also influential and the outreach to India's new age aspirations especially with the US post the second nuclear test was important. It is true that the relationship was taken forward by Dr. Manmohan Singh, who closed the India–US nuclear fuel deal. However, the foundations of the next step in building alliances with the US were built on the dreams of Atal Behari Vajpayee's dynamic leadership. It was also the first step in India and its leadership slowly using the internet space, although there was no social media presence then. The rise in the jump of Indian science, research and development was slowly making way in internet-based news. Nevertheless, India's future lies in moving forward. It was possible due to the personal leadership efforts of Atal Behari Vajpayee, who saw the need for the creation of a new India.

> The battle for power and the rising of the feeling of injustice or inequality fuels the failed state where the bonding of the citizenship is an important aspect for how much bonding one feels through the sacred connection of the state and vice versa.
>
> (Chandhoke, 2003)

Then came Narendra Modi, a man whose public outreach campaign had reached a sense of new dynamics. The dynamics of social media had evolved by his time and he was in charge of a country that wanted a change, a change into an authoritarian strong state, and the way that Modi has carried it forward has been based on his personal equation and most importantly his personal charisma and guile in using social media. It is true that irrespective of the dismal ranking of India in these sectors and the much-fancied ranking of many so-called "advanced economies" of the West, every economy has faltered terribly in this pandemic. "This comes in the form of the most important aspect of citizenship" (Ehrkamp & Leitner, 2009). The way of the Indian leadership changed with the dynamics of Modi coming in power in India, and it would probably not even be an exaggeration to say that he (Modi)fied India. The Western leaders from the US to European Union and even in Australia and Canada for the first time saw an Indian leader who was using his personal charm and the expertise of India to promote his nation. Not only that, but the quest to build a personal leadership has reached a new level and still continues to do. Modi has become one of the most followed world leaders and has been successful in starting the trend of Yoga Day and "Selfie with Daughter", banking on the expertise of India's soft power. This is where Modi has made his mark as a leader and created a new chapter of India's public outreach and external relationship building. Not only that, but the usage of social media to usher in a new image of India has also been done successfully under him through his new vigorous approach.

Discussion on the aspect of global power in terms of nation branding

Today, the world of public relations is intense and a very dynamic one. There is no denying the fact that social media today has a very important role in the top-notch global politics. "The concept of using media is increasingly important in the modern world of 21st century with increasing use of media in diplomacy" (Gallup, 2007). Therefore, the world of social media and foreign policy go hand in hand today. Never has there been a more important time for the dynamics of world politics and identity of every kind of political ideology. In a world fragmented as this new media and its constant churning of information as well messages, political messaging has taken a new order – an order which challenges the old system and strives to create a new one. India today has one of the most active social media presence through a lot networks, but the most important is the personal equation of the leadership. The concept of using media is increasingly important in the modern world of the 21st century with increasing use of media in diplomacy. Therefore, the idea is to understand the concept from the international relations perspective related to soft power, bringing it to the level of foreign policy projection to see how digital media is being used strategically under the purview of strategic communication and soft power. Looking to take the concept of soft power, which is a very malleable term, and use it mostly from the context of foreign policy and international relations where most of the work has been done in the area of soft power where new work is emerging in the form of nation branding and public diplomacy both overlapping each other. "The idea of the citizenship in itself is a very privileged concept albeit with many flaws depending on the country and it is not uniform" (Isin, 2008).

How the evolving understanding of soft power can be used in a new context such as nation branding and through digital media will add to a very new understanding with the added context of digital media. "The content is the king" is already being looked at from the management perspective; however, now it is time to look at it from the perspective of information, foreign policy usage and how to utilize the overall understanding for the evolution of nationalist policy at an evolving stage of today's world. The use of tourism, movies and other pop culture is also an important platform for digital usage related to foreign policy. "This brings to the fore the important context of how the migration in European continent had been shaped up" (Geddes & Scholten, 2016). Apart from that, the conventional use of digital medium for aid, charity and constructive development done by countries is also promoted. Public should get an idea on how to use digital platforms.

Constructs of Power and Nationalism

Work on the nationalist attitude is already being done through tourism campaigns and promotional advertisements, but the ideology of soft power and the strategic use of it related to policy-making would be a new addition to the body of knowledge. Also, as mentioned earlier, the "strategic" aspect and the models from "strategic management" and aligning it to nation branding through digital media would be a very new addition. There have been works based on the idea of soft power from the power projection and core foreign policy objectives, and YouTube as the source of foreign policy selling through public diplomacy. The whole new idea of putting diplomacy in the lines of digital marketing is an exciting area to look forward to. Soft power is a concept developed by Joseph Nye which involves the use of resources which would compel the thought process to change in favour of the nation. In the 21st century with fragile societies and the rising conflict scenarios the idea of the utilization of the soft power is very important for the successful projection of a country's image and selling. In the sphere of the public diplomacy, the information and the discourse via media, articles, newsletters are attempting to be a critical component for the country. "This is where the idea of the citizenship is important to understand apart from differentiating from naturalization and the immigration process" (Baubock & Cinar, 1994). There have been various components of measuring soft power, but they are very malleable in nature. However, the most important component for this research work is to focus on the application of digital media for nation branding. There is already a digital diplomacy index which talks about the impact of the digital sphere and the propagation of the message of various governments through public diplomacy discourse. However, now the present objective of the research is to find out the ways in which the element of "strategy of digital content" is important in the application of the soft power for nation branding through digital media. The research would involve the working of the digital media for assumed "positive influence". "Now the boundary of the soft power-public diplomacy which is known by the application of the information and the communication flow has been used in many diplomacy and negotiation channels" (Laroche et al., 2005). The areas of the application of soft power through public diplomacy implementation and practice should come with the course of the research work in the form of digital media discourse. Soft power is a malleable term and its exact use for diplomatic practice is still very much understudied, with most of the discourse lying around the US, Canada, the EU, etc. Today, public relation is in sync with digital media. The chapter works more on the building up of a broad idea already floated by Professor Joseph Nye and finding new measures through digital media. "Even the onset of human civilizational migration had started from the very idea of getting access to resources which were lacking in the place from where the migration started" (McNeill, 1984). There have also been models and reports which have mentioned the measurement metrics. It is to find out how much implementation of the tool is being looked at from the context of nation branding through the global diplomacy affairs and where the importance of strategic use of digital media lies. The point of implementing soft power (persuasion through money, culture and technology, etc.) perception and how it can be "strategically" used through digital media is the core.

> Usage of media channels such as Aljazeera from Qatar, DW from Germany, CNN, BBC and France 24 are prime examples of media diplomacy and information hegemony (assumed). This is where the very beginning of the essay points out that the creation of nation and nations states as per the European system.
>
> (Habermas, 1998)

Aspects of Global Power Projection and Understanding the Approach of India

The ultimate question would be to ask to a broad-based question, something like, "Whether digital media is effective for soft power projection and projecting nationalism through public diplomacy at all?" The emergence of new forms of digital media makes it a very interesting time to delve into the application of soft power public diplomacy practices. It must be specifically understood that the idea needs to be looked at from certain perspectives. Now the boundary of the soft power-public diplomacy, which is known by the application of information and communication flow, has been used in many diplomacy and negotiation channels. The boundaries of the soft power and their exact theory building for governance is where the various undefined boundaries of the soft power and use of public diplomacy can be synchronized to answer the question that the research work has set out for. The power advantage and the utilization for it to influence the thought process would bring out the possible factors for implementation of the tool. Soft power implementation looking from the context of the new and the old power structures such as the Union of India and the European Union could also be looked at as an example of the soft power approach. The reason for choosing these two geographic regions for research can have certain implications. First and foremost, the US is already considered a power, both in terms of hard and soft power. The concept which is a mix of the two is now termed as "smart power". However, the European Union, after the demise of Imperial Power, has been quite proactive in creating a new image of itself towards the postcolonial nations. Also, the EU in itself has come up as a hybrid model of being a soft power conclave focusing on the cooperation and development aspect of sovereign European nation states, especially after the crisis of the Second World War. The Union of India is a post-colonial nation but unique in its construction as a lot of different ethnicities and beliefs, languages, practices came together much like European Union as a country. This is because both of them have similar structures in terms of their diversity, structure of cooperative federalism and the most important aspect of stable democracy despite its possible flaws.

Theoretical Approach to the Chapter: An Introduction to Certain Variables to Understand the Concept of Indian Nation Brand over the Period of Time

The idea of this chapter has been based on the understanding derived from the literature review of the construct of India and its way of branding through the variables of tourism and culture as well as the way India has been envisioned in the times before the pandemic. The idea of the chapter has been to understand how India has been envisioned as a country and how the idea of the brand has been evolving in the past few years. "India has been evolving as a new nation since its independence and the idea of sustainable branding of India as a new nation brand entity is critical to understand especially in the age of nation branding" (Bosworth and Collins, 2008). The chapter looks to collect the ideas of how the branding of India has been looked at and what are the possible challenges for the branding exercise. The chapter has some limitations; although it is a literature review, the information has been collected from the variables. However, it tries to look at the adaptation of the branding of India over a period of time. "India as a nation that has evolved over the period of civilization changes and the historical evolution which also includes a new way of looking at the construct of India as a nation" (Bose and Jalal, 2009). The review tries to bring in various perspective to understanding the making of India from a nation-state perspective. This is exactly where the chapter tries to bring in the idea of the country as a brand and how it is evolving over a period of time. It tries to bring in multiple aspects from already published papers and does not try to build a theory as there are several theories which are already published, including the nation branding theories. The chapter just tries to attempt to take it forward and move it in the context of understanding the nation branding from the review of literature which will connect to the idea of sustainable branding over a period of time. This is where the idea of the chapter has been mainly constructed and how it has been finally shaped through the variables of the economic liberalization, tourism, social stratification, etc. These are some of the variables which have been taken into consideration in the chapter.

- ➢ Introduction to the concept of soft power and public diplomacy
- ➢ How the idea of soft power is evolving in the modern age of digital media

There were some assumptions set out for the proposed research work, some of which are:

1. Digital diplomacy is the new battlefront for asserting a country's soft power.
2. Nation branding and the digital medium are effective for bringing a balance between the smaller and the bigger nations in terms of marketing and projecting a country image.
3. A positive digital content actually helps to repair or complement the brand image of certain countries.
4. It is possible for the digital media diplomacy for soft power projection to transcend into offline spaces in terms of nation branding and the country of origin affects in a positive way.

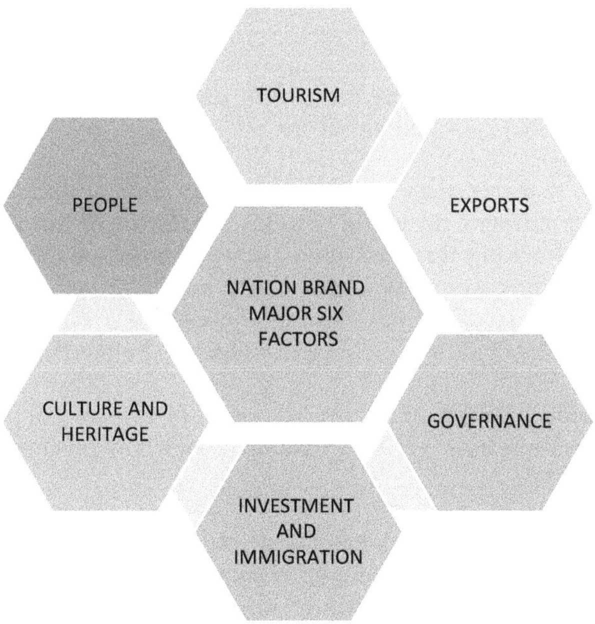

The above figure is a representation of Simon Anholt model which is used in real-life nation branding consultancies and also used for the hypotheses stated in the chapter.

Literature Review on the Aspect of the Nation Branding Evolution of India

"Now the boundaries of the soft power-public diplomacy which is known by the application of the information and the communication flow has been used in many diplomacy and negotiation channels" (Laroche et al., 2005).

> The freedom in the context of nations first and foremost could be difficult to explain as nation contain determining the more historical concept of the creation of the political boundaries and most of that who stays inside and outside the political boundaries.
>
> (Habermas, 1998)

The Covid-19 crisis was born in the already crumbling, if not completely shattered, times of globalization.[1] "The continent of Asia has had a rich history and had been at the forefront of the global cultural and political narratives for a very long time" (Khodabakhshi, 2011).

> If we look back at the history of global human civilization then be it the old civilization of *Indus, Mesopotamian, Sumerian, Chinese and even Egyptian civilization* considering Egypt an extension of the cultural and nation branding would be clear that it has been an important aspect of the global process of nation branding.
>
> (Fan, 2007, emphasis added)

The idea of nations has been born from the concept of the Westphalia Treaty that was incorporated in Europe.

> However, that treaty itself is a problem in terms of understanding the concept of nation in the world of today, the notion of Eurocentric world has moved a long time past and the emergence of the post-colonial countries albeit some of them least, moderate or very successful respectively.
>
> (Place Branding & Public Diplomacy, 2011)

"India as nation brand in the form of a country founded on principles of unique constitution however in a country which has diverse complexity" (Fernandes, 2004).

> The politics of India which has a very important connection in terms of the nation brand is still suffering from caste divide which is nevertheless a socio-economic phenomenon of so many years and would probably take a lot of time in aligning the internal policies of the domestic oriented process where the politics and the battle of power is related to development.
>
> (Mooij, 1998)

> The idea of skills development, usage of artificial intelligence as well as the development of the economic parameters in India is more of a policy-oriented politics in India. It may be the time to understand that mere rhetoric of the government or the figure head will not turn out to be that great for India.
>
> (Brass, 2004)

"Poverty in India has been there from centuries from a materialistic concept but India's political economy now has a hybrid form of take and emerging a stronger nation" (Varshney, 2000). "The system of British Raj colonial times has changed more into an Oriental-Occidental Hybridisation for India and in its system of political economy" (Tilak, 2007). "India despite remaining relatively calm after having huge disparity of income is really a surprise probably because of the fact that a democratic safety valve is still considered crucial" (Demetriades and Luintel, 1996). "India has very low GDP spent on Education and Health even amongst its BRICS peers which is a shame despite having shown improvements in certain health indicators but still lagging behind in many others areas of health" (Bosworth and Collins, 2008). "The idea of politics in India has a direct linkage to the question of marginalisation and the hierarchical power structures in India still dominating the political machinery" (Bose and Jalal, 2009). "Off late it is true that the nexus of politics and bureaucracy in India which is the most potent power structure in India seems to be the central focal point of the politics in India" (Jenkins, Kennedy, and Mukhopadhyay, 2011). "The mission of 70 years plus of branding India has been largely derived from the cacophony of Indian politics" (Mukerjee, 2007).

Research Design Methodology

Now on to the measuring part of the research objective it was based on certain keywords such as "Indian Diversity", "Culture of India", "Indian Tourism", "Indian Welfare State", "Indian Military Power", "Economic Growth of India", "India the Future Power", etc., for the content analysis in the form of comments on YouTube, Instagram, Quora and Facebook, which acted as the prime digital medium for a secondary data point, followed by focus group discussion of five people and also responses received from 18 people based on 22 questionnaire survey as a primary data point. Here it may be noted that the focus group discussion transcript is not being provided in full detail due to it lengthy nature. Apart from the content analysis, based on the digital platforms and pages and channels related to "Indian Foreign Policy", "Nation Brand Marketing", "Cultural Diplomacy", etc., another aspect of the data was collected from the vernacular newspapers covering Indian policy in terms of nation branding from the time period of June 2020 to November 2020. This included newspapers such as *AnandaBazar Patrika* and *Bartaman*, published in Bengali from Kolkata accessed from the e-paper version. The idea was to collect news based on articles related to India nation brand for the collection of data and the analysis of the content from the newspapers. Also, national newspaper portals such *The Hindu*, *Times of India*, and *Indian Express*, apart from think tank articles on Indian nation brand, were accessed from Vivekananda International Foundation, Institute for Defence Studies and Analysis, Gateway Council for Foreign Affairs and Strategic Foresight. In total, a collection of approximately 45-plus articles were studied related to the search. The questionnaire survey which was collected was added at the last minute, which is why only 18 people responded in the age group of 21–35. The use of mixed research methods in terms of the data collection was done as a last moment adjustment for the data to be more inclusive. The combination of the two should help understand the nation brand and the use of digital medium for that in terms of power projection. Sample biasedness could be an issue to consider. Now the idea for the proposed research work was to draw from the idea of digital media, especially in matters of nation branding. The harder conflicts from the aspects of war, politics and terrorism have been avoided. Softer aspects of power, which include the terms mentioned above, have been used. Now the question had been to understand and inspect the question of public diplomacy through digital media and how are they received. The perception of the people regarding the message they get or perceive in digital media will be the new addition. The codes had been divided into three broader headings. The content selectively put into the software had generated a few keywords in the form of a word cloud. Along with the repetition of words, the focus group discussion as well as questionnaire-based responses were recorded for the generation of three primary sections of the codes.

Codes have been added below manually from the software analysis of newspaper content and internet archived material on NVIVO trial version and divided as per sentiment analysis.

Positive Neutral Negative

- Nation Branding of India Indian and neighbours Media coverage of India
- India's Soft Power India in digital media Corruption perception
- International outreach Indian marketing of Tourism Religious dogmatism
- Economic Power Caste Divide
- Military Policy

Analysis Section of the Data

The use of discourse analysis is generally a systemic approach of identifying specific characteristics in the form of data which is qualitative. However, in the approach taken here the discourse analysis method had been used to identify certain themes in the matter of the response and the emotion attached with them. Generally, qualitive techniques in the form of content analysis, discourse analysis or thematic analysis take a lot of time. In qualitative approach, as already mentioned, the initial approach of coding, which is a time-taking process, requires several cycles of coding. That also includes the data to be cleaned based on certain filtering parameters. The chapter had earlier tried to approach the research design based on discourse analysis from the digital platforms as mentioned. However, the 45-plus articles or community-based posts which had been collected from the newspapers and the digital media channels were based on the aspect of covering the keywords as mentioned earlier and analysing them over a period of two months. As mentioned, the dimension of the coding process used in NVIVO was lagging in some aspects in terms of multiple coding cycles using more filters. However, the process of second cycle coding was done and to supplement the data reliability a focus group discussion of five people was conducted. The sample biasedness definitely could be considered as a major flaw as responses from the 18 known people based on a 22-question survey was also done. The sample size is low because the design had been adjusted at the last moment in terms of the methodology to include the mixed method approach. Also, the percentage of responses in terms of the positive codes were generated from revisiting the 187 responses from the 45-plus qualitative content in the form of comments, articles and community posts which had been generated. Then the broader divisions were done based on the keywords from the content. The elements of "subjective judgement" based on the interpretation related to the comments were used for broader classification of themes from the codes generated.

Therefore, now the defining boundaries as mentioned earlier was the task which show what it means for public outreach in the form of digital media. The keywords were selected based on the preliminary repetition in online search engines. *This was done based on the actual approaches of Google search of the most popular keywords entered in terms of soft power and using content in the digital media to achieve nation branding.* That was done to allow for the appropriate contribution related to understanding the content on how soft power application can happen over a period of time for "*effective*" use in nation branding, foreign policy and allied disciplines. However, there were some media, such as movies, documentaries, etc., which were excluded. Instead, as already mentioned Facebook posts AND YouTube channels of global news media were used in the search. However, as Marshall McLuhan said that the "world is now a global village" and "medium is the message"; therefore, the onset of the digital medium which transcends boundaries despite still having a digital divide was an aspect for the focus group discussion and the questionnaire was a supplementary aspect to find out the context of information diplomacy. The chapter tries to bring out the aspects of digital or new media in understanding the way we seem to be comfortable with in our perception of nation brand. However, the ever-increasing context of social media is what has transformed the public outreach of the older times into a new venture. *Move over entities and nations as it is back to the individualistic connection is what the questionnaire has been able to capture, which in turn collectively creates a halo effect.* Therefore, the world of today which has once again come a full circle from being a deglobalized world to a slowly emerging interconnected world has found most of the positive responses from the 45 plus articles in the form of keywords related to "attractive economy", "growth opportunities" as well as "infrastructure development" apart from the other keywords that were studied. The seven responses revealed that the branding of the nation holds more importance than public diplomacy. Then as understood from the focus group discussion the aspect of media biasedness operating from understanding specific country brand image is mostly already inherent in the way the nation brand was perceived by the respondents.

Discussion on Understanding Political Landscapes and Reforms for Sustainable Branding of India in Terms of Nation Branding

"The idea of politics in India has a direct linkage to the question of marginalisation and the hierarchical power structures in India still dominating the political machinery" (Bose and Jalal, 2009). "The nation brand of India is based on the nexus of politics and bureaucracy in India which is the most potent power structure in India seems to be the central focal point of the politics in India" (Jenkins, Kennedy, and Mukhopadhyay, 2011). India is an idea which has several political points with the dynamics of secularism not being compatible with the main reality where India's historical traditions have been built over a period for two millennia. "It is indeed true that India now has been portraying an image of a country as per western traditions which has been imposed and adopted for last 70 years" (Bhandari, 2020). "The idea of India has evolved and so has its politics over a period. However, the basic tenets of the politics have been functioning around regionalism as well as the caste and the religion" (Brass, 2004). The latest of such have just metamorphized in the form of NRC (National Registry of Citizens) away from the age-old politics of Ayodhya or Muslim sectarianism. Not to mention the marginalized-turned-violent revolt of the Naxals in the red belt of India stretching across the country as well as movements of secession politics on a larger canvas driving the politics of India. "The mission of 70 years plus of branding India has been largely derived from the cacophony of Indian politics" (Mukerjee, 2007). "It's the kaleidoscope of Indian politics that determines the approach of how India needs to look itself from the sense of supposed democratic politics" (Bhandari, 2020). It must be specifically understood that the idea needs to be looked from certain perspectives. "Now the boundary of the soft power-public diplomacy which is known by the application of the information and the communication flow has been used in many diplomacy and negotiation channels" (Laroche et al. 2005). "A growth in India over the last 70 years despite the constitutional welfare and the idea of poverty politics in India has still not managed to hit at the core of chronic poverty" (Kapur and Nangia, 2015).

> It does not mean that India did not pull people out of poverty, but those people are meagre in numbers and also form the chunk of the much-hyped India 'typical middle class' segment and not the high-end people including upper middle class.
>
> (Chopra, 2014)

"It's true that Indian politics has been constituted based on democracy but the permeation of politics in India derives itself from the structures of caste, religion. The power and politics in India also drive the idea of India" (Nandy, 1989).

Analysis of Finding and Discussion

The core idea for the research had been to understand what is the context of soft power through media and whether its application can be done in perspectives of foreign policy and power projection. As already given in the analysis section, the idea of the chapter had been to look into the nation branding space for use in diplomacy and how it is evolving through information sharing. Most of the data that had come out in the form of the questionnaire-based survey was used to understand the perception in the form of the data which had been earlier marked in the three headings of positive, neutral and negative. The study used already established data. The data was collected through first person responses. This included the response from the questionnaire survey as well. Nevertheless, the think tanks, experts and the media discourses which have been added here would have also been important for the data analysis based on certain codes from a broader section which had been later divided into certain themes.

These themes based on a widely different and diverse set of keywords, some of which have been mentioned earlier, were devised keeping in point with the core research objective, although being focused on the digital media spectrum the data collection option was kept on new media platforms. The use of information, especially through new media techniques in the form of tweets, official documentaries, videos, parallel news items and dedicated social media channels of foreign policy departments, were the most important data point sources for the study. The research objective was to bring forward how the policy of soft power can be used for the nation branding. The point of implementing soft power (persuasion through money, culture and technology, etc.) perception and how it can be "strategically" used through digital media was studied in the form of content based on the keywords sourced from YouTube channels based on news reports. YouTube media channels such as Aljazeera from Qatar, DW from Germany, CNN, BBC and France 24 are prime examples of media diplomacy and information hegemony (assumed). The question in this chapter had been to understand how India had been covered earlier and also how the policy of the Indian nation has also evolved towards it. The emergence of new forms of digital media makes it a very interesting time to delve into the application of soft power-public diplomacy practices. It must be specifically understood that the idea needed to be looked from certain perspectives for which the ideation of the discourse analysis based on the content related to the keywords were done. Now the boundaries of the soft power–public diplomacy, which is known by the application of the information and the communication flow, have been used in many diplomacy and negotiation channels. The question is "understanding nation branding in terms of positivity". The power advantage of the nations and the certain positive aspects utilization for it to influence the thought process were captured initially with the articles that were put in the NVIVO software for the initial coding. Soft power implementation has been studied looking from the context of the new and the old power structures such as the Union of India and the European Union where the latter had been more covered in terms of articles related to the positive aspects of tourism, nation branding as well as the "softer aspects of the power". The observation from the content studied along with the responses captured through the questionnaire and the focus group discussion was attempted to fill in the gap on the idea of nation brand of India although there is a possibility of response bias from Indians as respondents from abroad were not there. There is, however, an extension on the concept related to understanding the nation brand of India beyond tourism into other areas, as, for example, the European Union after the demise of the Imperial Power has been quite proactive in creating a new image of itself towards the postcolonial nations as an example of a region in terms of its respective nation states and collectively as well. Also, the EU in itself has come up as a hybrid model of being a soft power conclave focusing on the cooperation and development aspect of sovereign European nation states, especially after the crisis of the two world wars emerging from there. The Union of India is a post-colonial nation but unique in its construction as a lot of different ethnicities and beliefs, languages, practices came together much like the European Union as a country and that is how the nation brand of India has been found in terms of the literature review as well as the data findings. This is because both of them have similar structures in terms of their diversity, structure of cooperative federalism and the most important aspect of having a stable democracy despite possible flaws in capturing the responses related to nation brand of India.

Conclusions and Where the Future Work on This Topic Can Look Into

The research objective was to bring forward how the policy of soft power can be used for nation branding. The point of implementing soft power (persuasion through money, culture, technology, etc.) perception and how it can be "strategically" used through digital media was the core idea. Usage of media channels such as Aljazeera from Qatar, DW from Germany, CNN,

BBC and France 24 are prime examples of media diplomacy and information hegemony (assumed) in terms of new-age nation branding and the softer power aspects of the industrially advanced nations. The main question had been to limit the scope of the research to a broader understanding such as whether *digital media is effective for soft power projection and projecting nationalism through public diplomacy at all.* The emergence of new forms of digital media makes it a very interesting time to delve into the application of soft power–public diplomacy practices. It must be specifically understood that the idea can be extended from quite a lot of different perspectives.

> Now the boundaries of the soft power-public diplomacy which is known by the application of the information and the communication flow has been used in many diplomacy and negotiation channels as already mentioned however the aspect of the importance of this diplomacy in terms of nation brand is now being studied.
>
> (Yitzhak C, 2010)

The chapter tried to understand the response of the boundaries of soft power and the use of public diplomacy. The theory building aspect still needs to come up with a broader sample so that the responses can be synchronized in a better manner for answering the question that the chapter had originally set out with. The power advantage and the utilization of the nation brand could be done in terms of future research. Soft power implementation looking from the context of the new and the old power structures such as the Union of India and the European Union could also be attempted, although there is a possibility of response bias from Indians. Two geographic locations were selected due to one common phenomenon, i.e. second world war. Similar to the European Union as a country, many various ethnicities, religious beliefs, languages, and cultural practises came together to form the Union of India, a post-colonial entity that is unique in its construction. This is due to the fact that both of them share comparable structures with regard to their variety, cooperative federalism, and the most crucial component of stable democracy despite its potential shortcomings. Therefore, now the defining boundaries as mentioned earlier could be looked into for future research work. That will allow for proper contribution towards building knowledge as to how soft power application can happen over a period of time for "*effective*" use in nation branding, foreign policy and allied disciplines. The two different unions from two different geographic regions would make an interesting study in terms of the comparative analysis of their soft power application and how are they perceived through digital media. That could be in the form of movies, global news channels, documentaries, Facebook posts, meme, etc. This could build a way forward for theory building, which is limited in this chapter, on what exactly the limitation of public diplomacy and soft power application are and what exactly the role of digital media is in nation branding and the image build-up through digital diplomacy and soft power projection. Future research can look into comparative study between India and European Union for public diplomacy to help understand the dynamics of digital media usage and its relationship with nation branding.

Note

1 (Steven A. Altman, 2020) "Will Covid19 have a lasting impact on globalization?

References

Adejumobi S. (2001). Citizenship, rights and the problem of conflicts and civil wars in Africa, *Human Rights*, 23, 148.

Anderson, B. (2013). *Us and them?: The dangerous politics of immigration control*. OUP Oxford.

Baubock, R. and Cinar, D. (1994)). *West European politics*, Taylor and Francis.

Bhandari, B. Welfare schemes need tweaks to accommodate Covid 19 impact (Accessed from Business Line, 02/04/2020).

Bogardus, E. (1927). *Immigration and race attitudes*, New York: DC Heath Publication.

Bose, S. and Jalal, A. (2009). *Nationalism, democracy and development*, New Delhi: Oxford Univ. Press.

Bosworth, B. and Collins, S. (2008). Accounting for growth: Comparing China and India, *Journal of Economic Perspectives*, 22(1), 45–66.

Brass, P. (2004). Elite interests, popular passions, and social power in the language politics of India, *Ethnic and Racial Studies*, 27(3), 353–375.

Chandhoke, N. (2003). Governance and the pluralisation of the state: implications for democratic citizenship. *Economic and Political Weekly*, 2957–2968.

Chopra, D. (2014). *Development and welfare policy in South Asia*, London: Routledge.

Demetriades, P. and Luintel, K. (1996). Financial development, economic growth and banking sector controls: Evidence from India, *The Economic Journal*, 106(435), 359.

Fan, Yang (2007). Soft power: Power of attraction or confusion? *Place Branding and Public Diplomacy*, 4(2), 147–158.

Fernandes, L. (2004). The politics of forgetting: class politics, state power and the restructuring of urban space in India, *Urban Studies*, 41(12), 2415–2430.

Gallup. (2007). Perceptions of foreign countries. Acessed from gallup.com/poll/1624/Perceptions-Foreign-Countries.aspx

Geddes, A., and Scholten, P. (2016). *The politics of migration and immigration in Europe*. Sage. LONDON.

Habermas, J. (1998). Public Culture issue 10 (397–496), Accessed from pdf.semantischolar.org on 22nd November, 2020.

Isin, Engin (2008). *Theorizing acts of citizenship*, London, New York: Palgrave Macmillan.

Jenkins, R., Kennedy, L., and Mukhopadhyay, P. (2011). *Power, policy, and protest*, Oxford: Oxford University Press.

Kapur, D. and Nangia, P. (2015). Social protection in India: A welfare state sans public goods? *India Review*, 14, 73–90.

Khodabakhshi, A. (2011). Relationship between GDP and human development indices in India, SSRN Electronic Journal. https://dx.doi.org/10.2139/ssrn.1867887

Kunczik, M. (1997). *Images of nations and international public relations*, Mahwah, NJ: Lawrence Erlbaum Associates.

Laroche, M., Papadopoulos, N., and Mourali, M. (2005). The influence of country image structure on consumer evaluation of foreign products, *International Marketing Review*, 22, 96–115.

Mooij, J. (1998). Food policy and politics: The political economy of the public distribution system in India, *The Journal of Peasant Studies*, 25(2), 77–101.

Mukerjee, R. (2007). *India's economic transition*, New Delhi: Oxford University Press.

Nandy, A. (1989). The political culture of the Indian state. *Daedalus*, 1–26.

Mouzelis, Nicos (1999). Modernity: A non-European conceptualization, *The British Journal of Sociology*, 50(1), 141–159, Accessed from Wiley Online Library on 22nd April, 2020.

Leight, Naomi, Walton, Sherine Badawi, Ananian, Taleen, Cruz-Enriquez, Marissa and Jarwaharlal, Katherina (2011). Quarterly –Trends in public diplomacy: January, February and March, *Place Branding and Public Diplomacy*, [online] 7(2), 136–149.

Saari, Sinikukka (2014). Russia's Post-Orange Revolution Strategies to Increase its Influence in Former Soviet Republics: Public Diplomacy, *Europe-Asia studies*, [online] 66(1), 50–66.

SCHMIDT (2008). China's soft power diplomacy in southeast asia, *The Copenhagen Journal of Asian Studies*, [online] 26, 22–46.

Segal, U. A., Mayadas, N. S., Elliott, D., and Mayadas, N. (2010). The immigration process. *Immigration Worldwide: Policies, Practices, and Trends*, 3–16.

Hall, Ian (2010). The transformation of diplomacy: mysteries, insurgencies and public relations, *International Affairs*, [online] 86(1), 247–256.

Graham, Sarah Ellen (2008). US public diplomacy in the Asia Pacific: Opportunities and challenges in a time of transition, *Place Branding and Public Diplomacy*, [online] 4(4), 336–356.

Varshney, A. (2000). Is India becoming more democratic? *The Journal of Asian Studies*, 59(1), 3–25.

McNeill, William H. (1984). *Human migration in historical perspective*, *Population and Development Review*, 10, 1–18,

Yitzhak C. (2010). East and West in Jewish nationalism: Conflicting types in the Zionist vision? *Nations and Nationalism*, 16(2), 201–209, Accessed from Wiley Online publications.

4 India–China Bilateral Relations

From Nehru Regime to Modi Era

Vishal Singh Bhadauriya

Introduction

India and China have played an essential role in the Asian playground and have unknowingly shared borders since the advent of time. Both the countries were divided by the soaring Himalayan Mountain ranges and were the two major centers of the Asian civilization. Irrespective of the beginning, these two countries became the center of great attraction over time due to their cultural practices and the shared 'Silk Route', which was the prominent factor behind the evolution of both civilizations. In the 6th century CE, Buddhism went to China from India and flourished there. Buddhism enriched the development of bilateral relations in both countries. The role played by Tibet in the transmission of Buddhist philosophy was also very important, particularly in the 13th and 14th centuries.[1] In the later period, scholarly exchanges between both nations fortified their bilateral relationship even further. In the medieval period, there were fewer popular records of exchanges between the nations. In the colonial period, China became a huge market for the British to sell the opium produced in India. Also, during the First War of Independence against the Company, and in the Chinese Taiping Uprising, Indian soldiers and Chinese revolutionaries cooperated in fighting both the Company and the last Manchu-led ruler of the Qing Dynasty in a shared cause for the first time to oust foreign rule from the country.[2] Both countries underwent a significant change after World War II, and there were attempts to rekindle those lost ties on the grounds of ancient bonds shared between both nations.

Methodology and Literature Review

A qualitative methodology has been used in drafting this chapter. I have used the descriptive method with critical analysis of historical facts. Writings of a renowned person of their respective fields such as historians, international experts, and Sinologists have been widely used as a reference.

Old Bilateral Relations

While discussing India's neighborhood, Sir Girija Shankar Bajpai, the first Minister of External Affairs, articulated this. He spoke of the landmasses

DOI: 10.4324/9781003354703-5

between the Hindukush and the Arakan, but he was much more expansive when he spoke of the oceans and stated that "India's neighborhood extended from Suez to Shanghai."[3]

In April 1950, then Prime Minister Jawaharlal Nehru rekindled those forgotten bonds with China, thus making India the first country to enter into a diplomatic relationship with the PRC (People's Republic of China) and came in the famous catchphrase of "Hindi Chini Bhai Bhai". These bonds were further strengthened when Zhou Enlai visited India and signed the joint statement advocating five principles of peaceful coexistence, known as the 'Panchsheel'. In the same year, Nehru also visited China, becoming the first head of Government of a non-socialist country to visit the PRC. A year later, both attended the Afro-Asian Conference in Bandung in 1955, propagating a spirit of friendship and solidarity.[4]

Though diplomatic relations had started between both nations, many issues were yet to be resolved, and the border of both nations was the first. As the Great Himalayan Range separated the nations, so it was almost impossible to decide an LOC for both the nations; thus, LAC was being used for the time being, which later became an issue of dispute and thus began the border skirmishes between the army of both the countries, but no novel developments regarding border management had been achieved till then.

In his book, former Foreign Secretary Shyam Saran talks about the Chinese subtlety of deception through a famous Chinese classic known as Ruse of the Empty City. By this, he states the instances when India failed to see through these deceptions. Thus, China was successful in putting psychological pressure on India. The first was when Nehru approached Zhou Enlai on the border issue where a large part of Indian territory was depicted as a part of China. He explained that these maps were still to be revised and did not acknowledge they could be wrong. The second one was in the position of Kashmir, to which India was given a rhetorical answer in a very confusing way.

> When asked if China recognized Indian sovereignty over Jammu and Kashmir, Zhou had replied, rhetorically, "Has China ever said that it did not?" Now Zhou turned this same formulation on its head and asked Nehru, "Has China ever said that it did recognize Indian sovereignty over Jammu and Kashmir?"[5]

Even during the times of the Qing Dynasty, China saw itself as an epicenter of world politics, and thus in the later period, it became the "Chinese Dream" to restore China to that position. As stated by one of the four greatest historians of Modern China, Chen Yinke, "Mao's revolution never took its ultimate goal the communist seizure of the power in China rather at transforming China's state and reasserting China's central position in the world."[6]

In an interview, Dr. Jonathan Ward, a specialist in India–China relations, stated that they had to deal with Cold War and then the decolonization for this restoration. Both countries were competing for rising to the mantle of leading Asia. According to him, the motive behind the proposal of friendship from Zhou Enlai was that they wanted India's help in decolonizing the world. Their other motive was to use these newly decolonized countries as a containment zone for the U.S. in Asia. Like China, India also had some motives, but they were not anything like that of China. India's primary concern was peace in Asia and the war of China with the U.S., and it was also very inclined towards not letting anything like Korean War occur again. Nehru believed that the partnership of China was essential in executing this, thus 'Panchsheel'.[7] The Panchsheel was regarded as the height of the honeymoon period in India–China bilateral relations; however, the Indian Government failed to understand the nuance of Chinese statecraft.

Beginning of the Indo-China Conflict

After a few years of friendly relations with China, conflicts arose between the two nations, and the Tibet problem was the initial major cause. However, there were also many other extraterritorial reasons for it too. In 1906 when Tsarist Russia was very influential in the region and to save India from its clutches, the British entered into a treaty with Russia that recognized Chinese suzerainty over Tibet. However, later in the Shimla Conference in 1906, the British proposed that central and western Tibet would be under nominal Chinese suzerainty while the eastern region would be fully under their authority.[8] The border between the nations was later demarcated as the McMahon Line, but later China denounced it, claiming it to be an 'unequal treaty'. Before the few months of India's Independence, Tibet participated in an Asian Conference held in Delhi. In that Conference, Tibet's flag was flown with the flags of the other participating countries.[9] After the formation of the PRC, China annexed Tibet in 1950 as it claimed it to be theirs in the first place. The Indian Government strongly opposed the Chinese annexation of Tibet and sent a note of protest to the Chinese Government. Sardar Patel, who was then deputy Prime Minister of India, stated that "The tragedy of it is that the Tibetans put faith in us; they choose to be guided by us, and we have been unable to get them out of the meshes of Chinese diplomacy or Chinese malevolence."[10] In April 1954, India entered into a trade agreement with China with the five points of Panchsheel as its preamble. In that agreement of Trade and Intercourse between the Tibet Region of China and India, it first recognized Tibet as a region of China.[11] This trade agreement ended the centuries-old bilateral relationship between India and Tibet.

In 1958, Mao stated about a long-term plan to build up the economy and called it the "Great Leap Forward" and introduced economic reforms in the country, including Tibet. To connect Tibet with Mainland China, they decided to build a road through Aksai Chin, which they believed was their area, but India claimed it under its territory; thus the first seeds of mistrust, or at least confusion, were sowed in the minds of the Indian policymakers.

Another cause was that the territorial integrity of China was necessary for its restoration, and thus it started taking measures for consolidating its borders. Earlier its territory compromised three nations, Russia, Japan, and India. Also, there were some misconceptions aroused by the Chinese Embassy in India. They began to see India as an heir to British imperialism, which threatened the Chinese aspirations. Also, there was a portrayal that India was skillfully using both the world powers to tip the balance of power against China. Due to Kennedy's increased interest in India, these stories quickly caught fire. As stated by Ward in his interview, the Chinese Embassy said, "India is the hired thug of America's new Colonialism." They maligned India's image in front of other Afro-Asian nations by stating that Nehru was ready to implement the U.S. policy of using Asians to beat Asians.[12]

The Strife of 1962 and Its Repercussions

The skirmish of 1962 put the principles of Panchsheel to bed, and it sealed the fate of the Tibet issue as a source of eternal anxiety between China and India. China accused India of undermining its status over Tibet and of constantly budging into its internal affairs. The Dalai Lama's presence in India at that time made things even worse. According to former CIA agent Bruce Riedel, the main objective behind China's attack on India was to humiliate Nehru, who was gradually emerging as a leader among the Third World countries. He further stated that "India's implementation of the Forward Policy served as a major provocation to China in September 1962."[13]

In this war, Nehru sought help from the U.S. as he wrote in a letter to Kennedy, which was extracted from Kennedy Library. That excerpt stated:

> This is not a mere boundary dispute or a question of small territorial frontier adjustment. Apart from the vast, fantastic claims that China has made, China had already occupied 12,000 square miles of Indian territory during the last five years. This crisis is not only for India but for the world and will have far-reaching consequences. We cannot submit to this law of the jungle which affects our integrity and the honor of our motherland.[14]

By October 30, Kennedy agreed on giving India military assistance and reassured Pakistan, a very close ally of the U.S., that this did not mean granting any favor of the Indian position over Kashmir. The war officially ended on November 20, 1920, with China inflicting its greatest humiliations over the years. India suffered heavy losses in this one-month war, and by winning this one, China managed to give a setback to its other enemies. After the war, India immediately severed all its ties with China.

In the repercussions, the image of the Indian prime minister was badly hampered and most of his colleagues and parliamentarians spouted about Nehru's Shelleyan idealism on liberal values and socialist brotherhood (the Panchsheel). China managed to occupy the Aksai Chin region and claimed its right over Arunachal Pradesh, then known as NEFA. In 1963 China entered into a border agreement with Pakistan and constructed a highway joining Xinjiang to Gilgit. China also recognized Pakistan's position in Jammu and Kashmir.[15] Further, China conducted nuclear tests in 1964, adding to India's susceptibility.[16] The PRC also started meddling in India's internal affairs by openly supporting the Naga and Mizo movements. They were accused of providing them training within Chinese borders. It was believed that they were also involved in the Naxalbari uprising of West Bengal.

After becoming the prime minister, Indira Gandhi tried to normalize the situation and restore diplomatic relations in 1976. Since then, there have been many attempts made by the countries to resolve the border issue. In 1978 Atal Bihari Vajpayee was sent to China to hold talks with Deng Xiaoping in this regard. Later in 1988, Prime Minister Rajiv Gandhi visited China, where both sides agreed to look towards the future while seeking a mutually acceptable border solution. In 1991, Premier Li Peng visited India, thus restoring PM-level mutual visit. The most prominent solution came in 1993 when Prime Minister Narasimha Rao visited China, and an agreement on the maintenance of Peace and Tranquility along the Line of Actual Control in the India–China Border Areas was signed.[17]

The Confidence-Building Processes in the Military Field along the Line of Actual Control in the Sino-Indian Border Agreement of 1996 between the Republic of India and the Government of the People's Republic of China, As a result of this agreement, new protocols for securing the border and building confidence between countries have been formed. It calls for reduced troop levels and more communication between parties about border security and military exercises. When invited, either side may deploy observers within the other's territory to keep tabs on military operations and check for inspection. In 2005, the Protocol on the Modalities for the Implementation of Confidence-Building Measures in the Military Field along the LOC in the Sino-Indian Border, 2005, agreement was signed between the Government of the People's Republic of China and the Government of the Republic of India on the Political Parameters and Guiding Principles for the Settlement of the China–India Boundary Question. In 2012, a working mechanism was established for consultation and coordination on China–India border affairs, and in 2013, the Border Defense Cooperation Agreement was signed between India and China. These agreements manifested that India and China might work together and resolve their issues through dialogue.

Role of Multinational Organizations

Since the 1980s, there has been a beginning of various regionalist projects on a global scale. Many regionalist projects became visible in a relatively short period, with the expansion of the E.U. being the prime example. Other projects include NAFTA, ECOWAS, and SADC. Asia also joined this global huddle with the formation of ASEAN and SAARC, which in the later period paved the way for other regionalist organizations, thus ensuring the region's development.

Since its independence, India has shared close diplomatic relations with other ASEAN countries. It started expanding into the east during the 1950s and entered into many friendly alliances with the South-East Asian Nations. However, these relations got tarnished a bit due to India's involvement with the U.S.S.R. After its downfall, India started sorting out its priorities. It began mending its relations with these countries with its Look East Policy, and the concept of the extended neighborhood was popularized by leaders like I.K. Gujral and Jaswant Singh.

China's dominance in the region became the cause of uttermost tensions and required immediate actions. China, by the 1990s, had already become one of the most developing economies of the world and was providing military and economic aids to the surrounding South Asian nations, especially Pakistan, for its nuclear deal, which had become agitating for India. Thus, India also rekindled its lost relations with these nations as the country controlling this area will directly impact India. India changed its economic model in 1991 and changed its outlook from being an inward to more of an outward country. The results soon followed, as the bilateral trade flourished with the ASEAN nations' attempts to improve border relations post-1993.[18]

Indian political leaders realized the potential of this region and made it the focal point of their policies. India considers ASEAN to be the epicenter of the East Asian Region and emphasizes its interaction with the organization. India is also hoping for ASEAN to spearhead a multilateral security order in the Asia Pacific, which will also deal with its China issue. For other member countries, India was seen as an option to counterweigh China, but instead of doing that, India is looking to build a complementary relationship with them.[19]

BIMSTEC was formed in1997 to explore the economic initiative in South and South-East Asia, majorly around the Bay of Bengal. Its formation became more prominent in India's economic rise in the region as it was founded when India started opening up to the world. This organization stands to complement SAARC's efforts of free trade in the region. It also initiated and mended the jagged trading routes and built roads and rails connecting India, Thailand, Bangladesh, and Myanmar to ease trade. Except for Myanmar and Thailand, all the other members of this organization are also associated with SAARC. This organization has helped in consolidating those ties even further. Their field of work later expanded to enhancing information and intelligence sharing regarding terrorism and transnational crime and taking effective measures against individuals, groups, and entities involved in terrorism.[20] With BIMSTEC, India is better positioned to handle China as its policy seemed to be about hindering India's rise in the region as a rival Asian power. Since the collapse of the U.S.S.R., China's strategic importance has increased in the region. It has stabilized its external security and went into multiple alliances with Pakistan, the E.U. And with the U.S., its membership in the U.N. Security Council sets the standard for the settlement of its affairs with India.

SAARC was founded in 1985 and, since its inception, has been a significant organization in dealing with South Asian affairs. It was founded to tackle widespread poverty, strengthen energy cooperation and food security, promote trade, improve social welfare, provide educational opportunities, increase personnel exchanges, and fight against terrorism in the region. In the 1990s, SAARC introduced trading agreements among the member countries, which led to SAFTA (South Asian Free Trade Area) and its tariff reduction plan, which all the member countries accepted. Since then, trade in this region has been following this pattern. Besides trading, SAARC members have also reached a consensus over climate issues, environmental protection, and sustainable development. The major challenge for SAARC is to deal with poverty as five of its members are listed among the list of least developed nations by the United Nations.[21] SAARC has been a valuable entity for China in establishing its ties with the region as it had already established a number of exchange programs with other South Asian nations. This organization could help it achieve more engagement in the region. SAARC also has consolidated trading ties between China and India, which coincides with the fact that India has been a leading regional player in the organization over the years. There have been many programs between the two nations to mend that broken relationship, such as student exchanges, mutual investments, and rest. Apart from India, China also took a keen interest in developing trading ties with other South Asian nations like Sri Lanka and Bangladesh.[22]

Apart from these organizations, as mentioned above, India and China are members of the G20, BRICS, SCO, RIC, and other regional and international organizations. They all played a massive role in building the new strategic narrative for both countries and provided stability while addressing and eradicating their concerns and increasing regional cooperation.

New Strategic Narratives

Since the debacle of 1962, both nations have come a long way, and there has been tranquility over the border up until now. In fact, until 2016, there had been no firing across the borders in 25 years. Also, no casualty had occurred due to cross-firing for 40 years. The 1993 arrangement still held a relatively high ground for both nations regarding the border issue. China helped India in joining the SCO and supported its candidacy in APEC. There had been frequent talks over the issue of stabilizing Afghanistan in RIC.[23]

China started developing its ties with the E.U. and the rest of the world. It initiated economic changes around 1985 and soon became a heavyweight of the world on the economic front. Currently, it is the second-largest economy in the world after the U.S. China's relationship with the E.U. is more than one of trade and investment. Since the commencement of this newly formed partnership in 2003, the E.U. have been helping in China's transition towards a more plural and open society. Economic benefits were also humongous as the E.U. was China's largest trading partner in 2015, transacting 1.5 billion euros in two-way trade every day. In 2014, E.U. exports were 170 billion euros to China, with 350 billion euros exported back. In the same year, 15 per cent of all Foreign Direct Investment (FDI) into China came from the E.U., even though this only constituted 4.5 per cent of the stock of European outward investment globally (Brown, 2016). The U.S. was also very prominent and was the largest trading body with the PRC with an overall 625 USD up until 2014. Apart from trading relations with the western world, China was also very invested in developing the eastern sector. The inception of regional organizations saw it rekindle its relationship with other South and South-East Asian nations. India was among the top 20 trading partners of China back in 2004.

India opened up its economy in 1991 to the world and saw a massive development in its overall economic prowess. Now it has become the second-largest economy of Asia after China and marked its presence under the top 10 economies of the world. The Look East Policy played a huge part. The bilateral relations between the South-East Asian nations were consolidated due to the formation of ASEAN, SAARC, and BIMSTEC, making India a heavyweight of this region. As the external affairs minister said in the Raisena Dialogue:

> The India–China relationship, I think has a unique characteristic which is that, very rarely in history have two powers who are neighbours gone up in the international order in approximately the same timeframe. So, each of the countries is reaching a new equilibrium with the world and each other simultaneously. China is the number two globally, and India is number five or number six in the world. Probably, within the space of a decade, we would be two and three and maybe in the space of the next quarter of a century.[24]

The soft power that has been a prominent characteristic feature of both these nations was put to the mantle as India was among one of the few nations that possessed it, even when it lacked hard power in the second half of the 20th century as a democratic developing nation, a spiritual-cultural magnet also being one of the leaders of NAM added to its cause. To pounce on China's increasing influence in the region, it already had a cordial relationship with Pakistan through the agreement of 1965, whose primary beneficiary was Pakistan itself. China also signed a treaty with Sri Lanka in 1979 to improve cultural ties, which indirectly aided it over the Malacca issue for trade. The ICCR set up regional cultural centers and encouraged Hindi abroad by organizing the World Hindi Conference to overcome this deficit. Initiatives such as Brand India were started to lure the exporters by providing glimpses of India's culture and aesthetics. Pravasi Bhartiya Diwas was started to harness the resources of the Indian diaspora, which was much larger than that of China and is a significant contributor to India's economic growth through its remittances.[25]

New Strategic Partnership

In 2010 Chinese Premier Wen Jiabao visited India and brought the most extensive Chinese trade mission to India, consisting of a 300-member business delegation. The main motive behind Wen's trip was considered to promote pragmatic cooperation, but it had far more enormous implications. He stressed the bilateral economic and trade cooperation, which would have been mutually beneficial for both nations. At India-China Business Cooperation Summit, he said, "The two sides decided to establish China-India strategic economic dialogue and the CEO Forum strive to take bilateral trade volume to $100 billion by 2015, and further expand cooperation in investment, high-tech, energy, and other fields." The two sides also announced an exchange program through which 500 young people from each side would visit the other country and deepen exchanges and cooperation in media and education. He was very fixated that the future of the India–China relationship lied in the youth of the country.[26] In the following years, the celebration of this mended ties of friendship continued as 2011 was the "China-India Exchange Year" and the year 2012 was termed as the "Year of China-India Friendship and Cooperation"; between these years, the leaders of both the nations continued their friendly exchanges in their encounters in international summits. The year 2014 came with a change in Indian politics as Narendra Modi was appointed as the new prime minister of India. In September, President Xi Jinping paid a state visit to India and visited Indian Prime Minister Narendra Modi's home state of Gujarat. That year was called "China-India Friendly Exchange Year". In the following year, Prime Minister Modi visited China in the Xi'an province. While addressing at Tsinghua University in Beijing, Prime Minister Modi stated,

> *If we had to realize the extraordinary potential that exists between India and China for forging a very different power type partnership, we must be ready to discuss issues that lead to hesitations and doubts and distrust, and we must address this frontally.*[27]

That very same year, India entered into a joint vision statement with the U.S. for the Asia Pacific and the Indian Ocean. It accelerated infrastructure connectivity with Central Asia, South Asia, and Southeast Asia. Discordance came between the two nations over new security architecture as for India it was East Asian Summit while China believed more in the CHICA. The primary reason behind these newly formed strategic alliances with the U.S. is more robust defense security, economic cooperation, and bilateral naval exercises. After this, there were multiple meetings between the nations but they ended in vain. After this, the border tension resumed in 2017, which resulted in heavy casualties from both sides in Galway Valley, and the issue has elongated over time. China and Pakistan started 'Belt and Road', which heavily aided the failing Pakistani economy as India believed that China's real intention was to use Pakistan as a permanent source of pressure for India. While China was wary of the budding Indo-U.S. partnership and got the notion that India wanted to become a part of the China Containment Program initiated by the U.S., adding to their worst fears U.S. decided to change the name of their U.S. Pacific Command to U.S.-Indo Pacific Command.[28]

Political Shift

There was much happening around the world in 2020, and another instance of the skirmish between India and China added a new fold. Earlier it was the coronavirus or COVID-19; a China that went through a global pandemic that knocked the world off its feet. Almost every country was gravely affected by it except China; everyone else's GDP came tumbling down. Since May 5, there have been ongoing skirmishes over the China–India border in Ladakh, resulting in numerous casualties on both sides. In reaction to the last event, India adopted the policy of boycotting Chinese products, and since then, there has been an ongoing campaign for it. Several Chinese trade and sponsorship deals were cut off, amounting to billions of rupees. Initially, 61 Chinese mobile apps were also banned, and on September 2, 118 more were banned, which contained some of the heavyweight gaming apps having a multibillion turnover per year. Since the Galway Valley incident, the rules of engagement have also changed, and now the Army commander leading on the ground can decide on the tactics to counter any kind of aggression.[29]

In 2019 India's refusal to join the RCEP agreement raised some serious questions to which External Affairs Minister S. Jaishankar said in the inaugural session of the India-Singapore Business & Innovation Summit that

> *India remained concerned over the unfair market access to Indian products and the protectionist policies of Beijing that have created a significant trade deficit between the two nations. The trade deficit with India in 2018 rose to USD 57.86 billion from USD 51.72 billion in 2017 in about USD 95.54 total bilateral trade.* [30]

He concluded that this was an economic agreement, and it might as well have strategic implications but what is the most important here is the economic aspect.

There has been an economic shift in Asia as nations pool their manufacturing base from China and are looking to settle down in India and other regional countries. They believe China to be the main conspirator behind the pandemic, with the U.S. president openly calling it a 'CHINA Virus'. The president of USIBC recently stated that the companies that already have some manufacturing in India might be early movers in reducing output in plants in China and scaling up production in India. Nevertheless, it is easier said than done, as India might not be the obvious choice for global multinationals because of its toxic relationship with RCEP. Its broken relationship with FDI continues to bother the global MNCs. However, even after these severe concerns, if the shift manages to happen, it would be, as rightly said by Transport Minister Nitin Gadkari, "a blessing in disguise for India."[31]

The prime minister of India has also been vocal about using the local products and launched several schemes under 'Atmanirbhar Bharat', which will promote homegrown products instead of over-dependency upon foreign goods, especially that of China. This scheme up until now resulted in the states trying to replace goods with homegrown products. A revolution came in pharmaceuticals and the development of PPE kits essential in this adverse condition, with states like UP and Bihar leading it from the front.

Conclusion

Since the cold war, the relationship between China and India has been in a state of turmoil, and China has acted like a wolf in sheep's clothing. Our earlier stance of friendship with China resulted in the commencement of the Struggle of 1962, which bankrupted the liberal legacy of India's First Prime Minister Jawaharlal Nehru and is seen as an outcome of his incompetency in dealing with the issues regarding China. The Jan Sangh leader Deendayal Upadhyaya sarcastly remarked about Nehru's compliance with the "Panchsheel" and said that Nehru knew "How to emit smoke without fire how to arrest a conflagration in the Niagara of verbiage". In the era of globalization, there were efforts to mend the broken relationship, and after the 1993 agreement between India and China, things seemed to be settling down. With the help of its alliances and the more open policy of Deng Xiaoping, China soon became an economic superpower of the world and, at one moment, was one of the fastest-growing economies in the world. India started very late but was helped by China as slowly it became its largest trading partner. There were frequent visits of the leaders of both the nations, and there was a sense of tranquility coming in the relations, and it seemed like, finally, these two budding powers would settle the bad blood between them for good.

The U.S., too, saw them as the great competitors to its unipolar hegemony over the world and started taking much more interest in Asia. Before 2016 everything was going far too well until India entered into an agreement with the U.S. for its geostrategic stability in the region. However, China saw it as an attempt to contain its influence on Asia. In retaliation, China started the Belt and Road project with Pakistan and revived the failing Pakistani economy. Things went into ruins after the Galwan Valley incident of 2020, where numerous casualties occurred. Since then, the relations between both nations have gone downhill. The recent pandemic outbreak maligned China's reputation globally as many countries believe that the deadly coronavirus was manufactured in a lab in Wuhan. There was unanimity in the countries' voices against China, and many of them decided to relocate their manufacturing units, and India seemed like a plausible option.

However, the only question that remains is whether we are ready to undertake such an initiative. Once again, the fragile border relations became the focal point as the recent skirmish had vast implications with India boycotting and banning Chinese products from the Indian market. The electronic medium for retaliation is also being used. In three months, India has banned almost 200 Chinese software applications. In September 2020, India reacquired the disputed area along the Pan Gong Lake at LAC. Things seem far from overhand as there is profound distrust between the two nations. Since then, bilateral dialogues between the government officials and leaders of the two countries have been drastically reduced. The Indian prime minister's message was the exact opposite of when he visited Beijing in 2015 and gave emotional speech in Tsinghua University. The history of both the countries over the last 60 years indicates that China has successfully exploited India's political and ideological divisions to its benefit and shaped the narrative of the troubled bilateral relationship. China will remain an important part of the economic and technological ecosystem of the 21st century, and India's choices cannot be binary. The role of QUAD will also be vital in containing the Chinese threat in the region, and its members might look for broadening their structure by including other countries, giving it a QUAD+ structure. The question that remains unanswered is what the future holds for India and China. At the border, China is seemingly satisfied with the current status quo; however, India remains fixated that the border should go back to as it was in April 2020. The relations have been brought to a new normal. The possibility to return to the former status of bilateral relationship as they were before the skirmish is implausible as they will now be more adversarial, antagonistic, and contentious down the road.

Notes

1 Saran, S. (n.d.). How India sees the world: Kautilya to the 21st Century. Retrieved November 30, 2021, from https://books.google.com/books/about/How_India_Sees_the_World.html?id=rlU3tAEACAAJ
2 Indurthy, R. (2016). India and China: Conflict, competition, cooperation, and prospect for peace. *International Journal on World Peace, 33*(1), 43–108.
3 LKY School. (2016, April 07). [lecture] China–India relations in a changing world. Retrieved November 30, 2021, from https://www.youtube.com/watch?v=_fGwfbtO4w4
4 Final communiqué of the Asian–African conference of bandung (24 April 1955). (2017, March 1). Retrieved November 30, 2021, from https://www.cvce.eu/en/obj/final_communique_of_the_asian_african_conference_of_bandung_24_april_1955-en-676237bd-72f7-471f-949a-88b6ae513585.html
5 Saran, S. (2020, July 28). How India can counter china. Retrieved November 30, 2021, from https://www.rediff.com/news/column/ladakh-standoff-shyam-saran-how-india-can-counter-china/20200728.htm

6 China–India relations: The untold story. (2017, September 20). Retrieved November 30, 2021, from https://www.youtube.com/watch?v=grg8XqMHdCQ&feature=emb_logo.
7 Ibid.
8 Convention between Great Britain and China respecting Tibet (1906) [389]. (2009, September 12). Retrieved November 30, 2021, from http://www.tibetjustice.org/materials/treaties/treaties11.html
9 Mehrotra, L. L. (2000). India's Tibet policy. Retrieved November 30, 2021, from https://tibet.net/wp-content/uploads/2017/05/Inidas-Tibet-Policy.pdf
10 Sardar Vallabhbhai Patel's letter to Prime Minister Jawaharlal Nehru. (1950, November 7). New Delhi.
11 Lintner, B. (2015). *Great Game East India, China, and the struggle for Asia's most volatile frontier*. New Haven Connecticut: Yale University Press.
12 China–India relations: The untold story. (2017, September 20). Retrieved November 30, 2021, from https://www.youtube.com/watch?v=grg8XqMHdCQ&feature=emb_logo
13 PTI. (2016, May 06). Nehru sought U.S. help during 1962 Indo–China War: Book. Retrieved November 30, 2021, from https://www.thehindu.com/news/nehru-sought-us-help-during-1962-indochina-war-book/article7761071.ece
14 Papers of John F. Kennedy. Presidential Papers. National Security Files. Countries. India: Subjects: Nehru correspondence, November 1962: 11-19. JFKNSF-111-016. John F. Kennedy Presidential Library and Museum.
15 Dobell, W. M. (1964). Ramifications of the China–Pakistan border treaty. *Pacific Affairs, 37*(3), 283. doi: 10.2307/2754976
16 JFK, aides considered nuclear arms in China–India clash (2005, August 26). Retrieved November 30, 2021, from http://www.taipeitimes.com/News/world/archives/2005/08/27/2003269368
17 Menon, S. (2016). *Choices: Inside the making of India's foreign policy*. Washington, D.C.: Brookings Institution Press.
18 Anand, M. (2009, May 12). India–ASEAN relations: Analysing regional implications. I. Retrieved December 01, 2021, from http://scotomastudio.com/india-asean-relations-analysing-regional-implications/
19 Ibid.
20 Shrivastava, S. (2005). Bimstec: Political implications for India. Retrieved December 1, 2021, from https://www.jstor.org/stable/41856178
21 Jiali, M. (2012). SAARC: Achievements and challenges. Retrieved December 1, 2021, from https://www.jstor.org/stable/42922698
22 Gancheng, Z. (2012). China India relations and SAARC. Retrieved December 1, 2021, from https://www.jstor.org/stable/42922686
23 LKYSchool. (2016, April 07). [lecture] China–India relations in a changing world. Retrieved November 30, 2021, from https://www.youtube.com/watch?v=_fGwfbtO4w4
24 Room for two? India, China and the world order – YouTube. (n.d.). Retrieved December 1, 2021, from https://www.youtube.com/watch?v=wF4bnOZsO8g
25 Hajarika, B. & Mishra, V. (n.d.). Soft power consternation between India and China. Retrieved December 1, 2021, from https://www.jstor.org/stable/48505297
26 Chinese Embassy. (n.d.). Foreign minister Yang Jiechi talks about premier Wen Jiabao's visits to India and Pakistan – A journey of friendship and cooperation. Accessed September 4, 2020. http://in.china-embassy.org/eng/zt/wenindia/t780896.htm
27 Modi, N. (2015, May 15). *Address by Prime Minister at the Tsinghua University Beijing (May 15, 2015)*. Ministry of External Affairs, Government of India. Retrieved September 6, 2022, from https://mea.gov.in/outoging-visit-detail.htm?25242%2FAddress%2Bby%2BPrime%2BMinister%2Bat%2Bthe%2BTsinghua%2BUniversity%2BBeijing%2BMay%2B15%2B2015

28 Poghosyan, D. (2020, August 29). Evolving global order and the future of the India–China relations. Retrieved December 01, 2021, from https://www.indrastra.com/2020/08/Evolving-Global-Order-and-Future-of-India-China-Relations-006-08-2020-0064.html

29 Philip, S., Ghosh, A., & Taskin, B. (2020, June 20). India changes rules of engagement at Lac after galwan valley clash. Retrieved December 01, 2021, from https://theprint.in/defence/india-changes-rules-of-engagement-at-lac-after-galwan-valley-clash/445392/

30 YouTube. (2019, September 19). *Inaugural session by EAM dr. S Jaishankar at India - Singapore : Business & Innovation Summit*. YouTube. Retrieved September 6, 2022, from https://www.youtube.com/watch?v=JekI_BrAGv4

31 Inamdar, N. (2020, May 18). Coronavirus: Can India replace China as world's factory? Retrieved December 01, 2021, from https://www.bbc.com/news/world-asia-india-52672510

Part II

Financial and Infrastructural Perspectives

5 FDI Spillover on Domestic Firms in Developing Economies

A Systematic Review and Future Research Agenda

Kunwar Milind Singh

Introduction

Foreign Direct Investment (FDI) spillover is the channel of transmission through which FDI influences domestic firms. The larger debate in recent times has been whether FDI inflows in a developing economy can led to resource generation for the economy. The resource generation can be investment, consumption, technology, employment, output, human resource and exports. The spillover can be horizontal (within same industry) or vertical (inter-industry). In backward linkage, foreign firms receive supplies from domestic firms. In the forward linkage of FDI, foreign firms are supplier and local firms are customer. In any of backward, forward and horizontal linkages, the impact of FDI spillover on firms will depend on channel of transmission through which FDI will lead to resource generation.

Foreign direct investment is the most preferred form of foreign capital inflow for a developing economy since it is nonvolatile capital and FDI investment brings a series of benefits to the host country that includes transfer of technology, managerial knowledge, capital, development of ancillary units, backward and forward integration, employment generation and exports. Many studies have been conducted to study the impact of FDI on economic growth, but only a few have assessed the impact of FDI transmission on domestic firms in terms of output and efficiency. This study attempts to identify the different transmission channels of FDI spillover and its impact on domestic manufacturing firms in developing economies in the last two decades.

The findings of the study will be useful for policy implication as it will show which channels are more effective regarding FDI spillover so that industry-specific FDI policy can be made for larger output and productivity gain for the developing economy firms. The study will also help identify emerging research issues in the area of FDI spillover on domestic firms of developing economies.

Research Methodology

A systematic literature review method has been used to classify the existing literature on spillover effect of FDI on the domestic firm of developing economies in the last two decades. Research articles have been selected

DOI: 10.4324/9781003354703-7

using online databases, including the likes of business source Premier-EBSCO, Google scholar, Science Direct, Research Gate. The research articles have been identified using the keywords FDI, spillover, developing economies, MNE, domestic firms in either title, abstract or keywords. The review literature on the spillover effect of FDI on domestic firms has been divided into theoretical framework and division of research work on similarity and differences.

The theoretical framework of spillover effect of FDI includes various studies (Brems, 1970; Romer, 1993; Borensztein, De Gregorio and Lee, 1998; Javorcik, 2004; Lin, Liu & Zhang, 2009; Demena & Murshed, 2018)

The division of work on the spillover effect of FDI on domestic firms has been clubbed into four different tracks that include studies supporting both vertical and horizontal spillover, studies supporting vertical but not horizontal spillover, studies supporting horizontal but not vertical spillover and studies having alternative views on spillover effect of FDI on domestic firms. The studies having supporting conclusions related to a track have been placed under that track. Therefore, there is intratrack similarity and intertrack differences among studies.

Studies supporting both vertical and horizontal spillover effect of FDI on the domestic firm are Lin, Liu, Zhang (2009); Sahu and Solarin (2014); Wiboonchutikula, Phucharoen and Pruektanakul (2016); Moralles and Moreno (2020). Studies supporting vertical but not horizontal spillover are Javorcik (2004); Dua, Harrison and Jefferson (2012); Gorodnichenko, Svejnar and Terrell (2014); Liang (2017); Wiboonchutikula, Phucharoen and Pruektanakul (2016). Studies supporting horizontal but not vertical spillover are Blake, Deng and Falvey (2009); Lu, Tao and Zhu (2017); Demena and Murshed (2018); He, Kwan, and Fan (2019); Sur and Nandy (2018). Studies having alternative views on the spillover effect of FDI on domestic firms include Markusen and Venables (1999); Javorcik (2004); Lin, Liu and Zhang (2009); Behera et al. (2012); Blake, Deng and Falvey (2009); Dua, Harrison and Jefferson (2012); Sahu and Solarin (2014); Gorodnichenko, Svejnar and Terrell (2014); Liang (2017); Wiboonchutikula, Phucharoen and Pruektanakul (2016); Apostolov (2017); Demena and Murshed (2018).

Literature Review

Foreign direct investment is the most sought-after investment in developing and emerging economies, especially after the reform process started in these economies. Developing economies are one of the largest recipients of total global inward FDI inflows. FDI is one form of capital inflows that is non-debt creating and nonvolatile in nature. Therefore, it is the most preferred form of capital inflows for recipient developing economies. International economic institutions like the World Bank and International Monetary Fund also advise developing/emerging/transition economies to make open and transparent FDI policy. FDI is a preferred form of investment also because of its spillover effect on domestic firm. The spillover can be horizontal and vertical. The horizontal spillover is intraindustry whereas vertical spillover is interindustry. The spillover in intraindustry reflects in the form of a demonstration effect, labor turnover and competition effect, whereas spillover in interindustry happen through both backward linkage (upstream sector) and forward linkage (downstream sector). The spillover also depends on the absorptive capacity of the firms, technology transfer, ownership structure and geographical proximity. The absorptive capacity depends on R&D intensity, export status, trained employee in domestic firms.

The broad debate in this area is regarding the different channels of FDI spillover and mechanism through which FDI spillover to domestic industries and firms. There are broad agreements that FDI spills over through horizontal linkage (intra industry) and backward and forward linkage (inter industry). However, there are contrary views among researchers with respect to horizontal spillover. Some studies find that it is not significant; some others find that spillover is significant through horizontal linkage, while some others find that there is both positive and negative spillover and the net effect is very less through horizontal spillover. Another important issue is the endogeneity of FDI because foreign investors are expected to invest in those industries that are already high productivity industry, and therefore, we cannot say with certainty that productivity has increased because of spillover.

The literature review has been divided into different parts, which include channel of FDI spillover, theoretical framework, division of works, similarities and differences, conclusions and emerging research issues.

Channel of FDI Spillover

We can look at FDI spillover from two perspectives. One is the transmission channel through which FDI spills over to the domestic firm and characteristics of the industry/firm, which is receiving FDI.

Transmission channels of FDI spillover include horizontal linkages through intraindustry spillover. The entry of foreign firm within the same industry comes through FDI. In horizontal linkage, foreign firms do not have any incentive for knowledge spillover within the industry as other firms are the competitor and all firms, including foreign firms, want to retain their competitive advantage. The spillover in this channel can be explained through the demonstration effect, competition effect and movement of labor from the foreign firm to domestic firm. The demonstration effect is applicable when local firms imitate or replicate the technology, management structure and processes through observation. Labor turnover is the movement of labor/employee from foreign firm to domestic firm or employee opening its own venture that leads to spillover. The competition effect is more dominant in horizontal channel of FDI spillover. Foreign firms with large capital, superior resources and technology increase the level of competition in the industry and affect the industry concentration ratio. Competition also increases wages as the demand for labor and employees will increase. The situation leads to a decline in the sales of domestic firm and they are unable to spread the fixed cost over the revenue, which leads to losses and even the exit of the firm from the industry. This situation is known as crowding out. Therefore, horizontal spillover has both positive impacts and negative impacts on the domestic firm, which cancel each other out and finally lead to a net small positive or net negative effect on domestic firms.

Vertical spillover of FDI happens in form of input–output process through backward linkage and forward linkage. Backward linkage of FDI spillover got more support in academic literature compared to forward linkage. The reason is most FDI in developing economies is in the upstream sector compared to the downstream sector. The backward linkage of FDI spillover happens in the upstream sector where suppliers are domestic firms and foreign firms are the customer. In backward linkage foreign firm has an incentive to transfer technology or help improve productivity in the domestic firm as foreign firms are buying intermediate supplies and components from these domestic firms. The foreign firms will use these intermediate inputs in the manufacturing of the final product. Therefore, incentives for foreign firms are to get quality input from domestic firms for which they will be ready to share the knowledge. The high-quality input requirement by foreign buyers put pressure on the domestic firm to improve their processes and product as per international standards to meet the requirement of foreign firms. In case of forward spillover, foreign firms are suppliers and domestic firms are buyers in the downstream sector. Foreign firms mainly move in to developing economies to manufacture or assemble the final product. Therefore, forward linkage is less important compared to backward linkage. Forward linkages also have positive spillover to improve the processes of not only domestic firms but also other foreign firms.

It is not only market access of foreign technology that is important for developing economies, but many factors at industry and firm level also decide the extent to which spillover will percolate down and assimilated by the domestic firms. These include ownership structure, geographical proximity and absorptive capacity of domestic firms. The ownership structure is extent to which the foreign firms are having equity participation in domestic firms. Domestic firms having equity participation from foreign firms tend to spillover more than foreign firms coming as a wholly owned subsidiaries (WOS) that suggests that domestic firms with joint venture from foreign firms have higher spillover than WOS. Geographical proximity is the distance of foreign firms from domestic firms. Lesser the distance larger is the spillovers, which is more pronounced in industrial clusters where foreign firms have both forward and backward linkages. The absorptive capacity reflects the capacity of domestic firms to absorb spillover. It includes R&D intensity, export status of the firm, training of the employees, etc.

Theoretical Framework

The theoretical framework of spillover effect of FDI on domestic firms has been put forward by the authors in different ways.

Brems (1970) identified the reason for international direct investment. He says that if the assumption on which factor price equalization rest is relaxed, factor price equalization does not exist and therefore there are incentives for international investment. These incentives will be differences in the superiority of one country over the other in thriftiness, technology and consumer preference in the product offered by the entrepreneur of that country in a two-country model. This explains the reason for international direct investment. He defines international direct investment in the form of capital, technological and managerial knowledge from parent to subsidiary firms.

Romer (1993) assessed the impact of idea gaps and object gaps in the economic development of developing economies. The object gap talks about physical capital like factories, equipment investment whereas idea gap talks about sharing ideas by industrialized economies to developing economies. Idea sharing is not only in terms of manufacturing but host of other economic transactions that include marketing, packaging, distribution, inventory control, information system. The object gap between industrial and developing takes a long time before it can be bridged and has high opportunity cost. The idea gap that does not have the opportunity cost can be transferred to developing economies and the industrial economy at the same time. The idea gap can be minimized between the industrial economy and developing economy quickly and bring economic development in the developing economy.

Borensztein, De Gregorio and Lee (1998) look at the role of FDI in technology diffusion and economic growth in developing countries and find that a minimum threshold level of human capital is required in developing economy for higher FDI productivity. FDI will enhance economic growth when sufficient absorptive capacity to absorb advanced technology is available in the host country. Therefore, introduction of advanced technology and requirement of absorptive capacity in the host country are the determinants of economic growth in developing countries. The critical finding of this research is that the impact of FDI on economic growth depends on the level of human capital available in the host country.

Javorcik (2004) state that interindustry spillover is through backward and forward linkage. The determinant of the forward linkage are industry concentration and demand by the customers of host country firm whereas backward channel determinants are direct knowledge transfer from foreign customers to local suppliers. The product quality, online delivery introduced by MNCs and increasing demand by MNCs lead to supplier looking for economies of scale. Beside this spillover also depends on the foreign ownership in domestic firms in the form of joint ventures.

Lin, Liu and Zhang (2009) identify that FDI spillover happens both through horizontal and through vertical spillover. Vertical spillover happens through backward and forward linkage. Horizontal spillover is intraindustry, whereas vertical spillover is interindustry. In vertical backward spillover, domestic firms are supplier and foreign firms are customer in upstream sector, whereas in case of vertical forward spillover, foreign firms are supplier and domestic firms are customers in the downstream sector. Sahu and Solarin (2014) study the spillover effect of FDI on Indian manufacturing firms through total factor productivity by using Cobb-Douglus Production Function Framework. The firm-level efficiency is studied using stochastic production function approach. The estimation for the time invariant technical efficiency is based on Schmidt and Sickles (1984) and the time varying technical efficiency is based on Battese and Coelli (1988).

Demena & Murshed (2018) identify FDI spillover through knowledge and allocative efficiency spillover. The knowledge spillover happens through labor mobility, demonstration and imitation and allocative efficiency through competitive pressure. Size, importance and the presence of spillover depend on domestic firm absorptive capacity, technology level, geographical proximity and ownership structure.

Division of Works, Similarities and Differences

Studies Supporting Vertical and Horizontal Spillover

Many studies have found support for both horizontal and vertical spillover and within vertical spillover both for backward and for forward spillover. Lin, Liu and Zhang (2009) study 71 manufacturing industries of China to identify that foreign firms mainly from OECD countries have positive horizontal spillover on Chinese firms, whereas firms from HMT (Hong Kong, Macau, Taiwan) countries have negative horizontal spillover on Chinese firms. They find forward spillover from all types of FDI irrespective of motivation, source and ownership of FDI besides strong and robust vertical backward spillover from OECD foreign invested firms on state-owned enterprises (SOE) and not SOE firms in China. Jeon, Park and Ghauri (2013) study the spillover effect of FDI in China and find that vertical effects of FDI are found to be positive and significant across all industries and the effect of industries' technological levels on this effect is minimal. Sahu and Solarin (2014) analyze the effect of FDI spillover on the Indian manufacturing firms and find a positive and marginal effect of FDI on productivity spillover. The productivity spillover is due to the higher productivity and efficiency of foreign firms compared to domestic firms. Wiboonchutikula, Phucharoen and Pruektanakul (2016) analyze the spillover effect of FDI on domestic manufacturing firms in Thailand and find a negative spillover effect in upstream industries and positive and significant spillover effect in downstream industries. Moralles and Moreno (2020) examine the effect of FDI on firm productivity growth in Brazil and find that when FDI is set as the threshold and regime-dependent variable, Brazilian firms suffer from negative productivity spillovers, whereas local firms may collect positive spillovers if they are endowed with high absorptive capacity.

Studies Supporting Vertical but not Horizontal Spillover

Javorcik (2004) studies firm-level data from Lithuania and finds that productivity spillover occurs through backward linkage. He found no evidence of intra sectoral spillover and no indication of spillover from MNC presence in sectors supplying intermediate inputs i.e., forward linkage. Dua, Harrison and Jefferson (2012) in their study on Chinese firm-level data, find that all SOE and non-SOE firms with annual sales of more than 5 million yuan have weak or zero horizontal spillover whereas a positive and significant vertical spillover occurs through both backward and forward linkage. Gorodnichenko, Svejnar and Terrell (2014) study the spillover effect of FDI on transition economy and find the impact of FDI on the efficiency of domestic firms in the host country. They find that backward linkages have a consistently positive effect on the productivity of domestic firms, whereas horizontal and forward linkages don't show any consistent effect. Liang (2017) in his study on China's manufacturing firm finds positive spillover from multinational supplier to local firms and no positive spillover within the industry and from multinational customers to local firms. Wiboonchutikula, Phucharoen and Pruektanakul (2016) analyze the spillover effect of FDI on domestic manufacturing firms in Thailand and find no evidence of horizontal spillover on either total factor productivity (TFP) or technical efficiency of all firms.

Studies Supporting Horizontal but not Vertical

Blake, Deng and Falvey (2009) in their study of 998 Chinese manufacturing firms across five industries of China find transfer of labor and foreign firm presence affects spillover through horizontal effect. They also find that transfer of labor, horizontal demonstration and competition spillover to only Chinese SOE and not to private firms. They find vertical spillovers are not significant. Jeon, Park and Ghauri (2013) in their study on the spillover effect of FDI in China find that horizontal investment causes negative influences on local Chinese firms. Lu, Tao and Zhu (2017) in their study of all SOE and non-SOE firms in China with annual sales more than 5 million yuan find that FDI has a negative and significant effect on the productivity of domestic firms in the intraindustry spillover. They also analyze two underlying explanations of agglomeration and competition effects and their relative strengths, where agglomeration is moderated by the absorptive capacity of the local firms. Demena and Murshed (2018) in their study of eight sub-Saharan countries find that the demonstration effect is large and economically significant whereas labor mobility and competition are unstable on various specifications. He, Kwan and Fan (2019) in their study on horizontal spillover in China find that China gains more from horizontal spillover than world average and the average horizontal spillover effect in China is positive and economically significant. They also find that horizontal spillover varies across subgroups of firms characterized by the nature and origin of foreign-invested firms and ownership structure of domestic firms. Sur and Nandy (2018) analyze the spillover effect of FDI on Indian automobile industry and find that spillover effects through demonstration effect. The competition and information effects are not significant transmission channels of spillovers from foreign to domestic firms. Keshari (2018) in his study on channels of FDI spillovers, firm characteristics and the decision to export by domestic firms in selected Indian manufacturing industries finds evidence that domestic firms are benefitting in terms of decision to export from the competition effect of FDI.

Studies Having Alternative View on the Spillover Effect of FDI on Domestic Firms

The studies took ownership structure, absorptive capacity (R&D intensity, export status, training of workers), firm heterogeneity (size of the firm and extent to which they are affected by FDI spillover), geographical proximity (geographical distance of foreign firm from domestic firms), market orientation (export seeking or domestic market seeking) as important factors affecting spillover besides horizontal and vertical spillover. Markusen and Venables (1999) find that competition will lead to increase in wages and product costs result in a decline in profit, but supplier linkage will reduce input costs and profits will increase. They also find that FDI leads to the establishment of industrial sectors in which local production dominates and leads to the exit of foreign firms. Javorcik (2004) finds that productivity benefits are associated with partially owned foreign ownership. Lin, Liu and Zhang (2009) find that domestic market seeking FDI does not differ much than export oriented FDI in terms of spillover effect on Chinese firm. Blake, Deng and Falvey (2009) find that the absorptive capacity of domestic firms is important in determining the extent to which spillover is effective especially R&D expenditure per capita and export status. They also find that MNCs have a positive spillover effect on local firm exporting. Dua, Harrison and Jefferson (2012) find that Chinese firm heterogeneity influences absorptive capacity across the firms in responding to foreign investment. Firms who receive equity participation from OECD countries show a positive effect on firm productivity while foreign investment coming from HMT countries does not. Behera et al. (2012) find significant long-run relationship between labor productivity in large domestic firms and capital stock, capital intensity, foreign presence, technological gap, interaction between market concentration and foreign presence, R&D intensity of domestic and foreign firms and technology import intensity of domestic and foreign firms. They also find the presence of foreign firms in enhancing the level of technology of domestic firm through technology spillover. Hence, FDI brings a new level of knowledge and technology to domestic firms and enhances productivity and technology spillover. Sahu and Solarin (2014), in their study of spillover effect of FDI on Indian manufacturing firm, find significant impact of FDI on output growth. Gorodnichenko, Svejnar and Terrell (2014), in their study on spillover effect of FDI on transition economy, find that domestic firms not only benefit from its direct interaction with the foreign firm but also indirectly from other domestic firms' interaction with foreign firms. Liang (2017) finds that domestic firms R&D capital facilitates learning from foreign firms and local firm learnings comes from joint venture and wholly owned subsidiary, but more from WOS. Wiboonchutikula, Phucharoen and Pruektanakul (2016) identify that firm-specific factors such as age, size, imported raw material, location at industrial estate, R&D have a positive effect on firm TFP and technical efficiency in total industries. Apostolov (2017) examines the FDI influence on performance and entrepreneurship of domestic firms in southeast European economy of Macedonia and finds foreign ownership has helped restructure and enhance the productivity of domestic firms and creation of new firms and has had a strong impact on exports. Keshari (2018) studies the spillover effect of FDI on domestic firms in selected Indian manufacturing industries and finds that when firm-specific (size, experience, financial strength, capital intensity and product differentiation advantage) characteristics are strengthened, domestic firms are also in a position to take advantage of technological and information spillovers generated by FDI firms. Demena and Murshed (2018) find that the size and importance of spillover depends on firm's absorptive capacity, foreign ownership, geographical proximity and the level of technology.

Conclusions

Most of the studies conducted to study the impact of FDI spillover on domestic firms used three channels of FDI spillover, which include horizontal spillover, backward and forward spillover. Out of these channels, the horizontal channel of FDI spillover is debatable as contrary views have been identified in different studies. The forward vertical spillover is also not convincing as most of the MNCs in developing economies are in the upstream sector rather than the downstream sector. The only convincing spillover is backward vertical linkage. Many studies support this view on the context that MNCs in emerging economies are mainly in upstream activities where they are taking the required intermediate inputs from domestic firms. Beside this ownership structure, absorptive capacity (R&D intensity and export orientation), geographical proximity, technology transfer are other important determinants of spillover as identified in a number of studies. The limitation of this research includes different time periods have been taken in different studies and therefore concluding a specific type of spillover in a specific period is difficult to predict. A large number of factors related to firm-specific, institutional factors, liberalization policy of developing economies also affects spillover but sufficient literature could not be accessed. Most of the studies used for review have domestic firms as manufacturing units to study the spillover effect of FDI.

Emerging Research Issues

Javorcik (2004) suggests that instead of an input–output matrix to measure the interaction between sectors, data using individual firms as suppliers to multinational firms can be used. He also suggests that the host country and foreign investor characteristics will help determine the extent of spillover. Demena and Murshed (2018) suggest that in future studies each spillover channel requires a separate study to know the exact impact on domestic firms. The length of time a foreign company has a presence in the host country, firm heterogeneity, the mode of entry, source of FDI country and motive of foreign production need to be carefully studied to know the specific nature of spillover on domestic firms. Dua, Harrison and Jefferson (2012) suggest that future research should focus on the disaggregated level. The spillover effect on certain regions, along with the role of trade policy and heterogeneity across ownership types, can also be studied to see the spillover effect.

References

Apostolov, M. (2017). The impact of FDI on the performance and entrepreneurship of domestic firms. *Journal of International Entrepreneurship*, *15*(4), 390–415.

Battese, G. E., & Coelli, T. J. (1988). Prediction of firm level technical inefficiencies with a generalized frontier production function. *Journal of Econometrics*, *38*, 387–399.

Behera, S.R., Dua, P., & Goldar, B. (2012). Foreign direct investment and technology spillover: Evidence across Indian manufacturing industries. *The Singapore Economic Review*, *57*(2). DOI: 10.1142/S0217590812500117

Blake, A., Deng, Z., & Falvey, R. (2009). How does the productivity of foreign direct investment spill over to local firms in Chinese manufacturing? *Journal of Chinese Economic and Business Studies*, 7(2), 183–197. DOI: 10.1080/14765280902847676

Borensztein, E., De Gregorio, J., & Lee, J.W. (1998). How does FDI affect economic growth? *Journal of International Economics*, 45, 115–135.

Brems, H. (1970). A growth model of international direct investment. *American Economic Review*, 60(3), 320–333.

Demena, B. A., & Murshed, S. M. (2018). Transmission channels matter: Identifying spillovers from FDI. *The Journal of International Trade and Economic Development*, 1–28, DOI:10.1080/09638199.2018.1439083.

Dua, L., Harrison, A., & Jefferson, G.H. (2012). Testing for horizontal and vertical foreign investment spillovers in China, 1998–2007. *Journal of Asian Economics*, 23(2012), 234–243.

Gorodnichenko, Y., Svejnar, J., & Terrell, K. (2014). When does FDI have positive spillovers? Evidence from 17 transition market economies. *Journal of Comparative Economics*, 42(4), 954–969.

He, S., Kwan, Y. K., & Fan, H. (2019). In search of FDI horizontal spillovers in China: Evidence from meta-analysis. *Quality & Quantity*, *53*(3), 1505–1527.

Javorcik, B.S. (2004). Does foreign direct investment increase the productivity of domestic firm? In search of spillovers through backward linkages. *The American Economic Review*, *94*(3), 605–627.

Jeon, Y., Park, B. I., & Ghauri, P. N. (2013). Foreign direct investment spillover effects in China: Are they different across industries with different technological levels? *China Economic Review*, *26*, 105–117.

Keshari, P. K. (2018). Channels of FDI spillovers, firm characteristics and decision to export by the domestic firms in selected Indian manufacturing industries. In Partha Pratim Sengupta (Ed.), *Contemporary Issues on Globalization and Sustainable Development*. Serials Publications Pvt. Limited, New Delhi.

Liang, F. H. (2017). Does foreign direct investment improve the productivity of domestic firms? Technology spillovers, industry linkages, and firm capabilities. *Research Policy*, *46*(1), 138–159.

Lin, P., Liu. Z., & Zhang, Y. (2009). Do Chinese domestic firms benefit from FDI inflow? Evidence of horizontal and vertical spillover. *China Economic Review*, 20 (2009), 677–691.

Lu, Y., Tao, Z, & Zhu, L. (2017). Identifying FDI spillovers. *Journal of International Economics*, 107(2017), 75–90.

Markusen, J.R., & Venables, A. J. (1999). Foreign direct investment as a catalyst for industrial development. *European Economic Review*, 43(1999), 335–356.

Moralles, H. F., & Moreno, R. (2020). FDI productivity spillovers and absorptive capacity in Brazilian firms: A threshold regression analysis. *International Review of Economics & Finance*, *70*, 257–272.

Romer, P.M. (1993). Idea gaps and object gaps in economic development. *Journal of Monetary Economics*, *32*(3), 543–573.

Sahu, P. K., & Solarin, S. A. (2014). Does higher productivity and efficiency lead to spillover? Evidence from Indian manufacturing. *The Journal of Developing Areas*, *48*(3), 175–193.

Schmidt, P., & Sickles, R. C. (1984). Production frontiers and panel data. *Journal of Business & Economic Statistics*, 2(4), 367–374.

Sur, A., & Nandy, A. (2018). FDI, technical efficiency and spillovers: Evidence from Indian automobile industry. *Cogent Economics & Finance*, 6(1), 1460026.

Wiboonchutikula, P., Phucharoen, C., & Pruektanakul, N. (2016). Spillover effects of foreign direct investment on domestic manufacturing firms in Thailand. *The Singapore Economic Review*, *61*(02), 1640028.

6 Market Efficiency in Indian Stock Market

A Case Study of Covid-19 and the Financial Crisis of 2008

Mukesh Kumar and Md. Absar Alam

Introduction

Adjustment of prices in the secondary market caused by any event is a common phenomenon across the globe. Such adjustment is caused by information in market. Security prices fully reflect all available information that may be related to both internal and external environment influencing a business. Internal and external environments keep on changing, resulting in change in risk perception of investors. It also plays a pivotal role in the success of a business and wealth creation of shareholders. Internal environment consists of internal growth strategy adopted by businesses or their internal decisions. Announcement of such strategies or decisions may lead to adjustment of prices and volatility. Similarly, external environments such as government regulations, instability, recession or natural calamity may lead to adjustment of prices and volatility. The efficiency of the market is judged by the speed with which prices reflect any information or event. It is very difficult to earn abnormal return; however, sometimes due to anomalies, stock market prices may deviate from intrinsic value, resulting in abnormal returns.

After globalization, several measures such as dematerialization, reduction of transaction cost, reduction of settlement time, etc., were taken for transparency and efficiency of stock markets in India. This resulted in considerable growth of the Indian stock markets. But sometimes some events take place and stock markets start crashing. Similar situation took place in 2008 in the form of the subprime crisis and in 2020 due to Covid-19. Stock markets worldwide crashed due to the financial crisis and the Covid-19 pandemic, and in India also both BSE and NSE crashed starting from May 2008 and February 2020, respectively. The financial crises of 2008 and 2020 are also referred to as the subprime crisis and the corona virus crash, respectively. At one point of time, the United States future crude price reached below zero in 2020. Similarly, in 2008 the banking firm Lehman Brothers collapsed due to subprime crisis.

Several empirical papers have been written on event study that judge the efficiency of the market during the crisis period. Research in this field helps in formulation of strategies for the future. Market efficiency examines the

DOI: 10.4324/9781003354703-8

pace, degree and accuracy with which the information is being absorbed into security prices. There are three forms of efficiency, namely weak form of efficiency, semi-strong form of efficiency and strong form of efficiency. Weak form of market efficiency states that past information is already incorporated in security prices, which means abnormal gains or abnormal losses are not possible on the basis of past information; thereby, stock prices follow a random walk. Semi-strong form of efficiency states that all available public information is already incorporated into prices, meaning thereby that investors cannot make abnormal gains or incur abnormal losses based on publicly available information unless and until they have insider information. Strong form of efficiency states that both the forms of information sourced from public and insiders are already taken into account in current stock prices. This implies that no investor has special privilege to take undue advantage of the movement in stock prices. Traditionally, it was assumed that all stock markets are efficient and stock prices reflect the intrinsic value or true market value. But after many financial crises the traditional notion was challenged and debated by many authors and researchers. The Covid-19 and subprime crises present a great opportunity to measure the weak form of efficiency. They give an opportunity to compare market efficiency during the two events leading to economic downturn and stock market crash.

Review of Literature

An efficient market hypothesis is theoretically developed by Fama (1970) and empirically tested by Malkiel and Fama (1970) by examining the impact of information on 30 stock prices of Dow Jones. It was found that the effect of efficient market model is extensive and profound. Vasicek and McQuown (1972) examine the applicability of efficient market hypothesis by creating different portfolios and calculating return and risk for each portfolio and find that the theory could be usefully employed. Khalik and Rashad (1972) examine the relationships between efficient market hypothesis and quality of accounting data. Their paper concludes that the quality of accounting data affect the efficiency of market only if the quality of accounting data was known. Grubel (1979) argue that the talented portfolio managers over the years were able to generate superior performance and state that wizards exist in the capital market. On the other hand, French (1988) analyses market efficiency and crash and argues that researchers could never reject market efficiency; rather, they could only reject the joint hypothesis of market efficiency and a particular equilibrium model. This was also argued by Fama (1976, 1995). Fama (1995) explains that the empirical evidence support random walk theory explaining stock rice behaviour and this can be challenged only if analysts have better insight or new information which has not been fully considered in forming stock prices; otherwise fundamental analysis is of no use.

At the empirical level, the idea of efficiency market hypothesis and its different forms were tested with national-level data. Jagric and Strasek

(2005) examine the efficiency by taking real financial data from Slovenian stock index and conclude that the estimated Hurst exponent may be sensitive to the frequencies of the data employed. Cooray and Wikremasinghe (2007) examine the market efficiency of emerging markets from South Asian countries and conclude that there is weak form of efficiency in India, Sri Lanka and Pakistan, but not in Bangladesh. Mishra et al. (2009) examine the efficient market hypothesis in its weak form in Indian scenario by taking stock prices data from BSE and NSE using unit root test and conclude that there is weak form of inefficiency in Indian stock markets. Basu (1977) examines the impact of P/E ratio on stock returns of NYSE by taking data for 1,400 industrial firms and finds that P/E ratio information was not fully reflected in security prices as rapidly as stated by the semi-strong form of efficient market hypothesis. Laffont and Maskin (1990) examine the impact of insider information of large traders and small traders on stock return. They find that in the competitive market, large traders have rational expectations. In the case of small traders, the informational efficiency breaks down if a trader is capable of affecting prices. Renshaw (1984) examines the impact of misinformation on panic selling in NYSE and finds that investors sometimes panic due to misinformation reaching market. Tripathi and Kumar (2015) examine the sectoral efficiency of the Indian stock market and the impact of global financial crisis by taking data from 11 sectors from NSE for the period of January 2004 to January 2014 and find that overall market was weak form of efficient but some sectors such as banking were not efficient.

There have also been researches carried out to investigate the impact of financial crisis on stock markets. Limet al. (2008) empirically investigate the effect of the 1997 financial crisis on Asian stock markets. Their paper uses bicorrelation analysis for three periods of crisis, i.e. pre-crisis, post crisis and crisis. The result indicates that crisis adversely affected the Asian stock markets. Similarly, Anagnostidis et al. (2016) investigated the impact of the 2008 crisis on Euro Zone stock market using generalized hurst exponent method. Their paper finds that the crisis adversely affected the Euro Zone stock market. Ramkumar et al. (2015) examine the efficiency of sectoral indices by taking the top-5 sectoral indices from each BSE and NSE for the period of 1 January 2009 to 31 March 2014 and find that BSE and NSE IT indices earned highest return followed by other indices. Vashishtha and Hooda (2014) examine the semi-strong form of efficiency of the Indian capital market by collecting primary data from investors investing in the Indian capital market and find that the Indian capital market is efficient in semi-strong form. Moreover, Jethwani and Achuthan (2013) discuss the efficiency of Indian stock market during the crisis period. In the literature, the impact of a crisis is taken up by several researchers. However, there is a gap in presenting a comparison of the impact to two or more economic crises. Therefore, this research aims to fulfil this gap and presents the impact of Covid-19 crisis and the financial crisis of 2008.

Method and Data

For the purpose to analyse, stock price data from two different time periods was used. For the 2008 financial crisis, daily stock price data was taken from 2 January 2008 to 30 August 2008. In the case of the Covid-19 crisis, daily stock price data was taken from 1 January 2020 to 30 July 2020.The objective of taking data for these periods was to see the market efficiency in the short term, in particular when the impact of crisis was severe on the stock market. Daily data of 100 companies were taken from BSE and NSE websites for all working weekdays with the exclusion of Saturday and Sunday. If there was a public holiday, then the data used was based on the day before the public holiday.

Another reason for taking the data for this time period is that the objective of the chapter is to examine the form of efficiency of market during the period of the financial crisis of 2008 and the economic downturn during the Covid-19 pandemic. Besides, the chapter also intends to examine the efficiency of the market during the two different types of crisis when its effect was on peak. This chapter proposes that a continuous data from the financial crisis to the Covid-19 pandemic will be important to examine the market behaviour between the two crises.

In the selection of companies, it was taken care that the selected companies are the representative companies of their respective sectors. The company-level data was further grouped as sectoral data. Daily stock returns are calculated by using daily closing sector indices through calculating the differences in the natural logarithms of the indices (Mehdian and Perry, 2001).

$$Rit = \log\left(P_{t1} / P_{t-1}\right)^{*} 100$$

Where,

Rit = Daily percentage return of stock index i on day t;
P_{t1} = Closing value of stock index i on day t and
P_{t-1} = Closing value of stock index i on day t–1.

In the case of a trading day following a non-trading day, the return is calculated using the closing price index of previous trading day. For example, the Monday daily return of price index is calculated by using the previous closing price index on Friday.

Thereafter, the log return of sectoral indices were regressed on log returns of market index to obtain parameters of characteristic line, i.e., α, β, $T(\alpha)$ and $T(\beta)$. Two types of unit root tests are used to test the form of efficiency of the market during the two time period, i.e. during the Covid-19 crisis and the 2008 crisis. These tests are Augmented Dicky Fuller Test and Phillip Peron Test. Unit root tests are chosen to carry out the current analysis based on the hypothesis that there exists a unit root in the series. It helps in identifying the nature of data. It may be noted that stock prices follow random walk in the situation when stock prices reflect all available information. If there is a presence of unit root, the data is non-stationary. On the other hand, if unit root is not present in the series, then the data is stationary. The non-stationary series follow random walk. Therefore, the chapter uses ADF test in its AR (1) process. It may be noted that the ADF test corrects the higher order serial correlation in the series and the PP test enables the analysis to make corrections in t-statistics (Ibrahim et al., 2011).

Results

For the above analysis, we calculated return in percentage only using $((P_t - P_{t-1})/P_{t-1})$ multiplied by 100. This is all in percent form.

Table 6.1 gives the descriptive statistics of stocks for the period of the financial crisis of 2008 and lockdown during the Covid-19 outbreak. During the financial crisis of 2008, the entire sector has negative mean return, including stocks of private companies and public sector undertakings. On the other hand, during the Covid-19 crisis, sectors like chemical and fertilizers, infrastructure, information and telecommunications, media and entertainment and pharmaceuticals experienced a positive mean return. Likewise, stocks of sectors like automobiles, banking, consumer durables,

Table 6.1 Descriptive Statistics

	Financial crisis:2008					
Sectors	*Mean (%)*	*Standard deviation (%)*	*Variance (%)*	*CV (%)*	*Skewness*	*Kurtosis*
Automobile	−0.21	3.50	12.28	4.43	−0.58	4.51
Aviation	−0.39	3.64	13.27	4.69	−0.42	2.14
Banking	−0.23	3.77	14.23	6.63	0.25	0.68
Chemicals and fertilizers	−0.13	4.91	24.11	6.27	−0.24	1.37
Consumer durables	−0.27	3.47	12.05	3.44	−0.18	0.57
FMCG	−0.05	2.72	7.38	2.78	−1.00	7.26
Infrastructure	−0.37	4.53	20.56	7.97	0.28	1.32
IT	−0.10	3.95	15.60	5.54	0.08	2.33
Media &entertainment	−0.32	3.16	9.98	3.06	−0.23	3.61
Mining &minerals	−0.26	4.06	16.48	4.40	−0.38	1.13
Petrochemicals and natural gas	−0.21	3.49	12.15	5.01	−0.56	2.86
Pharmaceuticals	−0.01	2.74	7.49	2.78	−1.28	7.02
Steel	−0.19	4.11	16.91	5.62	−0.27	0.87
Public sector undertakings	−0.24	3.80	14.42	5.50	−0.20	1.61
Private sector	−0.16	3.75	14.06	4.79	−0.57	3.38
Market	**−0.17**	**2.40**	**5.73**	**4.93**	**0.05**	**0.59**

Table 6.2 Descriptive Statistics

	Covid-19:2020					
Sectors	*Mean (%)*	*Standard deviation (%)*	*Variance (%)*	*CV (%)*	*Skewness*	*Kurtosis*
Automobile	-0.14	3.95	15.62	6.9	-0.6	3.4
Aviation	0.11	4.53	20.49	2.5	-0.1	-1.7
Banking	-0.27	3.98	15.81	7.2	-1.0	4.5
Chemicals and fertilizers	0.18	5.58	31.13	5.1	-0.3	5.9
Consumer durables	-0.08	3.34	11.16	4.8	-0.9	3.3
FMCG	-0.02	2.78	7.71	4.4	-0.4	7.2
Infrastructure	0.11	4.03	16.26	4.4	-0.9	1.6
IT	0.08	3.79	14.39	5.5	-1.2	4.9
Media &entertainment	0.23	4.64	21.57	3.1	1.1	6.6
Mining &minerals	-0.15	3.84	14.76	5.2	-0.7	3.2
Petrochemicals and natural gas	-0.06	3.86	14.86	5.7	-1.0	5.9
Pharmaceuticals	0.25	3.60	12.98	4.2	-0.4	5.3
Steel	-0.01	4.39	19.24	6.9	-0.2	1.8
Public sector undertakings	-0.18	3.77	14.25	6.1	-1.0	4.8
Private sector	0.05	4.06	16.48	5.3	-1.5	6.3
Market	**-0.10**	**2.70**	**7.31**	**5.5**	**-0.9**	**5.7**

Source: Authors'calculations.

FMCG, mining and minerals, petrochemicals and gas and steel experienced a negative mean return. Stocks of the private companies experienced a positive mean return compared to the stocks of public sector undertakings. The highest return during the Covid-19 period was generated by the pharmaceutical sector. During the 2008 financial crisis, the lowest return was experienced by the aviation and infrastructure sector. During the Covid-19 period, the lowest return was noted in the stocks of the banking sector companies. Thus, the banking sector was the most risky sector for investment during the Covid-19 period and the infrastructure sector was the most risky sector during the financial crisis period, like the banking sector during the Covid-19 period and the infrastructure sector during the 2008 crisis with high covariance (CV) compared to other sectors.

The relative risk of stocks is measured by CV determining the volatility of the stocks. The CV is measured for return on stocks of individual sectors and overall market returns. The result explains that all sectors vary with variation in market during both the Covid-19 crisis and the financial crisis of 2008. There are some sectors thatindicate relatively more volatility than the others. Theskewness results indicate that the market for all the sectors except media and entertainment were skewed negatively during

Covid-19, while in 2008, there were some sectors skewed positively, like banking, infrastructure and information and technologies sectors.

The next task was to estimate parameters for characteristics line for all individual sectors. This was done using panel regression analysis of data for crisis period and also for the data during the Covid-19 period. In order to do regression analysis, we have calculated the index of return and have-taken natural log of them and carried out unit root tests for checking whether the series is stationary or non-stationary.

Tables 6.3 and 6.4 present results of Augmented Dickey Fuller (ADF) and Tables 6.5 and 6.6 Phillips-Perron (PP) unit root tests for 12 sectors. Tables 6.3 and 6.4 presents ADF results for the period of the 2008 crisis and the Covid-19 crisis, respectively. Similarly, the results of PP test for the 2008 crisis and Covid-19 is presented in Tables 6.4 and Table 6.5, respectively.

The null hypothesis in ADF test is that there is a presence of unit root in the series. The result of Tables 6.3 and 6.4 indicate the null hypothesis is rejected at 1% level of significance. Similarly, PP test also tests the null hypothesis that there is the presence of unit root in the series. Results in Tables 6.5 and 6.6 reject the null hypothesis.

In all the cases, results highlight the absence of unit root in the series, and therefore, the data is stationary and also suggest that the series is not a random walk. As a result, during both the crises, the Indian stock market tended to be not efficient in weak forms. It is important to mention that the market behaves similarly in the two time periods. However, the chapter does not attempt to compare the form of efficiency of market during crises and non-crises periods. It is suggested that after a normalcy in the stock market after the Covid-19 pandemic, a long period data should be analysed in order to examine the behaviour of market not only in the times of crises but also in the times of normalcy. The current study focused on comparing the two crises periods.

Conclusion

This research presents a comparative picture of the impact of the Covid-19 crisis and the financial crisis of 2008 on the Indian stock markets. In the beginning, a descriptive analysis was presented in order to understand the sectoral risks during both the crises. In order to do the test of market efficiency, unit root tests are used for data during the Covid-19 crisis and the 2008 crisis. During the financial crisis of 2008, the entire sector experienced negative mean return, including the stocks of private companies and public sector undertakings. During this period, the infrastructure sector was the most volatile sector for investors. On the other hand, during the Covid-19 crisis, sectors like chemical and fertilizers, infrastructure, information and telecommunications, media and entertainment and pharmaceuticals experienced positive mean return. The highest return during the Covid-19 period was generated by pharmaceutical sectors and the lowest return was generated by the banking sector companies.

Table 6.3 Results of ADF Test

Financial crisis:2008									
		P-value				*Estimate statistics*			
S. No.	*Sectors*	*P*	*Z*	*L*	*Pm*	*P*	*Z*	*L*	*Pm*
1	Automobile	0.000	0.000	0.000	0.000	519.948	-21.488	-48.283	83.658
2	Banking	0.000	0.000	0.000	0.000	538.101	-21.768	-47.357	81.919
3	Chemical and fertilizer	0.000	0.000	0.000	0.000	495.798	-20.618	-43.634	75.230
4	Consumer durables	0.000	0.000	0.000	0.000	365.790	-17.879	-38.624	66.482
5	FMCG	0.000	0.000	0.000	0.000	651.289	-24.262	-57.318	99.816
6	Infrastructure	0.000	0.000	0.000	0.000	383.182	-18.421	-40.460	69.769
7	IT	0.000	0.000	0.000	0.000	705.624	-25.276	-59.161	103.060
8	Media	0.000	0.000	0.000	0.000	131.910	-10.940	-26.762	45.223
9	Mining	0.000	0.000	0.000	0.000	266.298	-15.346	-33.432	57.310
10	Petrochemicals	0.000	0.000	0.000	0.000	616.533	-23.333	-51.691	89.629
11	Pharmaceuticals	0.000	0.000	0.000	0.000	585.995	-22.815	-51.572	89.492
12	Steel	0.000	0.000	0.000	0.000	367.128	-17.781	-36.205	62.071

Significant at 1% level.
P = Inverse chi-squared(20), Z = Inverse normal, L = Inverse logit t(54), Pm = Modified inv. chi-squared.

Table 6.4 Results of ADF Test

	Covid-19:2020								
		P-value				*Estimate statistics*			
S. No.	*Sectors*	*P*	*Z*	*L*	*Pm*	*P*	*Z*	*L*	*Pm*
1	Automobile	0.000	0.000	0.000	0.000	347.727	–16.547	–32.290	54.955
2	Banking	0.000	0.000	0.000	0.000	443.619	–19.545	–39.042	66.980
3	Chemical and fertilizer	0.000	0.000	0.000	0.000	388.253	–17.760	–34.168	58.226
4	Consumer durables	0.000	0.000	0.000	0.000	227.815	–13.530	–24.055	40.407
5	FMCG	0.000	0.000	0.000	0.000	384.588	–18.087	–33.847	57.647
6	Infrastructure	0.000	0.000	0.000	0.000	200.154	–12.298	–21.132	35.180
7	IT	0.000	0.000	0.000	0.000	388.085	–17.910	–32.538	55.190
8	Media	0.000	0.000	0.000	0.000	54.833	-6.606	–11.125	17.972
9	Mining	0.000	0.000	0.000	0.000	184.794	–12.404	–23.200	39.085
10	Petrochemicals	0.000	0.000	0.000	0.000	417.158	–18.617	–34.975	59.572
11	Pharmaceuticals	0.000	0.000	0.000	0.000	421.185	–18.725	–37.067	63.433
12	Steel	0.000	0.000	0.000	0.000	294.213	–15.483	–27.321	46.036

Significant at 1% level.
P = Inverse chi-squared (20), Z = Inverse normal, L = Inverse logit t (54), Pm = Modified inv. chi-squared.

Table 6.5 Results of PP Test

	Financial crisis: 2008								
		P-value				*Estimate statistics*			
S. No.	*Sectors*	*P*	*Z*	*L*	*Pm*	*P*	*Z*	*L*	*Pm*
1	Automobile	0.000	0.000	0.000	0.000	639.621	-24.189	-59.396	103.604
2	Banking	0.000	0.000	0.000	0.000	711.755	-25.518	-62.639	109.376
3	Chemical and fertilizer	0.000	0.000	0.000	0.000	660.323	-24.469	-58.113	101.244
4	Consumer durables	0.000	0.000	0.000	0.000	498.940	-21.366	-52.683	91.645
5	FMCG	0.000	0.000	0.000	0.000	720.873	-25.696	-63.442	110.818
6	Infrastructure	0.000	0.000	0.000	0.000	486.508	-21.068	-51.370	89.296
7	IT	0.000	0.000	0.000	0.000	792.960	-26.951	-66.483	116.227
8	Media	0.000	0.000	0.000	0.000	144.175	-11.492	-29.251	49.559
9	Mining	0.000	0.000	0.000	0.000	333.748	-17.358	-41.900	72.392
10	Petrochemicals	0.000	0.000	0.000	0.000	779.906	-26.704	-65.389	114.259
11	Pharmaceuticals	0.000	0.000	0.000	0.000	696.824	-25.190	-61.325	107.015
12	Steel	0.000	0.000	0.000	0.000	545.657	-22.264	-53.810	93.631

Significant at 1% level
P = Inverse chi-squared(20), Z = Inverse normal, L = Inverse logit t(54), Pm = Modified inv. chi-squared

Table 6.6 Results of PP Test

	Covidcrisis: 2020								
		P-value				*Estimate statistics*			
S. No.	*Sectors*	*P*	*Z*	*L*	*Pm*	*P*	*Z*	*L*	*Pm*
1	Automobile	0.000	0.000	0.000	0.000	575.830	–22.753	–53.472	92.972
2	Banking	0.000	0.000	0.000	0.000	678.831	–24.794	–59.742	104.170
3	Chemical and fertilizer	0.000	0.000	0.000	0.000	626.363	–23.183	–55.123	95.874
4	Consumer durables	0.000	0.000	0.000	0.000	379.943	–18.279	–40.118	69.157
5	FMCG	0.000	0.000	0.000	0.000	648.406	–24.202	–57.064	99.360
6	Infrastructure	0.000	0.000	0.000	0.000	357.994	–17.572	–37.801	65.009
7	IT	0.000	0.000	0.000	0.000	720.616	–25.433	–60.418	105.320
8	Media	0.000	0.000	0.000	0.000	83.945	–8.534	–17.031	28.265
9	Mining	0.000	0.000	0.000	0.000	300.199	–16.402	–37.688	64.890
10	Petrochemicals	0.000	0.000	0.000	0.000	704.258	–25.122	–59.046	102.854
11	Pharmaceuticals	0.000	0.000	0.000	0.000	654.325	–24.341	–57.585	100.296
12	Steel	0.000	0.000	0.000	0.000	578.616	–22.796	–53.731	93.436

Significant at 1% level.
P = Inverse chi-squared (20), Z = Inverse normal, L = Inverse logit t(54), Pm = Modified inv. chi-squared.

During the two crises, the Indian stock market was not efficient in weak form. One of the important constraints of these analyses is the use of the short run data. It is important to do such analysis on long run panel data. It can be construed that in the short run during both the financial crisis of 2008 and the Covid-19 crisis, the Indian stock market behaved in a similar fashion. The research suggests that long run analysis of the market data is needed in order to present a better comparison of the impact of the two crises on the Indian stock market.

References

Anagnostidis, P., Varsakelis, C., & Emmanouilides, C. J. (2016). "Has the 2008 financial crisis affected stock market efficiency? The case of Eurozone." *Physica A: Statistical Mechanics and its Applications*, *447*, 116–128.

Basu, S. (Jan1977). "Investment performance of common stocks in relation to their price-earnings ratios: A test of the efficient market hypothesis." *The Journal of Finance*, *32*(3),663–682.

Cooray, A., & Wickremasinghe, G. (2007). "The efficiency of emerging stock markets: Empirical evidence from the South Asian region." *The Journal of Developing Areas*, *41*(1), 171–183.

Fama, E. F. (1970). "Efficient capital markets: A review of theory and empirical work." *Journal of Finance*, *25*, 383–417.

Fama, E. F. (1976). "Efficient capital markets: Reply." *The Journal of Finance*, *31*(1), 143–145.

Fama, E. F. (1995). "Random walks in stock market prices." *Financial Analysts Journal*, *51*(1), 75–80.

French, K. R. (1988). "Crash-testing the efficient market hypothesis." *NBER Macroeconomics Annual*, *3*, 277–285.

Grubel, H. G. (1979). "The Peter principle and the efficient market hypothesis." *Financial Analysts Journal*, *35*(6), 72–75.

Ibrahim, J., Long, Y., Ab Ghani, H., & Salleh, S. I. M. (2011). Weak-form efficiency of foreign exchange market in the organisation for economic cooperation and development countries: Unit root test. *International Journal of Business and Management*, *6*(6), 55

Jagric, T., & Strasek, S. (2005). "Efficient market hypothesis in the capital market of a small transition economy-does it hold?"*ActaOeconomica*, *55*(4), 427–452.

Jethwani, K., & Achuthan, S. (2013). "Stock market efficiency and crisis: Evidence from India." *Asia-Pacific Finance and Accounting Review*, *1*(2), 35.

Khalik, A., & Rashad, Abdel (Oct 1972). "The efficient market hypothesis and accounting data: A point of view." *The Accounting Review*, *47*(4), 791–793.

Laffont, Jean-Jacques, & Maskin, Erik S. (Feb 1990). "The efficient market hypothesis and insider trading on the stock market." *The Journal of Political Economy*, 98(1),70–93.

Lim, K. P., Brooks, R. D., & Kim, J. H. (2008). "Financial crisis and stock market efficiency: Empirical evidence from Asian countries." *International Review of Financial Analysis*, *17*(3), 571–591.

Malkiel, B. G., & Fama, E. F. (1970). "Efficient capital markets: A review of theory and empirical work." *The Journal of Finance*, *25*(2), 383–417.

Mehdian, S., & Perry, M. J. (2001). The reversal of the Monday effect: new evidence from US equity markets. *Journal of Business Finance & Accounting*, *28*(7–8), 1043–1065.

Mishra, P. K., Das, K. B., & Pradhan, B. B. (2009). "Empirical evidence on Indian stock market efficiency in context of the global financial crisis." *Global Journal of Finance and Management*, *1*(2), 149–157.

Ramkumar, R. Rajesh, Selvam, M., Raja, M., Lingaraja, K., & Vasanth, V. (2015) "Efficiency of sectoral indices: A comparative study of BSE and NSE LTD."*International Business Management*, *9*(3), 258–266.

Renshaw, Edward F.(May–June1984). "Stock market panics: A test of the stock market hypothesis." *Financial Analyst Journal*, *40*(3), 48–51.

Tripathi, V., & Kumar, A. (2015). "Sectoral efficiency of the Indian stock market and the impact of global financial crisis." *Journal of Commerce & Accounting Research*, *4*(1), 46–62.

Vashishtha, S. D., & Hooda, Kalpana (2014). "Efficient market hypothesis: A study of Indian capital market." *International Journal of Social Science & Interdisciplinary Research*, *3*(2), 104–122.

Vasicek, O. A., & McQuown, John A.(1972). "The efficient market model." *Financial Analyst Journal*, *28*(5), 71–84.

7 Thai Canal Project

A Case Study of Regional Geo-economic Perspective

Mohd Faheem

Introduction

The Thai Canal is one of the major projects that would potentially connect Thailand with the Belt and Road Initiative (BRI). The Thai Canal would be a man-made canal proposed through five provinces in the southern part of Thailand on the Malay Peninsula. The canal would link the Andaman Sea to the South China Sea, which would shorten the distance from the Malacca strait to China by around 1,200 km or 3–4 days. However, in order to conduct the Thai Canal project, Thailand needed to consider national security and geopolitics. For national security, the north and the south of Thailand would physically be separated by the canal if the project is successful. The Thai government might find it difficult to govern the whole area of Thailand. Moreover, considering the geopolitical issue, Singapore and Malaysia, which are in the main area of the Malacca Strait, used for shipping, would lose the benefit if the Thai Canal project was completed. As a global comparison, the Thai Canal would be comparable in size to the Suez and Panama Canals. The Suez Canal stretches over 192 km and the Panama Canal is 77 km long, and the preferred route of the Kra Canal is 128 km long.

The excavation of the Thai Canal was a shortcut for maritime undertaking as part of a megaproject. The idea of the Thai Canal began under King Narai the Great. The objective of the excavation was to save time and facilitate trade with Western countries without passing through the Malacca Strait. However, the project was suspended at that time. The Thai Canal project was proposed many times because the excavation had many advantages. During the Rattanakosin period, the project was proposed in 1793 under King Rama I, in 1858 under King Rama IV, and in 1862 and 1882 under King Rama V. But there were no actions taken on the project.

In the year 1999, an extraordinary committee was set up to study the possibility of digging the Thai Canal. The senate collaborated with Management Limited and Japan's Global Fund Research Foundation. Under this collaboration, it was found that the 5A route was likely to be a suitable canal line. However, the 5A canal line was still an environmental issue as it needed to be cut through different geographical paths like

DOI: 10.4324/9781003354703-9

Songkhla Lake, which is the largest natural lake full of marine animals and resources.

In 2002, during the government of Pol. Maj. Thaksin Shinawatra, the Senate Extraordinary Committee conducted additional studies and found that there was a new route that might be better than the original route. The proposed new route, 9A, connected the Krabi Province and the Nakhon Si Thammarat Province (Ko Lanta District, Krabi Province; Sikao District; Wang Wiset District; Huai Yot District; Ratsada District Trang; Pa Payom District, Phatthalung Province; Cha-uat District; Ban Phru, Khuan Kraeng; Hua Sai District, Nakhon Si Thammarat Province). Therefore, it would not cut through Songkhla Lake like Route 5A. The committee, therefore, named the new line 'Thai Canal'. This period had the most potential to begin excavation for the canal, but there was a revolution in Thailand that caused the work on the Thai Canal to stop.

In 2017, the Thai–Chinese Cultural and Economic Association (TCCEA) and the European Association for Business and Commerce (EABC) held a convention to discuss the possibility of the Kra Canal or the Thai Canal project. In early February, the Thai Canal Association for Education and Development (TCA), which is a military seniority society, saw the benefits of the excavation of the Thai Canal. It was estimated that the Thai Canal project would cost approximately 28,000 million dollars (868,000 million baht) and would take about six years to complete. The Chinese authorities offered to provide both financial and technological support to Thailand for this project. There are two functional aspects to the Thai Canal project: (1) the canal connecting the South China Sea and the Indian Ocean, which would help avoid going through the traffic-high Malacca Strait and (2) the special economic zones which consists of cities and artificial islands in the area, for which the Thai Canal would act as a transportation intersection.

Recently, it was decided that this project would be included as part of China's mega-century project, the New Silk Road. The Silk Road was divided into two routes: the land and the road and rail routes from the west of China through Central Asia to Europe and the Maritime Silk Road from the east of China to the south through ASEAN to Africa, the Middle East, and Europe. Then China would be the headquarters of the world economy. For this project, China would be particularly benefitted if the Thai Canal was successfully excavated. For Chinese, they can face difficulties in trade through the Malacca Strait, where they would be faced with weather variability and the threat posed by pirates. It would be better to sail through the Thai Canal to the Andaman Sea and the Indian Ocean.

Despite its multiple benefits to Thailand, the Thai Canal project has not been launched. Therefore, this present study aims to analyze the barriers to the commencement of the Thai Canal project. The result of this study would benefit China to understand the difficulty of the Thai decision on launching the project as well as help in proposing solutions to start the excavation of the Thai Canal. If Thailand could start the project, the Thai Canal would be a suitable route for shipping. It would also help to reduce the air pollution of the world, which causes the greenhouse effect. Therefore, digging the Thai Canal will greatly benefit Thailand in many ways.

The objective of this chapter is to understand the geo-economic significance of the Thai Canal and China's global vision of a new Maritime Silk Road which leads directly through Thailand and opens the door for an economic opportunity. The chapter also aims to analyze the regional geo-economic impact of the Thai Canal.

This study is based on the secondary sources of data, particularly existing government reports, online information and published works on the subject in various journals. This study uses a case study method to analyze the impact of the Thai Canal on the regional economics in Southeast Asia.

Literature Review

Korkaew Jankingthong (2016) studied the impact and feasibility of the Thai Canal project (kor kot gra). The result revealed that people's opinions towards the impact of the Thai Canal project, Routes 2A, 5A, 7A, and 9A were different. Moreover, while people agreed to the construction of the Thai Canal project model 9A, they were uncertain about the construction of the canal models 2A and 7A. People didn't agree to construct the canal model 5A. Furthermore, a comparison of people's opinions towards the different routes of the Thai canal project (2A, 5A, 7A, and 9A) classified by personal factors found that people's opinions towards the implementation of the Thai Canal project differed depending on their levels of education, occupation, revenue, and whether they were residents of the country or not. Lastly, the opinions of executives and officers of public and private organizations regarding the implementation and the potential advantages and disadvantages of the Thai Canal project were different from that of the people.

Donhatai Jornwat (2016) conducted a study on "Thai Canal: Considerations and Legal Preparations" which aimed to study and scrutinize crucial issues. The study presented an argument against the Thai Canal by concentrating on the legal dimension and suggesting legal preparation for the future implementation of the project.

Wiwat Jankingthong (2017) investigated the impact of the Thai Canal project implementation in Route 7A (Trang-Songkhla). The results showed that the implementation of the Thai Canal project, Route 7A, had both positive and negative impacts. Overall, the average public was uncertain about the construction of the canal in Route 7A. In addition, their different careers, monthly incomes, and hometowns differentiated their attitudes towards the Thai Canal project implementation in Route 7A (Trang-Songkhla).

Importance of the Thai Canal Project

The purpose of the Thai Canal project is to connect the Gulf of Thailand to the Andaman Sea, which would make a better alternative to the Malacca Strait and help Singapore become an important global trade hub. The Thai

Canal is expected to have an estimated traffic volume of 84,000 ships, equal to around 30% of global trade (Shawn W. Crispin, 2018). The impact of a canal solution would be massive in several aspects. And many countries, such as Thailand, China, Japan, and other East Asian nations, will gain benefits from this project. Moreover, the Thai Canal would help China build a shorter route from the South China Sea to the Andaman Sea to avoid travelling around Malaysia over approximately 3–6 days or 1,200 km (M Kewalramani, 2019).

The advantage of the 9A route for Thailand is that it is located at the center of the southern part of Thailand, which is far from Myanmar and Singapore. This means that these two countries would not be able to build industrial companies to compete with Thailand. Thailand could also build a harbor to provide shelter from monsoon on both sides of the Thai Canal. The 9A line also has potential for urban development (Donhatai Jornwat, 2016).

If Thailand would start the Thai canal project, it will create a new world sea route. Ships from European and Middle Eastern countries will come directly to the Andaman coast past the Thai Canal to the Thai coast going to the South China Sea to go to China, Japan, Taiwan, and South Korea without having to pass through the three straits.

Thai Canal: Prospect for Thailand

The proposed construction of the Thai Canal is a great opportunity for Thailand to create huge financial benefits. Even when the global oil reserve runs out, sea transportation will still be important to every country in the world. Sea transport is the cheapest method of transportation for large amounts of goods. Every country that sea freight ships pass through will receive economic benefits. The Thai Canal will change the face of Thailand's economy enormously, as soon as the Thai Canal is finished, it will create 2–3 million stable jobs, benefiting many generations.

The Thai Canal would reduce poverty in Thailand, especially in the south of Thailand. It would develop to be the center of exchange goods and job opportunities for the local people. It would propel economic growth in southern Thailand. The primary income of the southern people is rubber and palm oil, but the prices are very low now, which has caused a downward economic turn. Therefore, the Thai Canal project would improve the economic situation as well as maintain the stability of the domestic politics. However, the Thai Canal had a very long time for debates, and at the same time, it is very much relevant to present for discussion. As Thailand is weak in terms of its political influence and lacks in budget and Navy, it would have to work on these weaknesses in order to support this project.

The Thai Canal will enhance the country's logistics and will save costs in sea transportation up to 200 billion baht every year. At present, oil refineries in Thailand use 800,000 barrels of crude oil; if we use a 120,000-barrel oil tanker, it would take 7 oil tankers to deliver crude oil to the refinery at Rayong or Chonburi every day.

The Thai Canal will create an opportunity for Thai fishing ships to use Thailand's oceanic boundaries in the Andaman coast, which is an abundant source of fish and has more area than the whole region of Thailand particularly with the boundaries to the Indian Ocean. More than 50,000 Thai fishing ships inside and outside the Thai coast will receive benefits from being able to travel and operate in both coasts, reducing the costs from fuel. These fishing ships will be free from being caught for invading the oceanic boundaries of neighboring countries.

Thai Canal: Prospect for China

In modern times, the Canal has been given serious reconsideration by China, which considers the route as part of the 21st-century maritime Silk Road. In this regard, China has shown keen interest with Thailand to build the Thai Canal. China can connect directly to the Pacific Ocean and the Indian Ocean, and go out of the country through the "Maritime Road" to become a true trading power. China is the largest oil importer. Eighty percent of China's oil is imported from the Middle East through the Malacca Strait. It would reduce the shipping cost, and someday if China is blocked by other competitor powers, this Canal might be a good alternative way (William Mellor, 2018). China supports the Thai Canal project because it is likely to improve economic power not only in China but also in the Southeast Asian region. China can also pursue multi-cooperation with other countries through it maritime power and support the freedom of sailing legally to guarantee the security of its sea paths. The BRI connected the land, infrastructure, finance and economy, which could help in the rise of China and to stability and advancement in the region. China can avoid the South China Sea dispute by supporting the Thai Canal project. Hence, this Canal is a logical alternative for China.

China will push to establish harbor facilities and manufacturing zones, and Thailand can collect sailing fees from tankers from the countries that use the canal line. For China, using the Thai Canal as a shipping line would reduce the cost of transportation of oil from the east to Thailand without having to pass through the Malacca Strait. Furthermore, China's rise would help the Thai military to be stronger because of the transportation. Sailing the ships to Thailand, China's ships would not need to sail past the Malacca Strait. This means the ships can sail quicker between the two coastlines.

With regard to the financial and economic aspects, the Canal is very weak. The real reason for China's interest in the Canal is strategic and military. Most of China's oil passes through the Malacca Straits, which is a convenient chokepoint to blockade, sometimes called "China's windpipe". This is a huge strategic weakness for China. This is why China has been trying to diversify oil transport routes, including this Canal and the "New Silk Road", while also building a Navy that can project power far enough to break a blockade on the Malacca Straits. The economic viability of the Canal is not an issue for the Chinese, who are the latest group to take a stab at the Kra Canal idea. It is a strategic play.

Thai Canal: Regional Geo-economic Implications

Natural infrastructure, particularly maritime canals and straits, play an important role around the globe during freight transportation. These two routes have become an alternative for the maritime transporter to reduce their navigation duration, fuel cost and fuel consumption, improving time bound delivery as well as preserving effective performance in order to avoid facing navigating risks and unpredictable conditions of the ocean. It is also claimed that the Canal will greatly benefit East Asian countries and littorals of the Indian Ocean Rim Association (IOR) since it would result in reducing maritime transportation.

In Southeast Asia, the Malacca Strait is an important route that connects the Indian Ocean to the South China Sea. It links major economic nations such as the Middle East, China, Japan and South Korea to the Western market. The Straits is 65 km wide and 800 km in length of shipping waterways, creating one of the world's chokepoints with the most traffic. There are more than 200 vessels passing the Malacca Straits on a daily basis, including 40–50 oil tankers carrying an estimated 15–16 million barrels of oil, transiting to and from Asian seaports (Ba, 2018). This is the reason that the Straits of Malacca have become one of the most important waterways in the world. Both Malaysia and Singapore reap enormous advantages from the Straits of Malacca to enhance and develop their economic performance by creating a lot of job opportunities locally and internationally through the seaports and seaport-centric logistics business along the Straits (Hayashi, 2002).

Along the Straits of Malacca, maritime industry, especially related to seaport, is growing efficiently, especially in Selangor (Port Klang), Penang (Penang Port), Johor (Port of Tanjung Pelepas and Johor Port) and Malacca (Port of Tanjung Langsat and Port of Kuala Linggi). The Straits of Malacca's crucial geopolitical location is one of the main factors influencing how competitive seaports are in global sea routes. The seaports that are located along the Straits become significant for shipping, labor migration and knowledge exchange, especially between neighboring countries (Evers and Darit, 2011).

An unclear argument exists that the construction of the Thai Canal is expected to reduce the number of vessels passing through the Straits of Malacca. However, the Straits of Malacca will still remain strategically salient for trade between the Persian Gulf and Indonesia or Australia, especially for containerships (Panda, 2013). Besides, the construction of the Thai Canal indirectly benefits Singapore and Malaysia by triggering an acceleration of economic development and trade in the entire region (Tennenbaum, 2014).

The Thai Canal can bring massive opportunities for maritime trade in the Southeast Asian region. It would be beneficial for the development among littoral countries, increase and boost the fishery industries and the tourism business. The Thai Canal would bring peace among the countries of Southeast Asian region, including with regard to the dispute of the South China Sea. Due to the heavy maritime traffic and pollution of the Malacca Strait, Singapore, Malaysia and Indonesia face the problems directly. The Thai Canal would reduce these problems. Myanmar and Indo-China nations can also gain benefits from the Canal.

The Thai Canal has a potential to change the political economy of the coastal countries in the ASEAN nations; it has a direct effect on Singapore, and might affect Port Klang of Malaysia. The Malacca Strait is 620 miles long in the area of the Sumatra Islands of Malaysia. The ships sailing from Western countries need to navigate through the Malacca Strait. Indeed, the Malacca Strait has been generating revenue for Singapore for a long time, so the excavation of the Thai Canal would reduce the number of ships navigating through Singapore. Singapore's economy is very diversified from the aerial hub, port, manufacture, tourism and finance, but it cannot be denied that the Canal project would reduce Singapore's income by around 30% of the shipping. Prime Minister Lee Hsien Loong declared that Singapore could stay above the competition due to the well-managed Changi Airport and even the fact that Thailand is in a better geographical position by using the Thai Canal project. The Malacca Strait can still remain a sailing path for the trade of Indonesia and Australia.

However, if the Canal is built, the estimated time duration to cross the Indian Ocean to the South China Sea may reduce the transportation cost, at the same time reducing the oil consumption compared to the inefficiency in using the Straits of Malacca. Besides, vessels can avoid the heavy traffic at the Straits of Malacca and can reduce the number of accidents of ship at the straits (Jeevan, 2016). By using the Thai Canal, vessels can reduce their journey by 2–3 days (instead of using the Malacca Straits). Further, the Thai Canal may reduce 4–5 days by circumventing the Sunda Straits, and finally 6–7 days can be reduced via the Thai Canal instead of using Lombok Strait in Indonesia. A concern has been aroused that the Thai Canal will not affect the Thai economy and not provide significant return benefits due to the attractiveness possessed by the primary seaports in Malaysia as well as in Singapore (Thongsin, 2002). This circumstance demonstrated that seaports' attractiveness was decreasing and was being kept from declining as a result of rivalry between or within regions' competitors.

In contrast, the development of the Thai Canal could possibly contribute a positive advantage to Thailand. For example, the Thai government will develop transportation infrastructure to allow for greater connectivity and substantial access to trade routes and to attract investors to invest in their region. Besides, the Thai government may generate revenue from activities related to the Thai Canal, such navigations, toll fees, tariff, space allocations and value-added services (Sulong, 2013). On the other hand, the construction of the Thai Canal might provide a negative impact to Malaysia. This is because Bangkok will have the advantage on the Canal because shippers would prefer to navigate through this new waterway for a shorter and faster journey from the east to the west and vice versa. However, the construction of the Thai Canal will not be a perfect choice for shipping lines because the toll fee for passing through the Thai Canal in addition to other charges would affect the freight chargers at the point of destination. Hence, shippers might prefer to utilize the Straits of Malacca as their preferable route due to its free toll passageway. The construction of the Thai Canal would actually provide mixed impacts to Malaysia. The negative impacts of the Canal to Malaysia would be the reduced ship traffic in the Straits of Malacca, reduced ship calls at local ports, decreased containers trade at local ports and a change in the trade and economic development of pattern. On the other hand, this Canal improves the overall security and navigation in the Straits of Malacca and the capacity to cater to the increasing traffic volume and the enlarging Malaysian manufacturing base and international trade and promotes regional trade and improves the port competitiveness (Khalid, 2006).

The Straits of Malacca has been bringing huge economic advantages for Singapore and Malaysia for many decades. In the case of Singapore, its transition from being a tiny fishing village to becoming the richest city in the world shows what a huge benefit the Strait is; most of world's container ships bypass Singapore, and even the Chinese, South Korean and Japanese economies has boomed in the past decades.

Singapore would be affected but not much due to construction of the Thai Canal and at the same time because of the Thai Canal is not the Suez or the Panama Canal. Also, Singapore does not depend that heavily on location in the shipping industry. Singapore's dominance in the shipping and trading industry is not only due to its location but also due to its political stability, contract predictability, logistical efficiency and trade openness.

Conclusion

The Thai Canal, also known as the Kra Canal, is a proposed canal that would cut across the Malay Peninsula in Southern Thailand. This manmade waterway would connect the Andaman Sea with the Gulf of Thailand, providing a maritime shortcut by rerouting shipping away from the Strait of Malacca. The Canal of approximately 100 km would save 1,200 km on the current journey via Singapore. The idea for a Klong Thai (Thai Canal) was first proposed by Thai King Narai in the 17th century, and the British East India Company showed interest in the early 19th century. The plan has been revisited over the centuries, but the financial and technical challenges involved in the project have prevented the project's inception. The Thai Canal might be a great economic prospect to Thailand and might strengthen its role in global trade transportation. The project is going to be beneficial in terms of tourism and developing special economic zones along the Canal. China has shown keen interest in developing the Thai Canal by financing the project, and it has also become a part of China's Belt and Road Initiative as it would strengthen geostrategic power of China in the Southeast region and at the same avoid the route of the Strait of Malacca. The geo-economic implications of the Thai Canal to the countries in the region of Southeast Asia and East Asia might be both positive and negative. An important impact of the Canal would be on the Strait of Malacca route, where the shipping traffic and trade of countries such as Malaysia and Singapore might be affected. But these implications are only possible if the Thai Canal is ready for execution.

Acknowledgement

I appreciate the support of Pridi Banomyong International College, Thammasat University, in presenting this work.

References

Ba, A. D. (2018). Governing the Safety and Security of the Malacca Strait: The Nippon Foundation between States and Industry. *Journal of Contemporary Asia*, 48(2), 252–277.

Er, Lam Peng (2018, February 01). Thailand's Kra Canal Proposal and China's Maritime Silk Road: Between Fantasy and Reality? *Asian Affairs An American Review*, 45, 1–17.

Evers, H. D., & Darit, S. (2011). Malaysian Maritime Potential and the Straits of Malacca. *Roczniki Socjologii Morskiej. Annuals of Marine Sociology, VOL. XX. Publisher: Polish Academy of Sciences - The Gdansk Branch Commission of Marine Sociology. ISSN: 0860-6552*, PP. 40–45.

Hayashi, R. (2002). Cooperation between Coastal State and User States in the Malacca and Singapore Straits. Unpublished Master Thesis, World Maritime University, 20–22.

Jankingthong, Korkaew (2016). The Impact and Feasibility of the Thai Canal Project (kor kot gra). Kingland Company, Hatyai.

Jankingthong, Wiwat (2017). The Impact of Thai Canal Project Implementation in Route 7A (Trang-Songkhla). Journal of Liberal Arts, Prince of Songkla University.

Jeevan, J., Chen, S. L., & Pateman. H. (2016). Implications of One Belt One Road for Malaysian Connectivity to International Trade Routes, *Proceedings of the "One Belt One Road" (OBOR) Conference*, December 1–2, 2016, RMIT University, Melbourne, Australia.

Jornwat, Donhatai (2016). Thai Canal: Considerations and Legal Preparations.

Kewalramani, M. (2019, April). The Kra Canal.

Khalid, N. (2006). Potential Effects on Malaysian Port and Shipping Sector. *Proposed Kra Canal Project*, 10–12.

Mellor, William (2018, January). Asian Panama Canal, a vision or a mirage.

Meon, Rheac (2018, April 06). Thailand's Kra Canal: China's Way Around the Malacca Strait.

Micallef, Joseph V. (2019). The Geopolitics of the Kra Canal, 2019, retrieved on 19 December,2020 from https://www.military.com/daily-news/2017/10/04/geopolitic-kra-canal.html

Panda, A. (2013, December 1). How a Canal Could Transform Southeast Asia.

Port Vision (2017, September 20), Thailand's Kra Canal: Game-Changer Waiting to Happen, retrieved on 15 December, 2020 from https://www.portvision.com/news-events/press-releases-news/thailands-kra-canal-game-changer-waiting-to-happen

Shawn, W. Crispin (2018, January 25). A Man, a Plan, a Canal Thailand.

Sulong, R. S. (2013). The Kra Canal and Southeast Asian Relations. *Journal of Current Southeast Asian Affairs*, 31(4), 109–125.

Tennenbaum, J. (2014, November). Fact Sheet on Kra Canal Project in Thailand.

Thomas, V. (2017, October 24), Kra Canal Can boost Asean Trade, retrieved on 19 December, 2020 from https://www.nst.com.my/opinion/letters/2017/10/294390/kra-canal-can-boost-asean-trade

8 An Indian Perspective on Sharing Economy for Development of Smart Cities

Dimple Vyas and Suman Pamecha

Introduction

In recent times, modern cities could become more sustainable and socially just by reinventing one of the basic age-old human traits, 'sharing'. Sharing efforts within collective groups facilitated our ancestors to group together for hunting, farming and creating shelter (Ridley, 1996). Belk (2007) defines 'sharing' as an alternative to individual ownership and elaborates that in sharing, multiple people may enjoy benefits that arise from owning a thing. The revival of sharing in our cities through latest developments in information and communication technologies (ICTs) could help rebuild sustainable communities, promote equity and cut down extensive resource use. Benkler (2004) describes sharing as 'nonreciprocal pro-social behaviour' and elaborates that 'social sharing' is not governed by rules of utility maximization but is instead oriented towards communal values arising from social relations.

The intersection of modern urban space and cyber-space paves the way for the emergence of a more inclusive and proficient form of economy such as a sharing economy. In recent times, the advent of new digital technological platforms over the internet, along with the widespread use of social media, has empowered citizens to conveniently call and track a ride, rent-out their homesand share idle goods instead of purchasing more than they need or can afford. The sharing economy lacks a shared definition and at times has also been referred to as 'collaborative consumption' or 'collaborative economy', which is generally defined as a socio-economic model based on the shared usage of underused or unwanted commodities (from spaces to skills to objects) either for monetary or for non-monetary benefits (Botsman & Rogers, 2011).

Sharing spaces, human interactions and transactions for goods and services have always been at the heart of cities. Digital *sharing* of unutilized assets over the internet not only enhances the *shareability* of resources; it also addresses the shortcomings of the commercial challenges of urban future. The quintessential feature of any smart city is that it must be open and receptive towards innovation; moreover, it must be adaptive to emerging economies and trends, letting the market decide which companies

DOI: 10.4324/9781003354703-10

benefit its residents and visitors. The results/changes the smart city outlook is aiming at might not be achieved with an overtly technical and economic approach. To a certain extent, social processes and personal attitudes must be considered as basic variables of change. The strategic vision that should encourage a city's growth in a smart, sustainable and shareable way is a dynamic depiction of the urban system with a long-term horizon encompassingtechnological, economic and social advances.

In order to contribute towards building a fair and sustainable world, cities must capitalize on building a sharing infrastructure and culture (Agyeman et al., 2013). Recently, 'sharing cities' is a term which has surfaced to express the amalgamation of sharing economy in urban areas (Agyeman et al., 2013; McLaren & Agyeman, 2015) and the notion of smart cities.With the rise in smartphone usage and higher internet penetration rate, the popularity of sharing economy platforms has also been augmented. As Airbnb and Uber succeed in making a grand impact over our existing societies, a lot of attention has been given to these two sectors (car rental and accommodation sharing) due to their dominance in online sharing (Chasin et al., 2018). However, community sharing at the local level engages the exchange of various things and is not confined to sharing of cars and apartments only. For example, Boyko et al. (2017) recognized 41 diverse sharing activities in a modern city, ranging from knowledge, food and plants to livestock, gardens, rides and others.

What Makes a City '*Smart*'?

Cities can be considered an intricate system wherein businesses, people, communication networks, transportations, services and utilities are all tangled with each other. As modern cities grow in size and evolve with time, the concept of economic and environmental sustainability is immensely jeopardized due to increasing technical, social, economic and organizational pressures (Bennett et al., 2017). In India, there are more than 55 cities with a population of one million or more and even the density of these cities is very high. For example, the city of Mumbai has around 20,000 people per square kilometer whereas the city of London has around 5,100 people per square kilometer (UN, 2012). It is quite clear that emerging markets like India must adopt innovative ways to deal with the intricacies of urban living. With the surge in urban population, a novel strategy must be adopted to pinpoint problems of overcrowding, congestion, energy consumption, resource management and environment protection. The concept of smart city emerged as an answer to this perspective which promises for better urbanization in the future by taking 'smart' strategic measures.

Literature review reveals that the notion of smart city has evolved from various concepts over a period of time, like 'networked city' (Castells, 1996); 'techno city' (Downey & McGuigan, 1999); 'cyber city' (Graham & Marvin, 1999); 'creative city' (Florida, 2005); and 'digital city' (Komninos, 2009). Furthermore, the inception of the idea of smart city dates back to the Smart Growth Movement around the late 1990s (Harrison & Donnelly, 2011).

There are six important dimensions (pillars) on which smart cities are structured. They are named as smart people, smart economy, smart mobility, smart living, smart governance and smart environment (Giffinger et al., 2007; Chatterjee & Kar, 2015; Chauhan et al., 2016). The Ministry of Urban Development, Government of India (MoUD, 2015), identifies ten core infrastructural elements of 'smart city':(i) adequate supply of water; (ii) secure supply of electricity; (iii) hygiene and sanitation; (iv) smooth urban mobility and efficient public transport; (v) housing for the poor; (vi) enhanced IT connectivity and digitalization; (vii) good governance, emphasizing e-governance and citizen participation; (viii) sustainability and environment protection; (ix) safety and security of citizens (particularly women, children and elderly); and (x) healthcare and education.

According to Nam and Pardo (2011), smart cities foster an environment where infrastructure and human and social capital permit sustainable economic growth and enhance the quality of life through collaborative governance. The adoption of latest 'smart' technology and ICT advances may transform a city's public and private services; real-time communication and data exchange not only enhances the livability of a city but also opens new gates of opportunities and wealth (Angelidou, 2014; Colldahl et al., 2013; Giffinger et al., 2007; Hollands, 2008; Washburn et al., 2010). PricewaterhouseCoopers (2015) selected three broad pointers and applied them on 30 global cities in order to find out the booming cities and resilient urban communities. These indicators are:

- Tools for ever changing world: Education, technology and universal access
- Quality of life: Aspiration for good life
- Economics: Paving the way for progress

In a true sense,a smart city offers its people the opportunity for a safer, satisfying and prosperous life by being better equipped to deal with the uncertainties of tomorrow. Coping with quick technological change efficiently and effectively may be the most complicated challenge that society and cities will have to face in the 21st century.

Conceptualizing a 'Sharing' City

The concept of a smart city and the phenomenon of a sharing economy are much talked about topics of this decade. As far as the connection between the two is concerned, both are aiming towards improving the quality of life and sustainable value generation. There are many factors that mark the diffusion of the two concepts, like surge in technological advances, easy access to internet and higher inclination towards social media. It is believed that difficult economic conditions, unemployment and scarcity of resources have also pushed citizen's behavior towards shared, sustainable and smart alternatives. Both smart city and sharing economy aim at the optimization of resources and reduction in wastage. With the rapid rise in urban population, resources are under tremendous pressure; sharing thus not only emerges as a smart alternative but is also the most logical choice for the public.

Smart cities and sharing economy have many common traits, like they are both communities oriented and driven by connectivity and network technologies. Real-time data exchange facilitates digital transactions and real-time funds settlement, which is one of the key features which reciprocate immediacy. On the one hand, smart city objectives are determined by public needs, while on the other hand, a sharing economy is driven by consumers'/citizens' needs. Online digital platforms play a very important role in both smart cities and sharing economy. Citizens and public not only can have access to civic information and government policies over these platforms but can execute various transactions as well. All this will attribute to generation of mammoth public database we usually know as 'big data', which in turn could be fruitfully used to finetune public policies and establish a grassroots-level reach in public systems. In sharing economy, these platforms act as typical 'matchmakers', who connect a person willing to share his/her unutilized asset with a person who is in need of one. This helps in utilization of idle capacities and is a win–win situation for all the parties involved. The lender generates some revenue out of an idle asset; the borrower gets temporary access and thereby avoids outright purchasing, while the 'matchmaker' (service-providing platform) gets its commission. Although there are multiple business models involved in sharing economy,whether a platform charges a fee or renders its services for free depends purely on the mode and type of organization. Improved usage of assets is another similarity among smart city and sharing economy; it leads to a variety of positive consequences like reduction in congestion, energy saving, pollution control and obviously financial profitability.

Environment protection and control is also one of the common goals of both smart city and sharing economy. For example, one car sharing vehicle has the potential to replace 9–13 vehicles on the road; moreover, car sharing services have fairly contributed towards lessening the transit cost and greenhouse gas emissions (E&Y, 2015).

Trust is another component which is vital in the functioning of sharing economy and smart city; as social and economic transactions take place over the internet among unknowns, 'digitization of trust' takes the center stage. Ratings, reputations and feedback creates a digital repository of database which helps create a virtual profile of users and acts as a foundation for futuristic transactions. In smart city framework, citizens trust public systems with regard to the use of their personal data, and moreover, public database can be materialized for drafting innovative public policies sensing citizens' social needs and aspirations. The government of China launched a social credit system in several cities of the country with an intention to merge a financial credit score system with the social and civic integrity of its citizens and corporations (Wong & Dobson, 2019). Chinese authorities have begun to apply a reward and punishment system that benefits those who fall in line with the Chinese government's ideals and punishes those who digress from them. These sorts of measures may attribute towards the establishment of smart governance and establish citizen's trust in good governance.As far as the establishment of trust and use of data and its protection and security are concerned,the smart city framework must set crystal clear guidelines to promote digital transactions in the future. Data-driven urbanism values data at par with currencies; the ability to collect and process data would definitely continue to influence socio-economic dynamics. As a matter of fact, the more data an organization possesses about its citizens/consumers, the better it can serve them. In a typical sharing city, there should be a clear-cut demarcation of public and private data, and furthermore, transparency of data must be ensured for winning the faith and loyalty of citizens/consumers.

Globally, the latest drafts concerning the design of a smart city highlight not only the use of technology but also economic concepts focused on collaborative consumption and moving further than a strictly linear economy. A linear economy at times is considered to be based on a 'take, make, and dispose' model of production which is causing increasing rates of consumption and pollution. A circular economy, on the flip side, is centered on co-creation or a regenerative system laying emphasis on cutting down all forms of waste, energy leakage and polluting emissions. A smart city framework should advocate long-lasting designs, maintenance, repair, reuse, remanufacturing, refurbishing and recycling. Gansky (2010) criticizes throwaway culture and tagging it as 'planned obsolescence' (products designed with the expectation that they will have a short life and be replaced) and advocates that the designers must produce timeless products that can be used over and over again. The physical and social pattern of a city takes shape in manner of sharing-based practices of its inhabitants; for instance, human association towards assets is gradually shifting from ownership-based to access-based (Salvia, Morello & Arcidiacono, 2019). As Figure 8.1 indicates, the evolution of sharing city connotes to the intermingling of two new-age phenomena, namely, smart city and sharing economy. Furthermore, sharing city are led by community initiatives aiming to harness shared prosperity and all round well-being by leveraging modern smart technologies of the future.

Impact of Sharing Economy over Indian Cities

The idea of sharing is mainly pertinent for fueling the Indian economic growth and could be establishing an adaptive operating model to trigger 'the winning leap' (PWC, 2014). According to the Nielsen Global Survey of Share Communities (Nielson, 2014), around 78% of Indians are expected to avail products or services from others in a shared community. A Boston

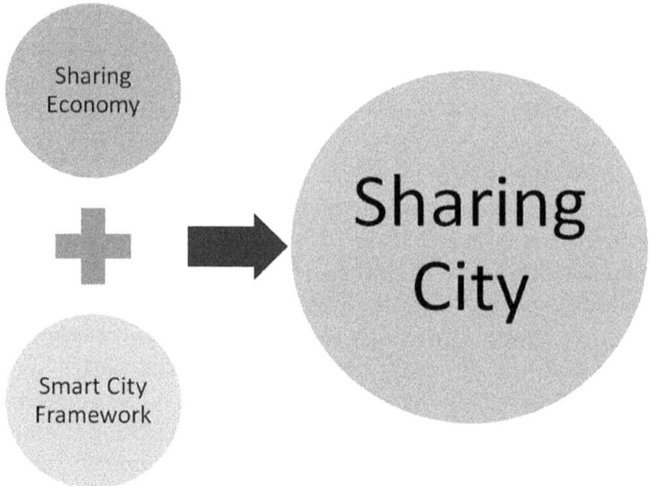

Figure 8.1 Conceptualizing a 'sharing city'.
Source: Author's own.

Consultancy Group (BCG) survey done in 2016 exhibits that around 85% of Indians would like to spend extra on a product with built-in features that simplifies sharing of the product in the future (Wallenstein & Shelat, 2017).

There seems to be manifold reasons behind the new attitudinal shift towards temporary access and sharing in India. The apparent economic reason is paying for what you use saves plenty of money in comparison to outright purchase while having a long-term view. Another reason has its source in the widespread usage of smartphone applications coupled with low-cost internet availability and deeper penetration rates of the internet. Indian millennials impulsively connect with the notion that 'ownership' represents repetitiveness, economic stagnation and responsibility (which arises from asset ownership) while 'temporary access' signifies effortlessness, freedom of choice, new experiences and change from routine.

The sharing economy may facilitate sustainable consumption and in turn help in achieving sustainable lifestyle to generate optimistic socio-economic and environmental impacts (Martin, 2016). Sharing has changed the format of urban dynamics and practices, be it utilizing the domestic space for peer-to-peer accommodation (Alexander, 2018), working in shared environments (Akhavan et al., 2018; Durante & Turvani, 2018) or moving aroundthe town through shared means (Vecchio & Tricarico, 2019). Figure 8.2 depicts the ubiquitous effects of sharing economy in myriad urban affairs and highlights the broad spectrums through which sharing economy is promoting new-age shared cities. The major impact areas of sharing economy which are profoundly stimulating the routine lives of city dwellers are p2p exchanges, emergence of social 'trust' as currency, focus on

Figure 8.2 Impacts of sharing economy.

Source: Author's own.

access-based systems, reduction in wastage, 'reusability'-centered product designs, rise of product-as-a-service models, rise in collaborative consumption practices, rapid 'platformization' of services, capitalization of under-utilized capacities and economic benefits. Not only this, sharing economy has also significantly influenced the culture of 'work' in recent times; 'gig economy', flat organizational hierarchies, co-working and workflexibility are in vogue, complementing sharing economy. Moreover, improved resource utilization, enhanced social mobility, increase in digital literacy and skill development are undoubtedly some of the perceived benefits of sharing economy (E&Y, 2015) which would, in turn,boost the smart city objective and lead society towards the development of sustainable 'sharing cities'.

In order to develop smart transportation under the 'smart city' movement led by the government of India,focus has been laid on the development of 'smart parking lots', wherein availability of parking space would be displayed on the driver's mobile phone (IBEF, 2018). On the same note, peer-to-peer platforms offering parking at private spaces based on the likes of JustPark (Stephany, 2015) are welcome ideas to solve parking problems in overcrowded cities.New sharing trends can merge with re-development and revitalization of the old neighborhoods of cities and may emerge as new shared spaces for social and economic activities. In the Indian context, the four most important features that facilitate in crafting a 'sharing city' are networked technologies, local governance, community-driven efforts and market orientation (Mishra & Madhav, 2020).

Regulatory Framework for Sharing Cities

The fundamental aspects regarding the mission, vision, structure and model of sharing cities crop up from commonalities among sharing economy and smart city; thus, even the competing and regulatory issues to be addressed regarding this phenomenon are to be dealt from a smart angle of innovation and technology. Intelligent management of disruptive technological trends could improve society's and consumer's welfare. The synergy between citizens, private companies and public actors creates a sharing triangulation, wherein interaction among local authorities and private partners yield mechanization of sharing city. For example, a smart traffic management system gathers relevant data from local transportation, social network, GPS (Global Positioning Systems) devices and car-sharing companies along with multiple arrays of sensors installed in cities to suggest alternative routes to prospective commuters on a real-time basis.

The business models concerning sharing economy and smart cities create various forms of unexpected frictions with existing traditional rules and regulations. The reason for the emergence of these frictions can be attributed to a misalignment between the traditional ways of providing consumer goods and services and the emerging new models. Local authorities and policymakers must make a balancing exercise; on the one hand, innovation should be encouraged, and on the other hand, they must ensure that sharing economy firms do not have anti-competitive advantage over conventional firms. For sustained development of sharing city, common standards, global principles and open innovative environment must be nurtured.

Conclusions

From the above discussion, it emerges that the amalgamation of two characteristically similar phenomena, namely,'smart city' and 'sharing economy,' would lead to the formation of 'sharing city'. In other words, a smart city framework must be drafted in such a way as to give ample amount of space to facilitate the proliferation of new-age economies (like sharing economy/circular economy/creative economy) to reap the benefits in the long term. The futuristic 'sharing cities' would definitely be the 'smart cities' with provisions for 'sharing' of resources, intellectual capital, skill, underutilized assets, idle capacities, capital, food and may be happiness.

The foremost prospective regarding the concept of sharing cities lies in the diverse set of benefits they pass on to the economic, environmental, social and democratic scope of urban communities. However, it should be noted that these benefits are highly subjective to the manner in which the notion of sharing is functionalized into service in cities. Depending on how this is realized, sharing may not only show the way to benefits but may even have unfavorable effects on employees, businesses and other stakeholders. The extent of 'disruptive' effect on local communities would prompt the city administration to craft a regulatory framework mechanism that is compelling in mitigating the negative consequences while safeguarding innovation.

References

Agyeman, J., McLaren, D., & Schaefer-Borrego, A. (2013). *Sharing Cities*. Thinkpiece for Friends of the Earth Big Ideas Project. Retrieved from http://www.foe.co.uk/sites/default/files/downloads/agyeman_sharing_cities.pdf

Akhavan, M., Mariotti, I., Astolfi, L., & Canevari, A. (2018). Coworking spaces and new social relations: A focus on the social streets in Italy. *Urban Science*, *3*(1), 2. https://doi.org/10.3390/urbansci3010002

Alexander, J. (2018). Domesticity on-demand: The architectural and urban implications of Airbnb in Melbourne, Australia. *Urban Science*, 2(3), 88. https://doi.org/10.3390/urbansci2030088

Angelidou, M. (2014). Smart city policies: A spatial approach. *Cities*, *41*,3–11.

Belk, R. (2007). Why not share rather than own? *The Annals of the American Academy of Political and Social Science*, *611*, 126–140.

Benkler, Y. (2004). Sharing nicely: On shareable goods and the emergence of sharing as a modality of economic production. *The Yale Law Journal*, *114*, 273–358.

Bennett, D., Pérez-Bustamante, D., & Medrano, M. L. (2017). Challenges for smart cities in the UK. In M. Peris-Ortiz, D. Bennett, & D.P. Yábar (Eds.), *Sustainable Smart Cities: Creating Spaces for Technological, Social and Business Development*(pp. 1–14). Cham: Springer, Switzerland.

Botsman, R., & Rogers, R. (2011). *What's Mine Is Yours: How Collaborative Consumption Is Changing The Way We Live*. London: HarperCollins.

Boyko, C. T., Clune, S. J., Cooper, R. F., Coulton, C. J., Dunn, N. S., Pollastri, S., Leach, J. M., Bouch, C. J., Cavada, M., De Laurentiis, V., & Goodfellow-Smith, M. (2017). How sharing can contribute to more sustainable cities. *Sustainability*, *9*(5), 701.

Castells, M. (1996). *The Rise of the Network Society: The Information Age-Economy, Society and Culture*. Oxford: Blackwell.

Chasin, F., von Hoffen, M., Cramer, M., & Matzner, M. (2018). Peer-to-peer sharing and collaborative consumption platforms: A taxonomy and a reproducible analysis. *IseB*, *16*(2), 293–325.

Chatterjee, S., & Kar, A. K. (2015). *Smart Cities in developing economies: A literature review and policy insights. IEEE International Conference on Advances in Computing, Communications and Informatics (ICACCI)*, 2335–2340.

Chauhan, S., Agarwal, N., & Kar, A. K. (2016). Addressing big data challenges in smart cities: A systematic literature review. *Info*, *18*(4), 73–90.

Colldahl, C., Frey, S., & Kelemen, J. E. (2013). *Smart Cities: Strategic Sustainable Development for an Urban World.* Karlskrona, Ruotsi: Blekinge Tekniska Högskola (BTH).

Downey, J., & McGuigan, J. (1999). *Technocities: The Culture and Political Economy of the Digital Revolution.* London: Sage.

Durante, G., & Turvani, M. (2018). Coworking, the sharing economy, and the city: Which role for the 'coworking entrepreneur'? *Urban Science*, *2*(3), 83. https://doi.org/10.3390/urbansci2030083

E&Y. (2015). *The rise of the sharing economy: The Indian landscape.* Retrieved from: https://www.ey.com/Publication/vwLUAssets/ey-the-rise-of-thesharing-economy/$FILE/ey-the-rise-of-the-sharing-economy.pdf

Florida, R. L. (2005). *Cities and the Creative Class.* New York: Routledge.

Gansky, L. (2010). *The Mesh: Why The Future Of Business Is Sharing.* New York: Penguin Group.

Giffinger, R., Fertner, C., Kramar, H., Kalasek, R., Pichler-Milanovic, N., & Meijers, E. (2007). *Smart cities—Ranking of European medium-sized cities.* Retrieved from http://www.smart-cities.eu/download/smart_cities_final_report.pdf

Graham, S., & Marvin, S. (1999). Planning cybercities: Integrating telecommunications into urban planning. *Town Planning Review*, *70*(1), 89–114.

Harrison, C., & Donnelly, I. A. (2011). A theory of smart cities. In *Proceedings of the 55th Annual Meeting of the ISSS 2011*, Hull, UK.

Hollands, R. G. (2008). Will the real smart city please stand up? *City*, *12*(3), 303–320.

IBEF. (2018). *India –Pushing the right levers.* Retrieved from https://www.ibef.org/India-Pushing-the-right-levers/index.html

Kar, A. K., Gupta, M. P., Ilavarasan, P. V., & Dwivedi, I. K. (2017). *Advances in Smart Cities: Smarter People, Governance, and Solutions.* New York: CRC Press.

Komninos, N. (2009). Intelligent cities: Towards interactive and global innovation environments. *International Journal of Innovation and Regional Development*, *1*(4), 337–355.

Martin, C. J. (2016). The sharing economy: A pathway to sustainability or a nightmarish form of neoliberal capitalism?*Ecological Economics*, *121*, 149–159.

McLaren, D., & Agyeman, J. (2015). *Sharing Cities: A Case for Truly Smart and Sustainable Cities.*London: The MIT Press.

Mishra, T., & Madhav, S. (2020). Envisioning Sharing Cities in India. *International Journal of Policy Sciences and Law*, *1*(2), 966–983. https://ijpsl.in/wp-content/uploads/2020/12/Envisioning-Sharing-Cities-in-India_Tarusha-Mishra-Sameeksha-Madhav.pdf

MoUD. (2015). *Smart Cities: Mission Statement & Guidelines.* A Ministry of Urban Development, Government of India report.

Nam, T., & Pardo, T. A. (2011). Smart city as urban innovation: Focusing on management, policy, and context. *5th International Conference on Theory and Practice of Electronic Governance, ACM*, pp. 185–194. Retrieved from http://www.ctg.albany.edu/publications/journals/icegov_2011_smartcity

Nielson. (2014). *Is Sharing the new buying? Reputation and trust are emerging as new currencies.* The Nielsen Global Survey of Share Communities. Retrieved from www.nielsen.com/global-share-community-report-may-2014.pdf

PricewaterhouseCoopers. (2015). *How smart are our cities?* Retrieved from https://www.pwc.in/assets/pdfs/publications/2015/how_smart_are_our_cities.pdf

PwC. (2014). *Future of India: The winning leap*. Retrieved June 26, 2016, from https://www.pwc.in/assets/pdfs/future-of-india/future-of-india-the-winning-leap.pdf

Ridley, M. (1996). *The Origins of Virtue*. London: Viking.

Salvia, G., Morello, E., & Arcidiacono, A. (2019). Sharing cities shaping cities. *UrbanScience*, *3*(1), 23. https://doi.org/10.3390/urbansci3010023.

Stephany, A. (2015). *The Business of Sharing: Making it in the New Sharing Economy*. Hampshire: Palgrave Macmillan.

United Nations. (2012). *World population prospects, the 2012revision*.https://esa.un.org/unpd/wpp/publications/Files/WPP2012_HIGHLIGHTS.pdf

Vecchio, G., & Tricarico, L. (2019). "May the force move you": Roles and actors of information sharing devices in urban mobility. *Cities*, *88*(September), 261–268. https://doi.org/10.1016/j.cities.2018.11.007

Wallenstein, J., & Shelat, U. (2017). *Hoping aboard the sharing economy*. BCG (Boston Consulting Group).Retrieved June 24, 2018 from http://imagesrc.bcg.com/Images/BCG-Hopping-Aboardthe-Sharing-Economy-Aug-2017_tcm9-168558.pdf

Washburn, D., Sindhu, U., Balaouras, S., Dines, R. A., Hayes, N. M., & Nelson, L. E. (2010). *Helping CIOs Understand "Smart City" Initiatives: Defining the Smart City, its Drivers, and theRole of the CIO*. Cambridge, MA: Forrester Research, Inc.

Wong, K. L., & Dobson, A. S. (2019). We're just data: Exploring China's social credit system in relation to digital platform ratings cultures in Westernised democracies. *GlobalMediaandChina*,*4*(2),220–232.https://doi.org/10.1177/2059436419856090

Part III

Business and Sociological Perspectives

9 Entrepreneurship Education in the Indian Context

Relevance and Limitations

Neha Taneja Chawla and Hitesh Bhatia

Introduction

Recently, the Government of India revised its 34-year-old Education Policy with some path-breaking recommendations. The New National Education Policy (NEP) 2020 focuses on reforms in planning and delivering contemporary education with more flexibility to students in terms of choice of courses and years of entry and exit. The NEP also emphasizes promoting industry-relevant vocational education at the school level along with interaction with local eminent entrepreneurs and incorporating critical thinking and design thinking courses in the curriculum (MHRD, 2020). These efforts will also help promote an entrepreneurial mindset among the participants. Even the London-based think tank Global Entrepreneurship Monitor in its reports published by the UNESCO on the 'Entrepreneurship Framework Conditions' emphasizes formal entrepreneurship education at the school, college, and university levels (GEM, 2020). Entrepreneurship is key to economic growth, as it contributes to job creation and enhances economic activity in the region. Entrepreneurs, like other professionals, add significant value to society and the economy at large. Thus it becomes imperative for the nation's education policy and framework to give adequate importance to formal education in entrepreneurship at least at the university level if not at the school level.

The world history of formal entrepreneurship education dates back to the early 20th century when the first formal course in entrepreneurship is believed to have been offered at the University of Michigan in 1927 (Entrepreneur India, 2014). Many studies also recognize Shigeru Fijii as the pioneer in teaching entrepreneurship at Kobe University, Japan, in 1938 (Alberti, Sciascia, & Poli, 2004; Edirisinghe & Nimeshi, 2016; Keat, Selvarajah, & Meyer, 2011). Another noteworthy entrepreneurship course was offered by Myles Mace in the MBA program at Harvard University in 1947. However, the real emergence of entrepreneurship education took place in the 1980s. And by 2005, more than 2,200 entrepreneurship courses were offered across 1,600 schools in the US alone (Kuratko, 2005). On the other end, though the seeds of the entrepreneurship education in the UK were sown in the 1970s and 1980s, driven by the consequences of the

DOI: 10.4324/9781003354703-12

economic crisis, employment pressure, and the philosophy of then Prime Minister Margaret Thatcher, who advocated private enterprise and celebrated individual empowerment, entrepreneurship education significantly entered the European curriculum only in the late 90s. The UK developed the world's first national-level guidelines on quality assurance in entrepreneurship education. By 2016, nearly 70% of the universities in the UK were members of 'Enterprise Educators UK' departing entrepreneurship education (CBBC, 2016).

In India, the Central Industrial Extension Training Institute (CIETI) was the first institute to provide training to budding entrepreneurs; it was established in New Delhi in 1960 and shifted to Hyderabad in 1962 as Small Industry Extension and Training Institute (SIET). In 2007, the institute broadened its objective and was rechristened as National Institute for Micro, Small and Medium Enterprises (NIMSME). The need, relevance, and impact of entrepreneurship education in India were established through the 'Kakinanda experiment' conducted by Harvard Professor David C. McClelland from the year 1964 to 1969 in different countries. The results of his experiment conducted in India and Spain revealed a significant impact of entrepreneurship training on the need for achievement and motivation to pursue an entrepreneurial career amongst the participants (Mohan & Revathi, 2012).

At the state level, Gujarat pioneered in imparting entrepreneurship knowledge by conducting the first-ever three-month entrepreneurship development program (EDP) for training new entrepreneurs in 1970, establishing the first Centre for Entrepreneurship Development (CED) in 1979 and setting up the Entrepreneurship Development Institute of India (EDII), Ahmedabad, in 1983 (EDII, 2016). By now, 15 states have established CEDs or the Institute of Entrepreneurship Development (IED) to promote entrepreneurship and deliver entrepreneurship training (DCMSME, 2016). The government established the National Science & Technology Entrepreneurship Development Board (NSTEDB) in 1982 to promote innovation and technology-centric entrepreneurship. NSTEDB initiated the establishment of STEP (Science and Technology Entrepreneurship Park) in 1984 and Entrepreneurship Development Cell (EDC) in 1986 to create an entrepreneurial culture in science and technology academic institutes. EDCs were rechristened to IEDC (Innovation and Entrepreneurship Development Cell) in 2009. In addition to the varied initiatives by the government for providing entrepreneurship training and education, a large number of colleges and universities are integrating courses on entrepreneurship in their curriculum. By 2016, more than 100 different departments at universities across India were offering courses in entrepreneurship at the undergraduate and postgraduate levels, and out of 620 universities and over 33,000 colleges in India, about 200 have Entrepreneurship Development Cells (Ilayaraja & Ganesh, 2016). Although, majority of MBA programs offer entrepreneurship as an elective course, the average percentage of students opting for this course is approximately 15% (Basu, 2014). Moreover, in the recent past, various renowned institutes across India have started offering one-year and two-year full-time post-graduate diploma/degree courses in entrepreneurship, family business, venture creation, and innovation, with EDII as the torchbearer and pioneer. In 2019, AICTE has introduced two years' full-time PGDM/MBA program in Innovation, Entrepreneurship, and Venture Development (IEV) and 15 colleges across Indian have been approved the same (AICTE, 2020).

The statistics from the Global Entrepreneurship Monitor measuring entrepreneurial ecosystem across the world indicates that the penetration of entrepreneurship education at post-school level in India has increased over the years. However, it is equally important that entrepreneurship education should meet its objective by making participants more entrepreneurial and increasing the chances of venture success. The current study, therefore, attempts to understand the effectiveness of the existing entrepreneurship education from the perspective of practicing entrepreneurs who have undergone entrepreneurship education. The scope of the study is limited to two-year full-time postgraduate courses in Entrepreneurship as they would offer the most in-depth insights into the domain of entrepreneurship education.

Literature Review

Schumacher, E.F, in his bestseller work, *Small Is Beautiful* published in 1973, propounded that with training, education, and support, individuals can regain their dignity, work towards self-employment, and become active members of the national economy (World Economic Forum, 2009). Over the years, the increasing focus on entrepreneurship education worldwide in the 21st century has inspired researchers to devise several frameworks for defining, understanding, and measuring the impact of entrepreneurship education.

The World Bank defines entrepreneurship education and training as "academic education or formal training interventions that share the broad objectives of providing individuals with the entrepreneurial mindsets and skills to support participation and performance in a range of entrepreneurial activities" (Valerio, Parton, & Robb, 2014). Another definition of entrepreneurship education as proposed by the European Commission (2017) states that entrepreneurship education refers to the development of skills, knowledge, and attitudes helping people in achieving their goals.

Hood & Young (1993) interviewed a hundred leading entrepreneurs in the US to understand the important components that should be included in entrepreneurship education to produce successful entrepreneurs. Their research suggested a combination of four components, including knowledge, skills, mentality, and personality as a requisite of successful entrepreneurs. Among the various content areas of knowledge, finance, marketing, strategy, and engineering were found to be of the most significance for entrepreneurs. Concerning the skills, leadership skills and communication skills were acknowledged as the most important skills for an entrepreneur by the majority of respondents. Creativity among the mentality factors and self-motivation and risk-taking among the personality factors were found to be the most relevant. It was suggested that an effective entrepreneurship curriculum should cater to all these factors with a primary focus on the specific areas of content knowledge. The research also reiterated that entrepreneurs can be trained to successfully pursue entrepreneurship. The components of entrepreneurship education as suggested by Liyan (2006) include building skills related to negotiation, creative thinking, new product development, leadership, and technological innovation as well as knowledge of intellectual property rights and sources of funding. The United Nations Conference on Trade and Development in 2010 proposed that effective entrepreneurship education can be imparted only through effective coordination between entrepreneurship educational institutions, government, and businesses. They suggested that the entrepreneurship education curriculum should focus on developing entrepreneurial attitude, self-confidence, self-efficacy, and leadership skills and provide knowledge regarding opportunity recognition, business planning, start-up, managing the SME, growth, and exit strategies (UNCTAD, 2011).

ASTEE (Assessment Tools and Indicators for Entrepreneurship Education) project by The Danish Foundation for Entrepreneurship – Young Enterprise developed a framework (depicted in Figure 9.1) illustrating the various dimensions to be included in entrepreneurship education initiatives and the dimensions for the assessment of the impact of entrepreneurship education initiatives (Moberg, et al., 2014).

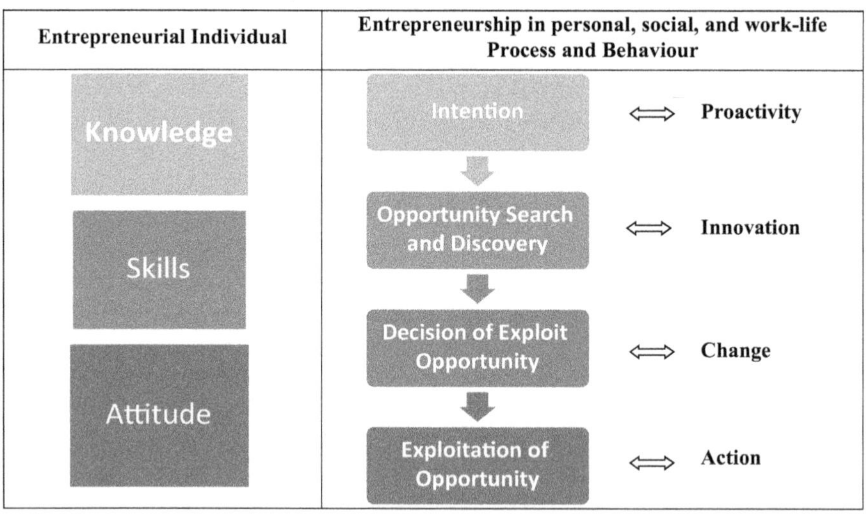

Figure 9.1 Dimensions of entrepreneurship education.

Source: A report of ASTEE project (Assessment Tools and Indicators for Entrepreneurship Education) by the Danish Foundation for Entrepreneurship – Young Enterprise (Moberg, et al., 2014).

The framework suggests that to measure the effectiveness of entrepreneurship education, the entrepreneurial self-efficacy of the participants in the identified skills, knowledge, and attitude should be measured as it indicates the closest proximity to their actions and success. The entrepreneurial skills in the framework include creativity, planning, financial literacy, resource marshaling, managing uncertainty, and teamwork. The proposed dimensions for measuring attitude in the ASTEE framework for fostering entrepreneurship include general self-efficacy, locus of control, and self-esteem. Lastly, it suggests that entrepreneurship graduates should know the assessment of business opportunities, availability of entrepreneurial career options, and the role of an entrepreneur in society (Moberg, et al., 2014).

Some of the critical elements of entrepreneurship education as identified in the previous studies are discussed in this section. Arthur, Hisrich, and Cabrera (2012) advocate for the importance of the appropriate content and the method of delivery for creating the right impact of entrepreneurship education. As the material taught in entrepreneurship education is derived from the various fields of management education like finance, marketing, operations, strategy, etc., developing a proper pedagogy for delivery of the course becomes pertinent (Albornoz Pardo, 2013; Basu, 2014; Fiet, 2001). The selection of the content by the faculty in teaching entrepreneurship should be based on the objective of the participants. The use of student-approved system for teaching entrepreneurial skills is more effective than a teacher-centric approach. Bechard and Toulouse (1991) also suggest that the pedagogical approach followed by most of the entrepreneurship courses should be replaced by a student-centric andragogical approach to achieve better outcomes. Pedagogical approaches are faculty-centric, whereas in an andragogical approach, students are more involved and interested as they feel the content that they are studying will be helpful to them in solving their problems or achieving their project goals. In addition, Sarooghi, Sunny, Hornsby, and Fernhaber (2019) suggest that entrepreneurship education can be made more effective by applying design thinking approach and principles in teaching entrepreneurship.

Another critical resource for teaching any course is the availability of robust textbooks in the domain. As entrepreneurship is a relatively new academic discipline, its content is mainly derived from various other disciplines. Fiet (2001) in his study found more than 80% of instructors teaching entrepreneurship were not satisfied with the available material and were using customized reading packets.

About India, the major hurdles in teaching entrepreneurship courses are related to a shortage of trained teachers, lack of indigenous experience, pedagogical limitations, lack of institutionalization and focus on short-term results, as identified by Shankar (2012). Several studies have thus concluded that to effectively deliver entrepreneurship education, special training programs should be organized for the faculty (Ramakrishna & Hulugappa, 2013; UNCTAD, 2011). Another significant challenge of entrepreneurship education in India is related to the absence of a standard and specific framework for teaching entrepreneurship. Entrepreneurship education mainly comprises of the courses taught in general management programs that are not found to be very effective in influencing the entrepreneurial spirit and intention (Rehman & Elahi, 2012). Agrawal and Thakur (2018) also emphasize the lack of standard framework for teaching entrepreneurship as one of challenges in imparting entrepreneurship education in the Indian context. The other challenges identified by them include cultural barriers, incomplete entrepreneurship education, and dependence on government. Ramakrishna and Hulugappa (2013) in their detailed study on the emerging trends and concerns of entrepreneurship education in India highlighted the cost of entrepreneurship education offered by the private institutions as one of the major challenges making it unaffordable for a large number of prospective entrepreneurs. Another study on challenges pertaining to entrepreneurship education specifically in developing countries by Mbeteh and Pellegrini (2018), in addition to above-mentioned challenges like cultural barriers, lack of experienced educators, and other difficulties, include a lack of adequate funding, government policies, lack of adequate system to develop curriculum and theory-driven approach for teaching entrepreneurship.

In an empirical study by Bharucha (2019) across 11 institutes offering elective or compulsory courses on entrepreneurship, it was found that nearly 47% of the participants were not satisfied with the entrepreneurship education offered to them, indicative of the gap for effective entrepreneurship education in India. Hameed and Irfan (2019) also emphasize on the key role of focused and 'learning by doing' entrepreneurship education in enhancing entrepreneurial intent and interest. They also suggest that every university should mandatorily offer a compulsory course on entrepreneurship to ignite the spirit of entrepreneurship across any nation.

Objectives

- To understand the contribution of entrepreneurship education in developing entrepreneurial skills, attitude, and knowledge
- To identify the limitations and scope for improvement in the existing entrepreneurship education program

Research Methodology

Sample

A total of 30 respondents who had undergone two-year entrepreneurship education were interviewed to understand their perception about the relevance and limitations of entrepreneurship education. Table 9.1 presents the sampling mix related to gender, current occupation, and prior experience before undertaking entrepreneurship education.

The sample was heterogeneous with respect to the representation from varied industries, including logistics, hygiene, event management, edu-tech, online puja services, food, real estate, hardware, online aggregation, etc.

Table 9.1 Sampling Mix

Gender	*Male*	*Female*	
	80%	*20%*	
Current occupation	Own venture 56%	Family business 27%	Job 17%
Prior work/entrepreneurial experience	Yes 6%	No 94%	

The data was collected through a combination of face-to-face interviews and telephonic interviews. All the interviews were audio-recorded for future reference with the consent of the respondents. A deliberate effort was made to ensure that respondents represented all the major institutes offering two-year entrepreneurship courses in western India. The data suggested that very few individuals have prior experience before pursuing entrepreneurship education.

Data Collection

To obtain in-depth insights from the respondents, detailed semi-structured interviews were conducted. The duration of each interview varied from forty minutes to ninety minutes. The respondents were asked about the role of entrepreneurship education in enhancing their self-efficacy in the various entrepreneurial skills about the four-stage venture creation model as well as in the development of entrepreneurial attitude.

The entrepreneurial skills and knowledge questions included tasks related to the searching, planning, marshalling, and implementation phases of the entrepreneurial venture creation model proposed by Stevenson, Roberts, and Grousbeck (1985).

- The searching phase tasks include opportunity recognition, idea creation, brainstorming, and basic market research.
- The planning phase tasks include the selection of appropriate idea, identifying an appropriate form of business, determining market segment, estimating prospective customer base, determining appropriate pricing, assessing the required start-up and working capital fund requirement.
- The marshalling phase entrepreneurial tasks comprise of identification of appropriate marketing strategy, writing a complete business plan, networking, liaising, and identifying the sources of funding and other resources.
- The implementation phase mainly includes tasks related to convincing investors (angels'/ venture capitalists/banks, etc.), obtaining finance, organizing financial assets, maintaining financial records, obtaining

required intellectual property rights, recruiting, training, supervising, and motivating employees. These tasks were identified based on the most prominent entrepreneurial self-efficacy scales developed by Chen, Greene, and Crick (1998); De Noble, Jung, and Ehrlich (1999); Lucas and Cooper (2005) and McGee, Peterson, Mueller, and Sequeira (2009).

- Besides, the respondents were also enquired regarding the role of entrepreneurship education in enhancing their internet and technological entrepreneurial skills and group interpersonal skills.
- With the advent of technology, Wang, Tseng, Wang, and Chu (2019) propose the indispensable need for internet entrepreneurial self-efficacy among entrepreneurs. The respondents were asked questions related to the use of e-commerce, digital marketing, and identification of required business management software.
- The entrepreneurial attitude–related questions included risk and uncertainty management and persistence as proposed in the scale developed by De Noble et al. (1999).

The range of questions was very comprehensive, including all the tasks performed by an entrepreneur and evaluating an individual's ESE related to knowledge, skills, and attitude possessed by him as proposed in the ASTEE framework as well.

Open-ended questions, including those on their overall experience with entrepreneurship education and their suggestions for making entrepreneurship education more effective, were also discussed and deliberated. All the interviews were audio-taped for future reference.

Data Analysis

About 15 codes were identified before transcribing the interviews. These codes were based on questions related to essential entrepreneurial knowledge, skills, and attitude that were asked during the interview. However, several unique codes emerged as we further analyzed the open-ended questions for each interview. At the end of transcribing 30 interviews, 134 new codes emerged, which were further deliberated for similarity and repetition. Similar codes were grouped, resulting in 43 distinctive codes that were further classified under five different themes. Figure 9.2 represents the process of content analysis used in the present study.

The respondents were asked to what extent the entrepreneurship education intervention helped them in improving their knowledge/skills/attitude on a Likert scale of 1 to 5, indicating *not at all helpful*, *less helpful*, *moderately helpful*, *highly helpful*, and *very highly helpful*. About 15 questions related to idea generation, feasibility analysis, business plan writing, market estimation, pricing, promotion, fund estimation, fund sourcing, human resource management, information technology, networking, risk-taking, perseverance, group-interpersonal skills, and problem-solving skills were asked to understand the role of entrepreneurship education. The responses

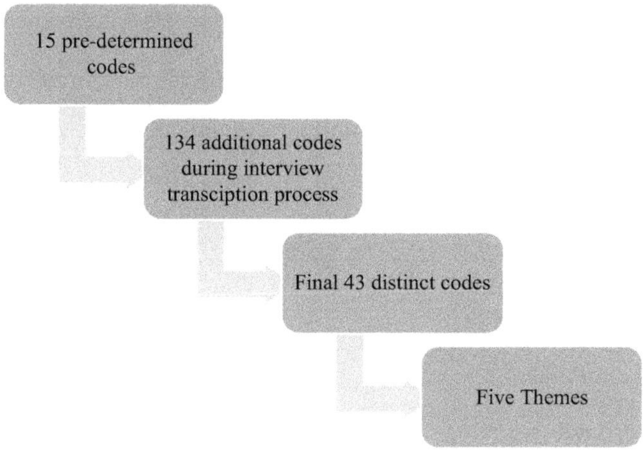

Figure 9.2 Content analysis process.

of the participant on 15 structured questions are summarized in the Table 9.2 below, and thereafter, insights of the respondents on each of the 15 questions are discussed in detail one by one.

Nearly 90% of the respondents felt that entrepreneurship education was moderate to extremely helpful in generating new ideas, whereas two of the respondents felt that the course was not at all helpful in idea generation. One of the respondents said:

> The course provides lots of tools and framework but no ways to apply them to match your passion as well as a market opportunity.

As far as evaluating the feasibility of the idea is concerned, most of the respondents found the course only to be moderately helpful. The insights revealed that though most of the programs offered the course on market research and even included market survey as a part of their pedagogy, that was not found to be sufficient to determine the actual feasibility of the idea. According to one of the respondents:

> Feasibility testing is very different from conducting market surveys. A much deeper customer-connect and continuous feedback process need to be undertaken for building feasible products/services. Qualitative discussions with prospective customers are much more beneficial than quantitative market surveys.

About marketing, most of the respondents found that the content offered through the entrepreneurship course was reasonably helpful in developing the promotional or marketing strategies but moderately helpful in estimating their customer base/market size and even lesser helpful in determining the appropriate pricing of their product. Similarly, in the financial aspect of the

Table 9.2 Summary of respondents' perception towards entrepreneurship education.

S. No.	*Role of entrepreneurship education on developing following knowledge/skills/ attitude*	*Not at all helpful (%)*	*Less helpful (%)*	*Moderately helpful (%)*	*Highly helpful (%)*	*Very highly helpful (%)*
1	Idea generation	5%	5	32		58
2	Feasibility testing			68		32
3	Market size estimation	17		61		22
4	Pricing	28	22	28		22
5	Promotion strategy			17	28	56
6	Networking	26		17		61
7	Estimation financial requirement	28	11	28		33
8	Identifying sources of funding	6	28	67		
9	Managing finances of business			44	11	44
10	IT for business	39	11	50		
11	Team building and managing employees	11	6	44	6	33
12	Risk-taking	44		17	6	33
13	Perseverance	6	11	1	37	45
14	Group-inter personal skills				44	56
15	Problem-solving		11	28	11	50

venture, most of the respondents felt they were more confident about maintaining the financial records of the business but not very confident about sources of obtaining funds after completing their entrepreneurship course. Most of them said they feel that more inputs should have been provided for financing a start-up and networking with investors as the current content only orients them to the available sources of funding like angels and venture capitalists in theory. Participants suggested inputs related to the valuation of start-up, pitching of their business idea, and the art of convincing the investors would have been much more helpful. There was uniformity in responses across most of the respondents regarding the content taught related to human resource management. The respondents found theories of human resource management to be completely irrelevant in the context of start-ups. They felt that greater focus should be on the nuances of building the initial team or finding the right co-founder for their enterprise. Few of the responses were:

> I found half of the content of the course similar to my undergraduate management course. It was like repetition for me.

> Case studies of multinationals like Tatas and Birlas are difficult to relate and gain from at the stage where we are still trying to finalize on our ideas.
>
> Concepts of marketing, finance, and HR taught to us may be helpful 8–10 years down for the line, but they first need to teach us how to reach there.
>
> In today's era, when most of the business runs on technology, the program offers very basic and theoretical inputs.

About networking, there was consensus among the respondents in terms of the opportunity entrepreneurship education program provided them to connect with like-minded people, which resulted in a lot of peer-to-peer learning, collaboration opportunity as well as enhanced their perseverance. But the networking opportunities provided with people outside the institute were found to be limited to batchmates and faculty. Though many of the respondents had several of their batchmates as customers, suppliers, and even business partners, they felt that if institutes had connected them to a wider network of people outside the institutes, it would have made their entrepreneurial journey much easier. Some of the responses in this regard were:

> The institute has a rich connection to corporates and other organizations. Helping students connect with them can help budding entrepreneurs in funding, customer acquisition as well as collaborations.
>
> No one knows us when we start our entrepreneurial journey but the institute is an established brand. If they can connect budding entrepreneurs to the required people and organization, it will be a great support to them.

Concerning the risk-taking attitude, the research revealed a mixed review; on the one hand, some of them felt entrepreneurship education improved their risk-taking capability, whereas others expressed they were more afraid of taking risks after knowing the failure rate and complexity of the entrepreneurial path.

Overall, the analysis of the responses reveals the following positive aspects of two-year full-time post-graduate entrepreneurship education.

1 Good networking opportunity with like-minded people who want to venture into entrepreneurship. This helped in getting relevant feedback from peers and many of them are still benefitting from that network symbiotically. One of the logistic entrepreneurs said, "My batchmate is my biggest customer, and I am among his top five customers."

2 Experience-sharing sessions by the entrepreneurs, especially failed entrepreneurs, were found to be inspiring and motivating by most of the respondents.

3 Course outcomes related to the domain of selling and promotion of business were also considered beneficial.
4 Courses on design thinking, idea generation techniques, lean management were also found to be helpful as respondents also found at least some improvement in their problem-solving skills after undertaking entrepreneurship courses.
5 All the respondents acknowledged the positive influence of entrepreneurship education on perseverance and group interpersonal skills.

Findings and Suggestions

The responses of the interviewees reveal that entrepreneurship education in the current state requires a lot of improvisation to make it relevant and effective for budding entrepreneurs. In the current context, it is more theoretical and very similar to regular management education which dilutes the entire objective of offering a distinct two-year entrepreneurship program. Various suggestions were requested from the respondents in this regard. The suggestions with sufficient backing from the respondents have been categorized under five themes, each of which is elaborated below.

1 **Student-centric Pedagogy**
The majority of the suggestions were related to improvising the existing pedagogy of entrepreneurship courses. As each student works on a different idea during the course, a student-centric pedagogy would be more effective as compared to faculty-driven pedagogy. The following inputs were received in this regard:

- Every respondent reiterated the scope for enhancing the *practical* approach towards the content taught. Some of the pedagogical interventions proposed for the same included *live case studies* and projects, more *field projects*, and a *studio teaching approach*. A combination of these methods will help participants understand real-life business problems in detail. However, in cases like risk mitigation or challenges where the above methods are inadequate, response *simulation* activities should be used at large.
- A more meaningful mentoring system should be developed. In the current system, adopted by most of the institutes, each student is allotted one faculty mentor. In addition to academic mentors, students should also be connected to *industry-specific mentors*. The students should also have the liberty to take benefit from the wider pool of faculty rather than just a single faculty.
- To enhance the practical understanding of running and managing a start-up, students should be provided an opportunity to undertake a minimum of three to four months of extended *internship* with the start-ups, preferably in the industry related to their idea of product or service.

- Entrepreneur *experience sharing* sessions should be more diverse and at regular intervals comprising a wide variety of speakers, including successful entrepreneurs, failed entrepreneurs as well as budding entrepreneurs. The focus of these sessions should not be restricted only to their entrepreneurial journey but also include the specific challenges and their coping strategies.
- To provide real exposure to entrepreneurial finance, demo as well as real *funding sessions* should be organized towards the end of the program. This will not only help some students to obtain funding in certain cases but also prepare them for future investor interactions in their entrepreneurial journey.
- Regular *networking events* should be organized by the entrepreneurship education institute to provide an opportunity for the students to connect with prospective customers, vendors, and entrepreneurs in their industry.
- Constant motivation, guidance, and connection to different *platforms of entrepreneurial exposure* like nation-wide business plan competitions, entrepreneurship conclaves, videos, podcasts, and specialized short-term courses should be provided.
- The overall pedagogy of the program should be more *rigorous*, disciplined, and demanding. Most of the respondents felt that in its current state entrepreneurship education is predominantly driven by the self-motivation of the student, and all of them are not able to sustain that motivation throughout the course. One of the respondents mentioned in the interview, "Two-year entrepreneurship education is like a paid holiday to a luxurious resort if the student is not self-motivated and pro-active."
- Though the focus of the course should be on the creation of a new venture, entrepreneurship programs may also provide *placement* assistance in start-ups or intrapreneurial positions for the participants who may not find an entrepreneurial career as a feasible option immediately after a two-year program.
- Few of the respondents experienced repetition and misalignment of the courses offered to them at foreign universities during the exchange program. The institutes offering semester-long *foreign exchange programs* as a part of entrepreneurship education should ensure proper alignment of objectives and pedagogy to the purpose of entrepreneurship education.

2 **Start-up Focused Content**

As stated earlier, the current content was found to be similar to regular management programs by the respondents. They recommended the following inclusions/modifications to make the content more relevant from the perspective of a start-up:

- Case studies used for class discussion should be of recent entrepreneurial ventures rather than classics from big multinationals. Moreover, *local and Indian case studies* would add more value as compared to case studies from Western countries as the socio-economic structures differ a lot.
- More and prolonged *workshops for idea generation* should be organized to give exposure to idea generation techniques, emerging industry trends, sectors with a window of opportunity, and assistance regarding aligning their passion with opportunity. Such workshops should be capable of assisting the students in the proper *articulation* of their ideas and thoughts.
- Courses related to *design thinking*, *problem-solving*, *lean management*, *creativity and innovation*, *communication*, and *soft skills* were found to be more relevant by the majority of respondents.
- It was recommended that further focus should be given to the courses related to *business development*, *creating a user interface* and user connect, *operations* and *marketing*.
- Content in the courses of finance and human resource was found to be primarily theoretical and more suitable for big business. The content in courses related to finance should primarily include start-up *fund estimation*, *bootstrapping* techniques, *sources of funding* for start-ups, *valuation*, and the art of *pitching* and presenting the financials of start-up to the investors.
- More detailed inputs related to the use of *technology* in business and the significance of *intellectual property rights* should be incorporated in the course. The technology-related inputs may include but are not limited to the use of available software, digital marketing techniques, basics of development of applications and websites, digitalization of business processes, and exposure to a large number of free and low-cost digital resources available for businesses.

3 **Necessary Institutional Ecosystem**

Institutes offering entrepreneurship education programs should also develop the required ecosystem to be able to extend the benefit of their resources and network to aspiring entrepreneurs. Some of the critical resources required for an entrepreneurship institute as recommended by the respondents are mentioned below.

- The institute must have an excellent *network* with local businesses, local start-ups, as well as big corporate all over the country.
- The faculty of entrepreneurship institutes should have some *entrepreneurial experience* as well in addition to the academic expertise and experience.
- The *location* of the institute should not be very distant from the main city as it becomes an impediment for continuous connect with the potential customers essential for product development and feasibility.

- The entrepreneurship program should be *residential* to provide greater opportunity for peer-to-peer learning and networking among the batchmates. It may also help entrepreneurship students connect with the regular management students at the institutes where both the programs are offered. Among the respondents, those with residential programs were found to have benefitted more from the course in their perseverance, group-interpersonal skills, and problem-solving skills.
- Entrepreneurship institutes must have their *incubators* to assist the students beyond ideation as well as after the completion of the course. The incubators should be accessible to the students as some of the respondents mentioned that though their institute had an incubator facility the entry barriers to incubators were very high.
- Sufficient in-house infrastructure or connect to external resources for assistance in *prototype development* should be available.
- Entrepreneurship institute should have a rich *repository* of relevant physical and digital books, videos, and podcasts related to the domain of entrepreneurship from across the world.
- The association of the entrepreneurship institutes with students should be strengthened and extended beyond the duration of the course for the mutual benefit that the institute may gain from *alumni network* and students may gain from their alma mater.

4 **Affordability**
The fee for a two-year entrepreneurship course at most of the institutes is currently exorbitantly high, making it unaffordable for a large number of candidates aspiring to take-up entrepreneurial careers. Scholarships, fee regulation, and government support may be helpful in this regard.

5 **Selection Process**
The majority of the respondents reiterated the need for the selection of the right candidates for entrepreneurship education programs. The current selection process was found to be less rigorous and very generic, diluting the quality of the over-all batch of students pursuing the course. A specific entrepreneurial aptitude test was recommended as a basic pre-requisite for the course. Moreover, most of the respondents suggested that only individuals with a minimum of two to three years of entrepreneurial or work experience should be admitted to the course to increase the e\fficacy of the course. Students with a business idea should be a preferred choice as they would be able to take the maximum advantage of the course.

Based on the above discussion, we propose the framework depicted in Figure 9.3 for developing and imparting effective entrepreneurship education programs.

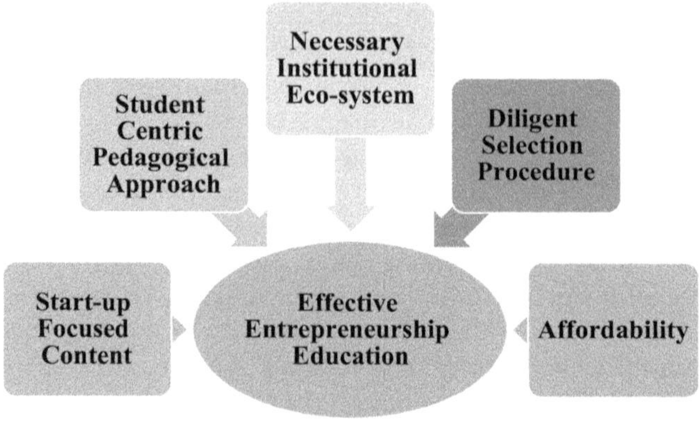

Figure 9.3 Proposed framework for effective entrepreneurship education in India.

Conclusion

After analyzing the responses from those who have undergone two-year full-time entrepreneurship education in some of the prominent institutes in western India, it can be said that the current framework of entrepreneurship education needs a considerable overhaul. The analysis depicts that the limitations in entrepreneurship education outrun its significance. To enhance the influence and efficacy of entrepreneurship education, the present study suggests pedagogical improvisation for enhancing the practicality of the course, creating differentiated content as compared to regular MBA programs, institutionalizing an eco-system for nurturing entrepreneurs, revising the selection process and fees as broad considerations. The responses were crucial in highlighting the importance of live case studies particularly from India, field projects in and around the region, studio teaching and simulation activities, extended internship programs, experience sharing sessions by successful and failed entrepreneurs as well as budding entrepreneurs as part of teaching methods. The respondents also pointed out that workshops on communication and soft skills, fund estimation and sourcing, valuation and pitching, and IPR would be very effective in grooming budding entrepreneurs during the two-year program on entrepreneurship.

To make entrepreneurship education a preferred choice amongst the students, it is important that it culminates into effective venture creation as an outcome and can offer significantly different propositions as compared to regular management programs of similar duration.

The current framework and research can be enhanced further by incorporating the inputs from entrepreneurship institutes and entrepreneurship faculty members as the present study is limited to the perspective provided by alumni and entrepreneurs of entrepreneurship education.

References

Abhyankar, R. (2014). The Government of India's role in promoting innovation through policy initiatives for entrepreneurship development. *Technology Innovation Management Review*, *4*(8), 11–17.

Agrawal, M., & Thakur, K. S. (2018). Entrepreneurship education and training in India: dimensions for success. *International Journal of Research in Management & Social Science*, *41*. DOI: 10.13140/RG.2.2.36686.20807

AICTE. (2018). *Model Curriculum for Management Program (MBA/PGDM)*. All India Council for Technical Education. Retrieved from https://www.aicte-india.org/sites/default/files/AICTE_MBA.pdf

AICTE. (2020). *List of HEIs offering MBA/PGDM in Innovation, Entrepreneurship and Venture Development (IEV) for the Academic Year 2020–21*. All India Council for Technical Education. Retrieved from http://cet.cbtexam.in/docs/list15.pdf

Alberti, F., Sciascia, S., & Poli, A. (2004). Entrepreneurship Education: Notes on an Ongoing Debate. *14th Annual IntEnt Conference University of Napoli Federico II (Italy)*.

Albornoz Pardo, C. (2013). Is business creation the mean or the end of entrepreneurship education? A multiple case study exploring teaching goals in entrepreneurship education. *Journal of technology management & innovation*, *8*(1), 1–10.

Arthur, S. J., Hisrich, R. D., & Cabrera, A. (2012). The importance of education in the entrepreneurial process: a world view. *Journal of Small Business and Enterprise Development*, *19*(3), 500–514.

Basu, R. (2014). Entrepreneurship education in India: a critical assessment and a proposed framework. *Technology Innovation Management Review*, *4*(8), 5–10.

Bechard, J. P., & Toulouse, J. M. (1991). Entrepreneurship and education: viewpoint from education. *Journal of small business & entrepreneurship*, *9*(1), 3–13.

Bharucha, J. (2019). Entrepreneurship education management in India. *International Journal of Business Excellence*, *17*(4), 456–468.

CBBC. (2016, February). *How British entrepreneurship education can inspire China*. Retrieved from The British Chamber of Commerce in China: http://www.britishchamber.cn/content/how-british-entrepreneurship-education-can-inspire-china

Chen, C., Greene, P., & Crick, A. (1998). Does entrepreneurial self-efficacy distinguish entrepreneurs from managers? *Journal of Business Venturing, 13* (4), 295–316.

DCMSME. (2016). *Schemes: DCMSME*. Retrieved January 2017, from Development Commissioner Ministry of Micro, Small and Medium Enterprises: http://www.dcmsme.gov.in/schemes/list_edi.htm

De Noble, A. F., Jung, D., & Ehrlich, S. B. (1999). Entrepreneurial self-efficacy: the development of a measure and its relationship to entrepreneurial action. *Frontiers of Entrepreneurship Research*, *1999*(1), 73–87

EDII. (2016). *EDII@Glance: EDII*. Retrieved January 2017, from Entrepreneurship Development Institute of India Web Site: http://www.ediindia.org/emergence.html

Edirisinghe, D., & Nimeshi, G. (2016). Entrepreneurial inclination among university students: with special reference to the University of Kelaniya, Sri Lanka. *IOSR Journal of Business and Management*, *18*(7), 7–12.

Entrepreneur India. (2014, September 15). The Oldest Entrepreneurship Programs in America. *Entrepreneur India*.

European Commission. (2017). *Entrepreneurship and SMEs: European Commission*. Retrieved January 2017, from https://ec.europa.eu/growth/smes/promotingentrepreneurship/support/education_en

Fiet, J. O. (2001). The pedagogical side of entrepreneurship theory. *Journal of business venturing*, *16*(2), 101–117.

GEM. (2020). *Global Entrepreneurship Monitor 2019/20 Global Report*. London: Global Entrepreneurship Research Association, London Business School. Retrieved from https://www.gemconsortium.org/report

Hameed, I., & Irfan, Z. (2019). Entrepreneurship education: a review of challenges, characteristics and opportunities. *Entrepreneurship Education*, *2*(3–4), 135–148.

Hood, J. N., & Young, J. E. (1993). Entrepreneurship's requisite areas of development: a survey of top executives in successful entrepreneurial firms. *Journal of Business Venturing*, *8*(2), 115–135.

Ilayaraja, & Ganesh, S. K. (2016). Entrepreneurship education in India and motivation to become entrepreneurs. *International Journal of Advance Research and Innovative Ideas in Education*, *1*(1), 372–376.

Jerome, K. (2003). The chronology and intellectual trajectory of American entrepreneurship education 1876–1999. *Journal of Business Venturing*, *18*, 283–300.

Keat, O. Y., Selvarajah, C., & Meyer, D. (2011). Inclination towards entrepreneurship among university students: an empirical study of Malaysian university students. *International Journal of Business and Social Science*, *2*(4), 206–220.

Kuratko, D. F. (2005). The emergence of entrepreneurship education: development, trends, and challenges. *Entrepreneurship theory and practice*, *29*(5), 577–598.

Liyan, Z. (2003). Entrepreneurship education within India's higher education system. Available at: http://www.asianscholarship.org/asf/ejourn/articles/zhang_l.pdf (accessed December 2019).

Lucas, W., & Cooper, S. (2005). Measuring entrepreneurial self-efficacy. *EDGE Conference: Bridging the Gap: Entrepreneurship in Theory and Practice* (pp. 11–13). Singapore.

Mbeteh, A., & Pellegrini, M. M. (2018). Entrepreneurship education in developing countries: A study of the key challenges in Sierra Leone. In Leo-Paul Dana, Vanessa Ratten and Ben Q. Honyenuga, (Eds.), *African Entrepreneurship* (pp. 89–116). Palgrave Macmillan, Cham.

McGee, J., Peterson, M., Mueller, S., & Sequeira, J. (2009). Entrepreneurial self-efficacy: refining the measure. *Entrepreneurship Theory and Practice*, *33*(4), 965–988.

MHRD. (2020). *National Education Policy 2020*. Government of India. Retrieved from https://www.mhrd.gov.in/sites/upload_files/mhrd/files/NEP_Final_English_0.pdf

Moberg, K., Vestergaard, L., Fayolle, A., Redford, D., Cooney, T., Singe, S., … Filip, D. (2014). *How to assess and evaluate the influence of entrepreneurship education: A report of the ASTEE project with a user guide to the tools*. The Danish Foundation for Entrepreneurship–Young Enterprise.

Mohan, R. S., & Revathi, R. (2012). Impact of training on entrepreneurial development. *IJEMR*, *2*(6), 1–6.

Ramakrishna, H., & Hulugappa, H. (2013). Entrepreneurship education in India: emerging trends and concerns. *Journal of Entrepreneurship and Management*, *2*(1), 28.

Rehman, A., & Elahi, Y. A. (2012). Entrepreneurship education in india-scope, challenges, and role of b schools in promoting entrepreneurship education. *International Journal of Engineering and Management Research (IJEMR)*, *2*(5), 5–14.

Sarooghi, H., Sunny, S., Hornsby, J., & Fernhaber, S. (2019). Design thinking and entrepreneurship education: where are we, and what are the possibilities?. *Journal of Small Business Management*, *57*, 78–93.

Shankar, R. 2012. *Entrepreneurship: Theory and Practice*. India: Tata McGraw Hill.

Stevenson, H. H., Roberts, M. J., & Grousbeck, H. I. (1985). *New Business Ventures and the Entrepreneur* (pp. 139–161). Homewood, IL: Irwin.

UNCTAD. (2011). Review of the technical cooperation activities of UNCTAD and their financing. *United Nations Conference on Trade and Development*. Geneva: United Nations.

Valerio, A., Parton, B., & Robb, A. (2014). *Entrepreneurship Education and Training Programs around the World: Dimensions for Success*. Washington DC: World Bank Publications.

Wang, Y. S., Tseng, T. H., Wang, Y. M., & Chu, C. W. (2019). Development and validation of an internet entrepreneurial self-efficacy scale. *Internet Research*, *30*(2), 653–675.

World Economic Forum. (2009). *Educating the Next Wave of Entrepreneurs: Unlocking entrepreneurial capabilities to meet the global challenges of the 21st Century-A Report of the Global Education Initiative*. Switzerland.

10 Growth of Store Brands in Uncertain Markets

Ipsita Padhi and B.B. Mishra

Introduction

COVID-19 has impacted the world in unprecedented ways and has dramatically changed the way we live and work. The pandemic has pushed economies of major countries downhill, with uncertainties looming large across many sectors throughout the globe. The situation has not been any better in India either. After the nation-wide lockdown was induced by the Government to keep a check on the rapid transmission of the virus, the retail sector went into a lunatic frenzy. The lockdown disrupted supply chain due to travel restrictions and impacted manufacturing and production units gravely due to the shortage of human resources. There has not been any market sector which has not been impacted by the hurdles of the pandemic. While there were few sectors crippled by the disruption due to the lockdown, specific sectors like consumer goods were less impacted. Amidst the pandemic leading to the economic crisis, a new standard of consumer behaviour has been witnessed. Consumers' buying pattern has been primarily curtailed; relatively newer products have become an essential part of the shopping list. There has been a sudden escalation in the buying behaviour of personal care items like sanitizers, hand washes, soaps, disinfectants and the like. Due to the gloomy market scenario, consumers have been averse to spending, leading to cutting down on unnecessary expenses and opting for readily available, cheaper alternatives. The current market chaos has led to new entrants or market players pitching in for a fair share in the consumer's buying list. Due to supply chain disruptions, retailers relied on store brands for sales, as manufacturer brands could not cater to consumer demand. In the present market scenario, the FMCG segment has seen a sudden spurt in store brands' rise across the country.

This study aims to check on the impact of the purchasing decision (Batra & Sinha, 2000; Karampour & Ahmadinejad, 2014) of store brands on specific consumer-specific parameters like price-consciousness, quality consciousness, brand awareness and store image (Fan et al., 2012; Gangwani et al., 2020). The objectives of the study include:

DOI: 10.4324/9781003354703-13

- To study the impact of crucial consumer attributes (price consciousness, quality consciousness, brand awareness and store image) towards the purchase of store brands.
- To analyze the consumption pattern of store brand in the FMCG sector.

Literature Review

The Indian retail industry dates back to olden times when village fairs housed independent retail units. The emergence of organized retailing has been instrumental in paving the way forward for the rapid growth in this sector (Cleggett, 2015). Over the past few decades, India's organized retail sector has experienced radical changes, most of which is directly proportionate to the consumer's changing buying patterns and demographics (Kakkar & Mathur, 2020). Store brands were one of the novel introductions to the retail sector. It is broadly understood as any brand manufactured and sold by the retailer exclusively in retailer's own stores (Private Label, n.d.). Store brands are also referred to as private labels or own brands. Earlier store brands were considered to be cheap and low-priced products (Harmancioglu et al., 2009). The increase in consumerism in the past few years and the change in the buying pattern has led to an increased number of buyers being inclined towards store brands (Baltas, 1997). The pandemic has seemed to have changed many expected norms to set a "new normal" for the retail sector (Sitaram, 2019; Somasekhar, 2018). To better understand the present study, it is imperative to have a conceptual understanding of store brands and consumer buying behaviour (Kumar & Steenkamp, 2007; Li et al., 2019).

Consumer purchasing behaviour has been defined as the sum of a consumer's actions when selecting and purchasing products or services to meet their needs, wants, or desires (Kotler & Keller, 2011; Schiffman & Kanauk, 1997). There are different divergent factors that contribute to the purchasing habits and the non-habitual, individual purchase decisions of each consumer (Chiranth & Kavitha, 2019; Shyam & Gupta, 2018). Over time, those factors have come to include product necessity, cost, availability, desirability, comparison to other products (whether they are very different or very similar), value (as well as perceived value), information, and the list continues. In a brick and mortar retail environment, some of these factors may play a more critical role in consumers' purchase decisions than other factors (Kotler et al., 2007). It has been proved that sensory consideration in a retail environment is a powerful tool used to drive customers to make positive associations with brands and products, which often leads to purchases and relationships with said brands and products.

It is essential to analyze the two most essential parameters of brand differentiation-price and quality and determine their association with each other (Boyle et al., 2018; Hoch & Banerji, 1993), which would help in understanding the consumer's buying behaviour. However, studies show that when the consumer is in a situation to choose between a store brand and a manufacturer brand with similar quality, price becomes the deciding factor for the purchase (Mbaye et al., 2013; Muruganantham & Priyadharshini, 2017). Some literature has also studied on the price consciousness of the consumer. It has been found that, in the case of store brands, there is a general perception of "low-priced-poor-quality" products among consumers (Lichtenstein et al., 1993; Liu et al., 2019; Richardson et al., 1996a). As a result, store brand consumers generally lack brand loyalty due to perceived risks associated with the brand. Being price sensitive, these consumers are often on the lookout for promotional offers, freebies, and discounts associated with store brands; since this gives them a valid excuse to buy store brands instead of manufacturer brands (Sayman et al., 2002; Semeijn et al., 2004). Extant literature has also found that the price-quality perception the consumer has towards a store brand is directly related to the store image where the store brand is available. Historically, consumers have turned to generic and store brand products during times of financial distress (Gupta et al., 2019). Despite the increase in store brands' consumer purchases, there are some products in which brand preference frequently trump price. Though many store brand personal care and hygiene products may be comparable to their national brand counterparts (in composition, variety, and efficacy), they have been unable to draw the same consumer attraction that store brand household goods and grocery items have since the recession. The economic event forced retailers to rethink their store brand portfolio strategies in order to remain relevant in a world where, more than ever, consumers seek brands that not only offer value but speak in a unique, identifiable voice and deliver substance with purpose. This value has been added by changes in product packaging and branding conventions for several retailers in the past decade.

In the Indian retail sector, store brands have emerged as a recent trend and are dynamically changing with the existing market landscape and consumer demographics (Liu et al., 2019). The demographic profile of Indian consumers is rapidly changing as a result of rising consumerism. Due to this change, some studies show that specific demographic parameters like age, gender, and income tend to influence store brands' purchase decisions significantly. Many authors have also studied store brand purchase decisions on the basis of the locations where they are being sold, like supermarkets and malls (Kartiwi et al., 2018; Nenycz-Thiel & Romaniuk, 2012). The recent activity in the store brand sector during the pandemic has prompted this study to analyze consumers' behaviors (Sharma et al., 2020; Sitaram, 2019). Based on the existing literature, the present study has been conducted to analyze consumers' purchasing decisions towards store brands, keeping in mind specific attributes like price consciousness, quality consciousness, store brand's awareness, and store image (Sonia San Martín Gutiérrez, 2006).

Methodology

The current study's scope is limited to store brand consumers in the FMCG sector. Therefore, this study's sample frame was derived from select consumers who have purchased and consumed store brands from the FMCG sector. The study was conducted to identify the impact of store brand buying behaviour among FMCG consumers during the uncertain market situation. To collect data, a quantitative study was conducted to analyze the impact of store brand purchasing decisions (Baxendale et al., 2015) against consumer-specific characteristics like price consciousness (Batra & Sinha, 2000; Burton et al., 1998), quality consciousness (Ailawadi et al., 2001), brand awareness (Hoyer & Brown, 1990; Richardson et al., 1996), and store image (Ailawadi et al., 2001; Collins-Dodd & Lindley, 2003; Kremer & Viot, 2012). For collecting the primary data, a closed-ended structured questionnaire was used with a 5-point Likert scale. The scale development for the questionnaire was done using an existing scale from the previous literature as mentioned in Table 10.1, and the Likert scale was used to measure responses over a range varying from 1 to 5, where 1 denoted strongly disagree and 5 denoted strongly agree. The Cronbach's alpha value of the questionnaire was found to be 0.72; hence, it was reliable. Data was collected through offline as well as online mode. In the offline mode, primary data was collected using the mall intercept method at selected departmental stores where there was a substantial concentration of FMCG store brands and a higher percentage of consumer footfall per day. In the online mode, the questionnaire set was distributed to various store brand consumers through Google Forms. A sample frame of 150 respondents was targeted for the study. The study timeline and the restrictions due to the pandemic situation posed a big challenge for data collection; hence only 128 valid responses could be collected for the study. The offline data consisted of responses from consumers intercepted at departmental stores in Bhubaneswar and Cuttack at Odisha; while the online data was collected via Google Forms from across the country. The data was arranged in digital format and analyzed using SPSS software. Statistical tools were used to test the hypothesis and analyze the relationship between the variables.

Table 10.1 Scale Development

Scale development	*Literature*
Price consciousness	Burton et al. (1998); Batra & Sinha (2000)
Quality consciousness	Ailawadi et al., (2001)
Brand awareness	Richardson et al. (1996); Hoyer & Brown (1990)
Store image	Ailawadi et al. (2001); Kremer & Viot (2012)
Demographics	Ailawadi et al. (2001)

Source: Litereature review.

Results

In this study, the relationship between the purchase decision of store brands (dependent variable) and other independent variables like price consciousness, quality consciousness, brand awareness, and store image has been explored.

Location for Purchasing Store Brand

According to the analysis of the responses, it was found that 58% of the respondents prefer to shop for store brands at supermarkets/departmental stores, 40% prefer e-commerce sites, and the rest 18% prefer shopping malls.

Spending Habits of Store Brand Consumers

Table 10.2 FMCG_Store Brand Consumer's Spending Habits

	Frequency	*Percent*	*Valid Percent*	*Cumulative Percent*
Valid FMCG_SB				
Grocery	15	60.0	60.0	60.0
Personal care	6	24.0	24.0	76.0
Other	4	16.0	16.0	100.0
Total	25	100.0	100.0	

Source: Author's analysis.

The table shows that consumers allocate 60% of their shopping budget for buying store brand groceries, while 24% buy store brand personal care items and the rest 16% is allocated for other FMCG store brand items like packaged food, beverages, and laundry items.

Factors Affecting the Purchase Decision of Store Brands

While filling the questionnaire, the respondents were asked to rank in ascending order the factors they felt they look for before making an FMCG store brand's purchase decision.

From Table 10.3, it was found that price was one of the primary factors contributing to store brand purchase decisions, followed by quality and discounts.

Table 10.3 FMCG_Factors Affecting Store Brand Purchase Decision

Factors affecting purchase decision of store brand		*Overall score*
Price consciousness		108
Quality consciousness		105
Brand awareness		98
In-store service	Store image	98
Ambience of the store	Store image	80
Sales and discounts at the store	Store image	100

Source: Author's analysis.

Regression

Table 10.4 is the model summary of a set of dependent and independent variables. The R square for the model (0.602) indicates that 60.2% of the dependent variable, store brand purchase decision, varies due to the independent variables, price consciousness, quality consciousness, brand awareness, and store image. Durbin-Watson statistic's desired value should be within the range of 1.25 to 2.5; hence, the value here is 2.001, which means that the assumption is valid about residuals not being correlated.

Table 10.5 describes the regression coefficients along with their significance levels. The table shows that brand awareness has the highest contribution to store brands' purchase, followed by price consciousness, quality consciousness, and store image.

Table 10.4 Regression Model Summary

Model	*R*	*R square*	*Adjusted R square*	*Std. error of the estimate*	*Durbin-Watson*
1	0.775[a]	0.602	0.595	0.645	2.001

a Predictors: (Constant), Store_Image, Quality_Consciousness, Brand_Awareness,Price_Consciousness
Dependent variable: SB Purchase decision
Source: Author's analysis.

Table 10.5 Regression Coefficients

		Unstandardized coefficients		*Standardized coefficients*		
Model		*B*	*Std. error*	*Beta*	*T*	*Sig.*
1	(Constant)	3.314	0.028		117.459	0.000
	Price_Consciousness	0.300	0.028	0.295	10.610	0.000
	Brand_Awareness	0.665	0.028	0.655	23.549	0.000
	Quality_					0.000
	Consciousness	0.228	0.028	0.225	8.070	
	Store_Image	0.179	0.028	0.177	6.351	0.000

Dependent variable: SB Purchase decision
Source: Author's analysis.

Thus, the regression equation is written as:

$$\text{SB Purchase decision} = 3.314 + 0.3^{*}(\text{Price\_Consciousness}) + 0.655^{*}(\text{Brand\_Awareness}) + 0.228^{*}(\text{Quality\_Consciousness}) + 0.179^{*}(\text{Store\_Image})$$

Correlation

It is imperative to check for multi-colinearity to understand the interdependence of the variables among each other.

Table 10.6 Inter-Construct Correlation

Constructs	*Price consciousness*	*Quality consciousness*	*Brand awareness*	*Store image*
Price consciousness	1	0.543	0.478	0.488
Quality consciousness	0.543	1	0.424	0.464
Brand awareness	0.478	0.424	1	0.300
Store image	0.488	0.464	0.300	1

At 5% level of significance
Source: Author's analysis.

As seen from Table 4.5, the inter-variable (construct) correlation has low values, meaning that the constructs are interdependent. Here, the correlation between store image and brand awareness has the weakest correlation of 0.300. Hence, from this we can draw an inference that consumers consider each variable separately while making a store brand purchase decision. Since all the other correlation values are also less than 0.05, there is no relationship between the variables, and they do not showcase any signs of multi-colinearity. The p-value is <0.05 at 5% level of significance.

Cross Tabulation

From Table 10.7, we infer that the p-value is less than 0.05; hence all the demographic variables have a significant relationship with the store brand purchase decision. Age is the most significant factor responsible for the store brand purchase decision with a value of 50.070, followed by income at 46.62, occupation at 29.73, qualification at 25.699, and gender at 11.128, in descending order of values.

Table 10.7 Demographics vs SB Purchase Decision

Demographics	*Pearson chi-square value*	*df*	*Asymp. sig. (2-sided)*
Age	50.070	12	0.000
Gender	11.128	4	0.025
Occupation	29.737	12	0.003
Income	46.623	12	0.000
Qualification	25.669	12	0.012

Source: Author's analysis.

Discussion

- As more people are frequently purchasing store brand products, it is apparent that store brands are achieving better patronage from consumers.
- The availability of store brands across varied platforms, both offline and online, speaks volumes about consumer preference to buy these brands.
- Due to the pandemic, store brands have forayed their entry into digital platform to increase their visibility. Hence, the present study projects almost 40 % consumers as buying store brands online.
- Brand awareness of store brands is going to attract more consumers in the future.
- The USP of store brands is their affordable price yet durable and good quality product, making it a good choice for the price-sensitive consumer.
- There is a positive correlation between demographics, especially the respondents' age group, and purchase of store brands.
- Different age groups of consumers have different choices and hence have different buying patterns of store brands.
- Consumers' preference towards store brands has increased, as can be seen from the present study since consumers now buy store brands from many categories in the FMCG segment like groceries, personal care, packaged goods, and laundry items.

Hence, it could mean that store brands have come off the age to shed the "cheap substitute" tag. They are ready to take the competition head-on with manufacturer brands across product categories.

Limitations

Although there has been an attempt to achieve the study's objectives with the utmost earnestness, there are limitations to the present study. The data was collected over three weeks during September 2020, when lockdown rules had been slightly relaxed in Odisha, yet there was a restriction in moving out. Hence, this has badly affected the data collection process, as a result of which the total responses collected could not go beyond 128. An extended timeline and conducive market conditions could have benefited in collecting an adequate number of responses for the study. Since the data collection has been restricted to only two cities in Odisha-Bhubaneswar and Cuttack, the study might not project an exact geographical representation of other cities. Another limitation is that this study concentrates on store brands in the fast-moving consumer goods sector only. The primary data included responses collected from consumers, but statistical data or percentage growth of store brand consumption figures could not be fetched from the retailers due to internal policies. The presence of such data would have significantly enhanced the credibility and authenticity of the present study.

Conclusion

An uncertain market environment like the one we are facing now due to the pandemic always leads to stressful situations for companies. However, the silver lining is, in the backdrop of the chaos in the market, there is also a wave of change in the air that has seeped in due to altered consumer buying behaviour, slump down in consumption pattern and migration to better-valued substitutes. These are times when companies should tap into newer opportunities and harness their efforts to grab market share and brand equity (Agyapong, 2017).

In the study, brand awareness was one of the critical attributes for store brand purchase decision; hence, companies should look for ways to promote their store brands through exciting promotional deals that could also help towards brand creation. Price and quality consciousness were also attributed to influence the sale of store brands; hence companies could invest in more research to position store brands in niche categories and quantities not available with manufacturer brands, to leverage on the price-sensitive consumer while also achieving competitive advantage in terms of quality. Store brands could look for novel ways to provide value-for-money categories while keeping in mind the consumer's changing preferences and tastes (Falahat et al., 2018). The improved labelling and packaging of the store brands could also make them stand out in the competition (Sarkar et al., 2016; Sharma et al., 2020).

The crisis due to COVID-19 has seen a shift in consumers' shopping pattern towards e-commerce and digital payments. However, there is much potential in the online channels that companies can harness to allure potential consumers (Hu & Chaudhry, 2020). A recent market survey conducted by the global consulting firm McKinsey emphasizes the accelerated growth of online marketplaces, particularly the FMCG segment, in the last few months. This is a clear signal for marketers to push their efforts in enhancing their operational complexity by focusing on renewed value, reducing on the potential demand for store brands during customer traffic and migrating their sales towards such online marketplaces (Vahie & Paswan, 2006; *COVID-19: Implications for business*, McKinsey Executive Briefing, October 21, 2020).

Thus, store brands have had a steady growth in the FMCG categories, even amidst uncertain markets during this pandemic, and there is a way forward for store brands' future.

Recommendation and Scope for Future Research

As already mentioned in the limitation section, this study has been conducted to keep in mind store brands in fast-moving consumer goods; hence, future studies could be conducted to study store brands' growth in other product categories. Future studies could make up for the present study's limitations and widen the study's scope to a better geographical representation. According to literature, in the last few years, online marketplaces have been booming, leading to the steady growth of store brands on the online platforms, with a good assortment being available across different categories in various e-commerce sites (Lian & Yen, 2014; Rajyalakshmi, 2015). Future research could look into the growth of store brands on online platforms.

References

Agyapong, H. A. (2017). *Exploring the influential factors of online purchase* (Thesis). Business Economics and Tourism International Business, Finland. Retrieved from https://core.ac.uk/download/pdf/161426026.pdf

Ailawadi, K., Neslin, S., & Gedenk, K. (2001). Pursuing the value-conscious consumer: Store brands versus national brand promotions. *Journal of Marketing*, *65*(1), 71–89.

Baltas, G. (1997). Determinants of store brand choice: A behavioural analysis. *Journal of Product and Brand Management*, *6*(5), 315–324.

Batra, R., & Sinha, I. (2000). Consumer level factors moderating the success of private label brands across product categories, *Journal of Retailing*, *76*(2), 175–191.

Baxendale, S., Macdonald, E. K., & Wilson, H. N. (2015). The impact of different touch points on brand consideration. *Journal of Retailing*, *91*(2), 235–253. http://dx.doi.org/10.1016/j.jretai.2014.12.008

Boyle, P. J., Kim, H., & Lathrop, E. S. (2018). The relationship between price and quality in durable product categories with private label brands. *The Journal of*

Product and Brand Management, *27*(6), 647–660. http://dx.doi.org/10.1108/JPBM-09-2017-1590

Burton, S., Lichtenstein, D. R., & Garretson, J. A. (1998). A scale for measuring attitude toward private label products and an examination of its psychological and behavioral correlates. *Journal of the Academy of Marketing Science*, *26*(4), 293–306.

Chiranth, K. M., & Kavitha, B. N. (2019). Factors influencing purchase of private labels. *Journal of Emerging Technologies and Innovative Research*, *6*(2), 1–7. Retrieved from http://www.jetir.org/papers/JETIR1902B08.pdf

Cleggett, C. C. (2015, Summer). Making over the retail industry. *The Crisis*, *122*, 36–37. Retrieved from https://search-proquest-com.library.britishcouncil.org.in:4443/magazines/making-over-retail-industry/docview/1699263853/se-2?accountid=145163

Collins-Dodd, C., & Lindley T. (2003). Store brands and retail differentiation: The influence of store image and store brand attitude on store brand own perceptions. *Journal of Retailing and Consumer Services*, *10*(4), 345–352.

COVID-19: Implications for business. (2020, October 21). McKinsey. Retrieved from https://www.mckinsey.com/business-functions/risk/our-insights/covid-19-implications-for-business

Falahat, M., Chuan, C. S., & Kai, S. B. (2018). Brand loyalty and determinates of perceived quality and willingness to order. *Academy of Strategic Management Journal*, *17*(4), 1–10. Retrieved from https://search.proquest.com/docview/2124080642?accountid=172344

Fan, X., Qian, Y., & Huang, P. (2012). Factors influencing consumer behaviour towards store brand: A meta-analysis. *International Journal of Market Research*, *54*(3), 407–430. https://doi.org/10.2501/ijmr-54-3-407-430

Gangwani, S., Mathur, M., Chaudhary, A., & Benbelgacem, S. (2020). Investigating key factors influencing purchase intention of apparel Private Label brands in India. *Academy of Strategic Management Journal*, *19*(3), 1–8. Retrieved from https://www.abacademies.org/articles/Investigating-key-factors-influencing-purchase-intention-of-apparel-private-label-brands-in-India-1939-6104-19-3-549.pdf

Gupta, K., Kaur, J., & Duggal, V. (2019). Private brands waiting to be purchased-the store image story. *Asian Journal of Marketing*, *14*, 1–9. Retrieved from https://scialert.net/fulltext/?doi=ajm.2020.1.9

Gutiérrez, Sonia San Martín (2006). A model of consumer relationships with store brands, personnel and stores in Spain. *The International Review of Retail, Distribution and Consumer Research*, *16*(4), 453. Retrieved from https://search-proquest-com.library.britishcouncil.org.in:4443/scholarly-journals/model-consumer-relationships-with-store-brands/docview/219434503/se-2?accountid=145163

Harmancioglu, N., Finney, R. Z., & Joseph, M. (2009). Impulse purchases of new products: An empirical analysis. *Journal of Product and Brand Management*, *18*(1), 27–37. https://doi.org/10.1108/10610420910933344

Hoch, S., & Banerji, S. (1993) When do private labels succeed? *Sloan Management Review*, *34*(4), 57–67.

Hoyer, W. D., & Brown, S. P. (1990). Effect of brand awareness on choice for a common, repeat-purchase product. *Journal of Consumer Research*, *17*(2), 141–148.

Hu, M., & Chaudhry, S. S. (2020). Enhancing consumer engagement in e-commerce live streaming via relational bonds. *Internet Research*, *30*(3), 1019–1041. http://dx.doi.org/10.1108/INTR-03-2019-0082.

Kakkar, S., & Mathur, S. (2020). Organized retail in India and consumer buying behaviour: A review of literature. *Journal of Critical Reviews*, *7*(6), 1–8. Retrieved from http://www.jcreview.com/fulltext/197-1588228678.pdf

Karampour, A., & Ahmadinejad, B. (2014). Purchase intention for a private label brand: Direct impact of factors including price sensitivity, understanding brand, image of private brands and mental image of store; (case study: etka chain stores). *Kuwait Chapter of the Arabian Journal of Business and Management Review*, *3*(7), 417–426. Retrieved from https://search.proquest.com/docview/1510284049?accountid=172344

Kartiwi, M., Hussin, H., Suhaimi, M. A., Jalaldeen, M. R. M., & Amin, M. R. (2018). Impact of external factors on determining E-commerce benefits among SMEs in Malaysia. *Journal of Global Entrepreneurship Research*, *8*. http://dx.doi.org/10.1186/s40497-018-0105-7

Kotler, P., & Keller, K. (2011). *Marketing Management* (14th ed.). London: Pearson Education.

Kotler, P., Keller, K. L., Koshy, A., & Jha, M. (2007). *Marketing Management: A South Asian Perspective* (12th ed.). New Delhi: Pearson Education.

Kremer, F., & Viot, C. (2012). How store brands build retailer brand image. *International Journal of Retail and Distribution Management, Emerald*, *40*(7), 1–8. Retrieved from https://hal.archives-ouvertes.fr/hal-01803720/file/kremer_viot_store_brands_2012_IJR%26DM.pdf

Kumar, N., & Steenkamp, J. (2007). *Private Label Strategy: How to Meet the Store Brand Challenge*. Boston, MA: Harvard Business School Press.

Li, C., He, Y., Peng, L., & Yuan, D. (2019). How manufacturer brand erosion shapes consumer assortment perceptions. *Asia Pacific Journal of Marketing and Logistics*, *32*(4), 922–939. http://doi.org/10.1108/APJML-04-2019-0235

Lian, J.W., & Yen, D. C. (2014). Online shopping drivers and barriers for older adults: Age and gender differences. *Computers in Human Behavior*, *37*, 133–143. https://doi.org/10.1016/j.chb.2014.04.028

Lichtenstein, D. R., Ridgway, N.M., & Netemeyer, R.G. (1993 May). Price perceptions and consumer shopping behavior: A field study. *Journal of Marketing Research*, *30*, 234–245.

Liu, Y., Xiaojun, F., Li, J., & Dong, X. (2019). Extrinsic cues, perceived quality, and purchase intention for private labels. *Asia Pacific Journal of Marketing and Logistics*, *31*(3), 714–727. http://dx.doi.org/10.1108/APJML-08-2017-0176

Mbaye, F. D., Chandon, J., Cliquet, G., & Philippe, J. (2013). Factors influencing consumer behaviour towards store brands: Evidence from the French market. *International Journal of Retail & Distribution Management*, *41*(6), 422–441. http://dx.doi.org/10.1108/09590551311330816

Muruganantham, G., & Priyadharshini, K. (2017). Antecedents and consequences of private brand purchase. *International Journal of Retail & Distribution Management*, *45*(6), 660–682. http://dx.doi.org/10.1108/IJRDM-02-2016-0025

Nenycz-Thiel, M., & Romaniuk, J. (2012). Value-for-money perceptions of supermarket and private labels. *Australasian Marketing Journal (AMJ)*, *20*(2), 171–177. Retrieved from https://search.proquest.com/docview/1027770396?accountid=172344

Private Label. (n.d.). https://en.wikipedia.org/. Retrieved October 15, 2020, from https://en.wikipedia.org/wiki/Private_label

Rajyalakshmi, N. (2015). Factors influencing online shopping behavior of urban consumers in India. *International Journal of Online Marketing*, *5*(1), 38–50. http://doi.org/10.4018/IJOM.2015010103

Richardson, P., Jain, A., & Dick, A. (1996a). Household store brand proneness: A framework. *Journal of Retailing*, 72(2), 159–185. https://doi.org/10.1016/S0022-4359(96)90012-3

Richardson, P., Jain, A. K., & Dick, A. S. (1996b). The influence of store aesthetics on the evaluation of private label brands. *Journal of Product and Brand Management*, *5* (1), 19–28.

Sarkar, S., Sharma, D., & Kalro, A. D. (2016). Private label brands in an emerging economy: An exploratory study in India. *International Journal of Retail & Distribution Management*, *44*(2), 203–222. http://dx.doi.org/10.1108/IJRDM-07-2015-0102

Sayman, S., Hoch, S., & Raju, J. (2002). Positioning of store brands. *Marketing Science*, *21*(4), 378–397. Retrieved January 8, 2021, from http://www.jstor.org/stable/1558072

Schiffman, J. B., & Kanauk, L. L. (1997). *Consumer Behavior* (6th ed.). Upper Saddle River, NJ: Prentice Hall.

Semeijn, J., van Rieb, A., & Ambrosini, A. (2004).Consumer evaluations of store brands: Effects of store image and product attributes. *Journal of Retailing & Consumer Services*, *11*(4), 247–259.

Sharma, V., Kedia, B., Yadav, V., & Mishra, S. (2020). Tapping the potential space-positioning of private labels. *Journal of Indian Business Research*, *12*(1), 43–61. http://dx.doi.org/10.1108/JIBR-09-2019-0263

Shyam, H., & Gupta, M. (2018). A study on consumer buying behaviour for shopping FMCG in large retail outlet. *ANVESHAK-International Journal of Management*, 7(2), 82–94. http://dx.doi.org/10.15410/aijm/2018/v7i2/122575

Sitaram, K. (2019, January 27). *Indian Recipe For Private Labels*. https://www.Businesstoday.In/. Retrieved from https://www.businesstoday.in/magazine/special-reports/food/indian-recipe-for-private-labels/story/307496.html

Somasekhar, G. (2018). Key retail store attributes determining shoppers' perception and satisfaction: An empirical study of organized retail stores located in Tirupati, AP. *International Journal of Multidisciplinary, Special Issue* (July), 1–8. ISSN: 2455-3085 (Online). Retrieved from https://rrjournals.com/wp-content/uploads/2018/08/54-61_GBMPETC20180710.pdf

Vahie, A., & Paswan, A. (2006).Private label brand image: Its relationship with store image and national brand. *International Journal of Retail and Distribution Management*, *34*(1), 67–84.

11 Rural Marketing in India

A Case Study of Consumer Durables

Rahul Kumar and Md. Shahnawaz Abdin

1 Introduction

Any country can make a shining mark on the world map only if it is characterized by continuous economic growth and development in this cut-throat competitive era. There has been tremendous pressure on the economies to go in tandem with the world and make their presence felt on the world map. To keep an economy running and to further its growth and development, the role of trade and business cannot be ignored. Trade and business provide an economy a platform to achieve its economic objectives. Moreover, trade and business bring in with them a tremendous opportunity for an economy to change its fate. India is an excellent example of how trade and business can change the fate of an economy. India took a bold and courageous decision and reformed its economy in 1991 that has opened up tremendous opportunities for India. Given its lucrative business environment, every businessman in the world sees India as an ocean of opportunity.

It's said that marketing is an essential element to operating in an economy. Over the years, marketing has played an important role in the development of countries. It is marketing that facilitates bringing final products and services to people from the factories. Marketing brings in new opportunities and makes the lives of individuals easy. Marketing facilitates the exchange of goods and services among individuals and groups and helps marketeers achieve organizational objectives (Kotler & Armstrong, 2011). The role of marketing is everywhere, from individuals to organizations to governments. It is because of marketing that people make use of new goods and services. With the changing times, marketing also keeps on changing and it develops itself according to the need of time. Over the years, marketing has witnessed a sea change. Many old techniques of marketing have become obsolete with the passage of time and there is emergence of new and advanced methods of marketing in the present scenario. With the onset of 21st century, marketing has seen a sea change and traditional methods of marketing are not going to bring much success to organizations. Organizations need to come up with new and innovative methods of marketing in order to offer their goods and services to consumers so that consumers buy the same.

DOI: 10.4324/9781003354703-14

In order to survive in an ever-evolving and cut-throat competitive era like that of today, business organizations need to look for alternative markets that can prove to be profitable for them. One of such alternative market that provides ample opportunities to organizations is rural marketing (Abdin & Kumar, 2020a). The very reason for business organizations resorting to rural marketing is the saturation of urban markets (Kashyap, 2012; Kumar & Abdin, 2021a). The term "rural marketing" traces its history back to about a hundred years ago, but it has gained importance in the last 20–30 years. There have been many studies (e.g. Jha, 1988; Rao & Tagat, 1985; Sarwade, 1998) that have explored the potential of rural marketing in India. The growing income of rural people, aspirations for quality and branded products, and growing awareness among the masses make the rural markets of India a lucrative place for marketeers (Ali et al., 2012; Kashyap, 2012; Kumar & Abdin, 2021b; Kumar & Bishnoi, 2007; Tyagi, 2017). Moreover, rural youth exhibit the same purchase behaviour as their urban counterparts do and aspire for branded, trending, quality products (Kashyap, 2012). It should also be kept in mind that around 70% of the population in India resides in its rural areas (Census of India, 2011), and further, it is predicted that half of India's population will be residing in rural areas even in the year 2050, which simply signifies that the rural marketing in India has a very prosperous scope in the time to come. But entering the rural markets of India is not as easy as one may think. It requires lots of analysis and understanding of the psyche of rural consumers (Abdin & Kumar, 2020b). It has been found that the rural people are more tradition bound (Kumar & Abdin, 2021a; Kumar & Bishnoi, 2007; Kashyap, 2012) and they do not want to detach themselves from their cultures and traditions, which makes marketing in rural areas difficult. Lack of infrastructural facilities and development works also makes rural marketing in India extremely difficult (Kumar & Abdin, 2021b; Singh, 2003). The biggest hurdle that one may face in entering the rural markets is the languages spoken by rural people and the dialects that they use (Abdin & Kumar, 2020b; Desai, 2021; Kashyap, 2012), which makes the promotion and sale of goods and services very difficult in rural areas. Thus, it is necessary that the marketeers come out with appropriate promotional strategies to advertise and sell their goods and services in rural areas.

Keeping all these in mind the authors have developed this chapter as a case study which attempts to give a historical background of rural marketing world over in general and in India in particular. The chapter explores how the definition or concept of rural marketing developed over the years and what changes occurred in it with the passage of time. It also makes an attempt to outline the current issues and future scope of rural marketing in India, with a special focus on consumer durable products. The study finds out that the term "rural marketing" traces its origin to about a hundred years ago in the US and then it developed world over. As far the as the case of India is concerned, the first mention of the term "rural marketing" was made in 1947. Rural marketing in India evolved through four phases and different phases had different implications and accordingly, different goods and services were bought and sold in it. The importance of rural marketing in India has grown in the last 20–30 years and it is attracting business organizations given its mammoth size and untapped potential, which has also been highlighted in previous studies like Singh (2003), Kumar and Bishnoi (2007), Kashyap (2012), Abdin and Kumar (2020a), Kumar and Abdin (2021a). There are some hurdles like poor infrastructure, lack of communication facilities, scattered markets, illiteracy, irregular income, etc., that make rural marketing in India extremely difficult. However, there exists a prosperous future of rural marketing in India. The World Economic Forum (2019) predicts that the rural per capita consumption will grow to 4.3 times by 2030, compared to 3.5 times in urban India, which simply confirms that it would be fruitful to invest in the rural markets of India. The size of the durable goods market in rural India is more than half of the total durable goods market in India. It accounts for 59% of the total durable goods market share of India, which again confirms the growing importance of rural marketing in India. All these factors highlight the importance and role of rural marketing in India and indicate that the rural market of India is surpassing the urban market. On these grounds, it can be said that rural marketing in India has a prosperous future.

Literature Review

1.1 History of Rural Marketing

The history of rural marketing has been in itself a very interesting story as well as a topic of debate for many marketeers and authors as the term "rural marketing" suffered, and is perhaps still suffering, a lot to establish its identity and dimensions. The origin of rural marketing can be traced back to 1925 where Egger made the first use of the term "rural marketing" in the context of rural marketing societies in the US (Sarkar et al., 2016). After that, McFall analyzes the information generated from the first census of agricultural distribution in the US. Based on this, he appreciated the benefits of this information for the participants in the domain of "agricultural and rural marketing" in 1930 (Sarkar et al., 2016).

In the case of China, the discipline of rural marketing is said to have started as a separate subject in 1964 in a seminal paper of G. William Skinner, who analyzed rural marketing in China. G. William Skinner wrote about agricultural marketing. Porter (1993) finds the development of rural marketing in Africa around 1960s.

In Bhutan, nothing much is known about rural markets, although approximately 70% population of Bhutan resides in rural areas. The reason for this lack of clarity is that no serious attempt has been made by scholars to write on rural marketing in Bhutan (Sarkar & Pareek, 2013).

As far as the case of India is concerned, India is well known for its popular rural markets called village *haats* or *mandis* since ancient times. Here, people exchanged goods for goods, popularly called as the barter system of trade. This practice is prevalent in some parts of country even today. However, Sarkar et al. (2016) find the first mention of the term "rural marketing" by K. T. Shah in 1947 in the reports of a sub-committee set up in 1937 by the National Planning Committee.

1.2 Defining Rural Marketing

There is little consensus on the definition of rural marketing (Walmsley, 2012). Various authors have defined the term "rural marketing" as per their understanding of the subject. Rao and Tagat (1985) saw rural marketing from the lens of developmental marketing and defined it in the context of developmental marketing (Rao & Tagat, 1985). "Developmental marketing refers to the need for marketeers to generate wealth among rural inhabitants by employing their abilities and entrepreneurial skills in marketing efforts that in turn will enable the villagers to consume more of marketeers' products" (Rao & Tagat, 1985). So in this way the onus of developing the rural markets lies on the marketeers.

Jha (1988) defines "rural marketing" as all the flows from urban to rural areas, from rural to urban areas, and from rural to rural areas. As per this definition, rural marketing may be interpreted as any flow of goods and services that simply has at least one rural player, be it customer or marketeer, on either side. In a similar vein, Vaswani et al. (2005) suggest that the domain of rural marketing should cover all market relationships that are part of growing rural–urban linkages. Sarkar and Pareek (2013) suggest that if anything is produced in rural areas and supplied to urban areas then it should be termed as "agricultural marketing". In this way, the second of Jha's (1988) definition of rural marketing, that it flows from rural to urban areas, doesn't fall under rural marketing; it falls under agricultural marketing. Here is a topic of debate for the authors of marketing as to whether they should consider rural marketing as a synonym to agricultural marketing and vice versa. As a result of this, agricultural marketing and rural marketing were used interchangeably; there was no clear boundary between the two. In India, too, both the terms were used interchangeably until 1980s when a boundary was drawn between the two (Kashyap, 2012). The most surprising fact was that even up to economic liberalization, rural marketing was treated as a step child. It was only after the economic liberalization of the Indian economy in 1991 that the term "rural marketing" got its new identity.

In the Indian context, the definition of rural marketing given by Iyer (2010) is accepted and agreed upon by most of the researchers and authors in the field. Iyer (2010) defines rural marketing as a function that manages all the activities involved in assessing, stimulating and converting the purchasing power of rural consumers into an effective demand for specific products and services and moving these products and services to the people in rural areas to create satisfaction and a better standard of living and thereby achieving organizational goals. A similar definition of rural marketing is given by Walmsley (2012) who studied the touring theatres of rural Scotland. Adapting from Kotler and Armstrong's definition of marketing, Walmsley (2012) proposes that "rural marketing means the determination of specific needs and desires of rural communities and it works in tandem with these communities to deliver their needs effectively and promote their general wellbeing". These two definitions of rural marketing give us some clarity on the subject of rural marketing.

Rural Marketing in India

Rural marketing in India has evolved a lot to its present form. Rural marketing in India has been classified into four Phases (Kashyap, 2012): Phase 1 (before 1960s); Phase 2 (1960–1990); Phase 3 (1990–2000); and Phase 4 (after 2000). In Phase 1, rural marketing was treated as synonymous to agricultural marketing, where selling of rural products in rural and urban areas and agricultural inputs in rural markets was referred to as rural marketing. This was an unorganized market where local business people dominated.

Phase 2 dealt with the demand for agricultural inputs due to green revolution. Here the basic items that were sold in rural markets were agricultural inputs like tractors, pump-sets, fertilizers, etc. Here, too, "agricultural marketing" and rural "marketing" were synonyms to each other.

Phase 3 focused on the marketing of household consumables and durables to the rural markets. It was only after Phase 3 that "rural marketing" was separated from conventional "agricultural marketing". Also, India's industrial sector gained in strength and maturity, signifying the transition of an agricultural society into an industrial one; economic reforms further accelerated the socioeconomic progress, thereby resulting in the growth of rural markets for household consumables and durables (Kashyap, 2012).

Phase 4 (after 2000) has taken the centre stage as companies that were focusing on urban markets earlier have started planning to enter the rural markets. Here the modern marketing practices came into play. It is in this phase that most companies have made their way into rural marketing (Kashyap, 2012). Here, new experiments like Project Shakti, e-choupal, etc., took place in the rural markets of India.

1.3 Studies on Rural Markets of India

Sarwade (1998) makes an analysis of rural markets and consumer behaviour in rural India. The author finds that the Green Revolution has created tremendous opportunities in rural markets as the rural consumers have more purchasing power. The author concludes that factors like price, availability of product and the harvesting prosperity affect the behaviour of rural consumers, and the rural consumers are more price conscious than quality of the product. Singh (2003) studied the environment of rural marketing in India. The author found that the rural marketing in India grew because of growing rural population, growth in rural income, government expenditures on rural development programs and considerable expansion of rural retail networks. However, lack of infrastructure facilities, lack of proper physical communication facilities, illiteracy, transport problems, etc., were some of the factors that made rural marketing difficult. Jain and Hundal (2007) went on to discover the factors influencing the mobile services adoption in rural India. They found the need for consumer education as an integral part of rural marketing strategy. They found that rural consumers wanted to move towards modernity despite having low income and knowledge. Moreover, rural consumers were value driven and wanted to make optimum utilization of their hard-earned money, the study concludes.

Kumar (2009) studied the rural marketing system in India and analyzed how rural consumers were making purchase decisions. The author found that the rural consumers made purchases from unorganized retailers in case of FMCGs, and in case of durables, they purchased it from both unorganized and organized retailers. Unavailability of branded products, unethical and unsocial practices adopted in rural markets, lack of after-sales services were the problems that rural consumers faced. Gaurav et al. (2011) studied the behaviour of rural consumers towards the adoption of rainfall insurance products. The study concludes that difficult products such that rainfall insurance will only be successful in rural areas if awareness for these products, financial literacy, and insurance in this case, is brought among the rural consumers. Falguni et al. (2012) analyzed the behaviour of rural consumers by taking demographic factors as variable. The study focused on rural women as target group of study. The study revealed that consumers in rural India have a mind of their own and do not blindly follow their urban counterparts; cultural and other dimensions do impact their behaviour. Kashyap (2012) underlines the changing scenario of rural markets in India. He says that the rural consumer is becoming more literate, and value driven and the greatest change is taking place amongst the rural youth, who are rapidly getting exposed to urban products and services. The same has been found by Abdin and Kumar (2020). Upadhyaya (2012) says that rural marketing in India actually offers an opportunity for the companies to come out of the current economic crisis.

Maheshwari (2013) in her study of rural marketing strategies relating to durable products in Rajasthan finds the price of the product as the third most important factor impacting the purchase of the product. The company or brand name was the first important factor impacting the purchase of the product. The study concludes that for overall rural development, rural marketing is essential. Mishra (2014) studied the consumer behaviour towards FMCG products in the rural markets of Uttar Pradesh. The study revealed that around 32% of the rural markets can be reached out and a whopping 68% of rural markets remains untapped due to various reasons that range from inaccessibility to lack of awareness. Chiru (2017) studied the rural consumer behaviour in Manipur and found that alternative markets were not available in rural areas; there was mass adulteration in products that was experienced by 80% of the rural consumers, manipulation by the sellers was prevalent and the prices were shooting up.

Rangith (2018) finds poor marketing system, finance problems, poor information access, lack of infrastructure, lack of distribution and lack of communication as the main factors hampering the rural marketing. However, the study sees an opportunity in growing urbanization and growing income levels in the rural areas. Sharma (2019) analyzes rural marketing strategies of FMCGs in Rajasthan. The study shows that the price of a product has a strong bearing on the behaviour of rural consumers, who prefer price over brands. The widely scattered rural markets, poor infrastructure facilities, seasonal and irregular demand, poor literacy and high distribution cost in rural areas were impediments to the rural markets. Desai (2021) found the after-sales service, brand image, electricity consumption, image of the retailer, warranty, product features and product quality as strongly impacting the durable product purchase behaviour of rural consumers. The study listed advertisement, family and friends as most influencing factors for consumer behaviour. In line with the findings of Desai (2021), Kumar and Abdin (2021a) in their study of consumer durable products found that the price of the product, advertisements, word of mouth, the family and friends had an important bearing on the behaviour of rural consumers. The study concluded that the brand name, product attributes, warranty of the product, and the culture and tradition had a very strong impact on the durable product purchase behaviour of rural consumers.

Objectives of the Study

The present chapter is an attempt to give a historical background of rural marketing world over in general and in India in particular. The chapter explores how the concept of rural marketing was developed over the years and what changes are taking place in it with the passage of time. This study has the following research objectives:

1. To explore the historical background of the term “rural marketing”
2. To explore the developments of rural marketing in India
3. To identify the current issues of rural marketing in India
4. To explore the future prospects of rural marketing in India with special reference to durable products

Research Methodology

The research methodology for the study has been designed keeping in the mind the specific nature of the research objectives. The research is based on the case study approach, wherein the authors review various research papers that focus on the development of the term “rural marketing” and give the historical aspects of rural marketing; research articles that define the term "rural marketing". Through this, the authors try to trace the origin of the term "rural marketing" and explore how it evolved world over in general and in India in particular in order to give a historical background of the term "rural marketing" and understand the definition of the term "rural marketing". The authors also highlight the development of rural marketing and various phases of it in the Indian context. In order to shed light on the future scope of rural marketing in India, the authors collect the required data from various prominent secondary sources of data like previous research papers, government reports, business reports, and industry reports. Based on the analysis and interpretation of the data, the chapter analyzes and discusses extensively and draws relevant conclusions.

Analysis of Data and Discussion of Results

4.1 Historical Perspectives on Rural Marketing

The history of rural marketing has been in itself a very interesting story as well as a topic of debate for many marketeers and authors as the term "rural marketing" suffered, and is perhaps still suffering, a lot to establish its identity and dimensions. As we all know, the earlier societies in ancient times were based on barter system of trade, where they exchanged goods for goods. In some parts of the world, village *haats* or *mandis* were prevalent, wherein rural people bought and sold goods and consumables. These village *haats* or *mandis* had a very limited area of operation and dealt with items of daily use. This practice is prevalent in the world even today. India is a good example of that. As far as the term "rural marketing" is concerned, its origin can be traced back to 1925 where Egger made the first use of the term "rural marketing" in the context of rural marketing societies in the US (Sarkar et al., 2016). After that, McFall analyzes the information generated from the first census of agricultural distribution in the US. Based on this, he appreciated the benefits of this information for the participants in the domain of "agricultural and rural marketing" in 1930 (Sarkar et al., 2016).

In the case of China, the discipline of rural marketing is said to have started as a separate subject in 1964 in a seminal paper by G. William Skinner, who analyzed rural marketing in China. G. William Skinner wrote about agricultural marketing. Porter (1993) finds the development of rural marketing in Africa around 1960s. Porter (1993) studied the rural marketing accessibility and reorganization in Western Africa. In Bhutan, nothing much is known about rural markets although approximately 70% population of Bhutan resides in rural areas. The reason for this lack of clarity is that no serious attempt has been made by scholars to write on rural marketing in Bhutan (Sarkar & Pareek, 2013).

As far as the case of India is concerned, India is well known for its popular rural markets called as the village *haats or mandis* since ancient times. Here, people exchanged goods for goods popularly called barter system of trade. This practice is prevalent in some parts of country even today.

However, Sarkar et al. (2016) find the first mention of the term "rural marketing" by K. T. Shah in 1947 in the reports of a sub-committee set up in 1937 by National Planning Committee. Rural marketing in India occupies a special space. India is known for its villages wherein around 70% population resides in rural areas. It is said that true India lives in her villages. India's villages have a very decent system of society as well as of marketing since ancient times. Indian rural markets have become lucrative places because of their immense potential.

So, as far as the historical background of rural marketing is concerned, it can be said that the term "rural marketing" originated around a hundred years ago in the US. Thereafter, it developed in other parts of the world with the passage of time. In different parts of world, it was referred to on different times. But what is most important today is the fact that it has become a centre stage of marketing because of various reasons. We live in an era where modern marketeers are facing a stiff competition. In urban markets, most of the markets have saturated or are near to saturation levels. In this context, rural marketing is proving to be a successful alternative.

4.2 Development of Rural Marketing in India

Rural marketing in India has evolved a lot to its present form. There have been lots of changes with the passage of time in rural marketing of India. Various authors (e.g. Kashyap, 2012; Kumar & Abdin, 2021) broadly see the development of rural marketing in India in four phases as discussed below.

Rural marketing in India is classified into four phases (Kashyap, 2012). The first phase (before 1960s), the second phase between 1960 and 1990, the third phase ranges between 1990 and 2000 and the last phase starts after the year 2000. The first phase is characterized by dominance of local business people in the market which was unorganized in nature. Also, sale of rural products in urban-rural markets and sale of agricultural inputs like tube-wells, pump-sets, etc., in rural markets was known as rural marketing. In short, there was no distinction between agricultural marketing and rural marketing.

Phase 2 saw the demand for agricultural inputs which was the result of green revolution. This was the phase where basic agricultural inputs like fertilizers, pesticides, pump-sets, tractors, etc., were the main products sold in rural markets, and in this phase, too, there was no distinction between rural marketing and agricultural marketing.

With the onset of Phase 3, the marketing of household consumables and durables to the rural markets started in India. An important development of this phase was the separation of "rural marketing" from conventional "agricultural marketing". The strength and maturity was witnessed in the industrial sector of India which signified the transition of Indian agricultural society into an industrial one; the economic reforms stimulated the socioeconomic progress, which accelerated the demand for household consumabland durables in rural markets (Kashyap, 2012). As the rural income was wholly dependent on the agriculture, the performance of agriculture had a direct impact on the income of rural people and the rural economy of India (Abdin & Kumar, 2020a), which in turn had an impact on the spending capacity of rural people that ultimately affected their buying behaviour. After economic liberalization of Indian economy in 1991, the agriculture sector of India didn't perform well for a few years (Abdin & Kumar, 2020a) because of reduced expenditure on rural economy of India by the government.

The fourth phase is said to have taken the centre stage in rural marketing wherein the companies have started to look into the rural markets. One can find application of modern marketing practices in this phase (Kashyap, 2012) wherein new experiments like Project Shakti, e-choupal etc., were done during this phase in the Indian rural markets. It is in this phase that multinationals have entered into the rural marketing in India and rural marketing has become a favourable destination for marketeers world over.

So as far the development of rural marketing in India is concerned, it has seen a sea change over the years. From a small concept of village *haats* or *mandis*, it has evolved itself to the present day of modern marketing.

4.3 Current Issues in Rural Marketing in India

Rural marketing in India has gained importance in the recent past and has become the centre stage of marketing in this cut-throat competitive era. Rural markets of India offer an excellent opportunity to marketeers and they account for half of their incomes for many FMCG businesses. However, there are certain issues that make marketing in rural India extremely difficult. The scattered markets, poor infrastructure, unequal and irregular distribution of income, illiteracy, sale of spurious products, etc., are some of the hurdles that make rural marketing in India extremely difficult (Chiru, 2017; Kashyap, 2012; Mishra, 2014; Rangith, 2018; Singh, 2003; Sharma, 2019). In addition to this, it has been found that rural consumers are very attached to their culture and tradition (Abdin and Kumar, 2020a; Falguni et al., 2012; Kashyap, 2012; Kumar & Abdin, 2021a; Kumar & Bishnoi, 2007); they don't want to let anyone play with their culture and tradition. This attachment of rural consumers makes it extremely difficult for marketeers to sell their goods in rural markets of India as it is near impossible to understand the culture and tradition of rural consumers. Moreover, language and dialects change every 5–10 kilometres in India, which further adds to the difficulty of rural marketing. Also, the level of education is low among rural masses in India (Mander, 2018).

4.4 Future Prospects of Rural Marketing in India

As far as the future prospects of rural marketing in India is concerned, there are many researches and industry reports that indicate towards the prosperous future of rural marketing in India. The World Economic Forum (2019) predicts that the rural per capita consumption will grow to 4.3 times by 2030, compared to 3.5 times in urban India. The report of IBEF (2018) on Indian consumer durables and FMCG industry predicted the rural FMCG market size to reach US$ 220 billion by 2025 from US$ 29.4 billion in 2016. The most favourable prediction is of the Census of India that says that more than 50% of India's population will reside in villages, i.e., rural areas, till the year 2050 (Kumar & Abdin, 2021). This prediction of the Census of India makes marketeers think of the potential of rural marketing in India that lies ahead.

Future Prospects of Rural Marketing in India with Special Reference to Durable Products

The size of the durable goods market in rural India is more than half of the total durable goods market in India. It accounts for 59% of the market share. The consumer durables industry has been divided in two parts: consumer electronics (brown goods) and consumer appliances (white goods). The two in India are predicted to grow at CAGR of 9% over the years 2017–2022 (IBEF, 2020). This CAGR of Indian appliance and consumer electronics industry in India will be over 11% and will grow at CAGR of 11.7% during the period 2019–2025 (IBEF, 2020).

In the light of above prediction, it can be said that the durable products industry in India will be having better future prospects. In rural markets of India, too, this prospect is reflected as the size of the durable goods market in rural India is more than half of the total durable goods market in India. It accounts for 59% of the market share. Previous studies (e.g. Kumar & Abdin, 2021b; Maheshwari, 2013) also support this result.

5 Conclusion

The aim of this chapter was to give a historical background of rural marketing and explore how the term "rural marketing" originated world over as well as how this term was first mentioned in India. In addition to this, the chapter explored how the development of rural marketing in India occurred over different phases of time. Last but not the least, this chapter also explored the current issues of rural marketing in India and also the future prospects of rural marketing in India with special reference to durable products. We here conclude that the term "rural marketing" traces its origin to about a hundred years ago in the US and then it developed world over. As far the as the case of India is concerned, the first mention of the term "rural marketing" was made in 1947. There is little consensus on the definition of rural marketing, but various authors have tried to establish the definition of rural marketing as per their understanding of the subject of rural marketing.

As far as rural marketing in India is concerned, it has a very prosperous future. The rural marketing in India evolved through four phases and it has become a favourable destination for every marketer. The different phases of rural marketing in India had different implications accordingly, different goods and services were bought and sold in it. There are some hurdles in rural marketing in India like poor infrastructure, lack of communication facilities, scattered markets of rural India, illiteracy, irregular income etc. that make rural marketing in India extremely difficult. The government and private players need to invest in the further development of the rural marketing in India.

Many studies and industry reports have favourable indications for the prospects of rural marketing in India. The World Economic Forum (2019) finds 4.3 times growth in rural per capita income as compared to 3.5 times in urban per capita income by 2030. IBEF (2018) predicts the rural FMCG market to be to the tune of US$220 billion by 2025, which was to the tune of US$ 29.4 billion in 2016. The durables market size in rural India is 59% of total durables market of India. Most importantly, more than half of the Indian population will be living in rural areas of India even in the year 2050. All these factors make the rural marketing in India a favourable destination for marketers. To grasp these opportunities of the rural markets of India, understanding rural marketing and subsequently the behaviour of rural consumers is imperative.

References

Abdin, M.S., & Kumar, R. (2020a). Marketing Across Cultures: A Study on Rural Consumer Behaviour in India. Accessed from https://www.researchgate.net/publication/343193358 on 20th October, 2020.

Abdin, M.S., & Kumar, R. (2020b). Rural Economy of India Helping India Become a 5 Trillion Dollar Economy: Contribution, Opportunities and Challenges. *Journal of Interdisciplinary Cycle Research, Volume XII, No. V*, 1006–1024.

Ali, M.A., Thumiki, V.R., & Khan, N. (2012). Factors Influencing Purchase of FMCG by Rural Consumers in South India: An Empirical Study. *International Journal of Business Research and Development, Volume 1, No. 1*, 48–57.

Census of India, 2011. www.censusindia.gov.in

Chiru, P.R. (2017). Consumer Behaviour in Rural Market: A Study on Buying Behaviour of Rural Consumers in Manipur. *International Journal of Contemporary Research and Review, Volume 8, No. 7*, SC20206-20254.

Desai, Y.B. (2021). Consumer Buying Behaviour Towards Consumer Durables – A comparative study of Urban and Rural areas of Surat District. Accessed from http://hdl.handle.net/10603/320298 on 28th November, 2021.

Falguni, V.O., Nagraj, A., & Krishna, Y. (2012). Marketing to Rural Women: How Various Leading Brands Are Doing It? *The IUP Journal of Brand Management, Volume IX, No. 2*, 7–17.

Gaurav, S., Cole, S., & Tobacman, J. (2011). Marketing Complex Financial Products in Emerging Markets: Evidence from Rainfall Insurance in India. *Journal of Marketing Research*, Accessed from https://www.jstor.org/stable/23033473?seq=1 on 17th October, 2020.

IBEF (2018). Indian Consumer Durables and FMCG Industry Analysis. Accessed from https://www.ibef.org/pages/37298 on 04th December, 2021.

IBEF (2020). Consumer Durables September, 2020. Accessed from https://www.ibef.org/industry/indian-consumer-market.aspx on 30th October, 2020.

Iyer, V. (2010). Rural Marketing. *SIES Journal of Management, Volume 6, No. 2*, 104–111.

Jain, A., & Hundal, B.S. (2007). Factors Influencing Mobile Services Adoption in Rural India. *Asia-Pacific Journal of Rural Development, Volume XVII, No. 1*, 17–28.

Jha, M. (1988). Rural Marketing : Some Conceptual Issues. *Economic and Political Weekly, 23(9)*, M9–M16.

Kashyap, P. (2012). *Rural Marketing*. 2nd Edition. Dorling Kindersley (India) Pvt. Ltd. Pearson.

Kotler, P., & Armstrong, G. (2011). *Principles of Marketing*. New Delhi: Pearson Prentice Hall.

Kumar, A. (2009). An Evaluation of Rural Marketing System in India. Accessed from *Shodhganga* http://hdl.handle.net/10603/244575 on 18th October, 2020.

Kumar, R., & Abdin, M.S. (2021a). "Rural Marketing in India: Impediments, Issues and Prospects for Consumer Durable Products", in Sunayana and Saif Siddiqui, eds, *Management Functions in COVID-19 Era*, New Delhi: Bloomsbury India.

Kumar, R., & Abdin, M.S. (2021b). Durable Product Purchase Behaviour in India: A Study of Rural Consumers of Western Uttar Pradesh. *PIMT Journal of Research, Volume 13, No. 4(A)*, 83–87.

Kumar, S., & Bishnoi, V.K. (2007). Influence of Marketeers' Efforts on Rural Consumers and Their Mindset: A Case Study of Haryana. *The ICFAI Journal of Brand Management, Volume IV, No. 4*, 28–50.

Maheshwari, M. (2013). Rural Marketing Strategies Relating To Consumer Durables (A Case Study Of Rajasthan). Accessed from *Shodhganga* http://hdl.handle.net/10603/102713 on 10th October, 2020.

Mander, H. (2018). 25 Years of Economic Reforms : A Blotted Balance Sheet. *VIKALPA: The Journal for Decision Makers*, *43*(1), 1–23.

Mishra, N.K. (2014). A Study of Consumer Buying Behaviour in Rural Markets of Fast Moving Consumer Goods (FMCG). Accessed from *Shodhganga* http://hdl.handle.net/10603/248737 on 18th October, 2020.

Porter, G. (1993). Changing Accessibility and the Reorganization of Rural Marketing in Nigeria. *Journal of Macromarketing*, 54–63.

Rangith, M. Josephin (2018). Problems and Prospects of Rural Marketing – A Study with Reference to Southern Districts of Tamilnadu. Accessed from *Shodhganga* http://hdle.handle.net/10603/237500 on 10th October, 2020.

Rao, K.L.K., & Tagat, Ramesh G. (1985). Rural Marketing: A Developmental Approach. *Vikalpa, Volume 10, No.* 3, 315–324.

Sarkar, D.N., Kundu, K., & Chaudhari, H. R. (2016). Conceptual Expansion of the Discipline of Rural Marketing: An Objective Analysis. *Vision*, *20*, *No.* 3, 1–14.

Sarkar, D.N., & Pareek, G. (2013). Rural Marketing Mix in Bhutan: An FMCG Perspective. *IUP Journal of Management Research, Vol. XII, No.* 3, 7–28.

Sarwade, W.K. (1998). A Study of Rural Marketing with Special Reference to Marathwada Region in Maharashtra. Accessed from *Shodhganga* http://hdl.handle.net/10603/147013 on 10th October, 2020.

Sharma, V. (2019). Rural Marketing Strategies of Fast Moving Consumer Goods in Rajasthan. Accessed from *Shodhganga* http://hdl.handle.net/10603/298700 on 18th October, 2020.

Singh, S.B. (2003). Rural Marketing Environment, Problems and Strategies. Accessed from *Shodhganga* http://hdl.handle.net/10603/167792 on 10th October, 2020.

Tyagi, V. (2017). Analysis of Marketing Mix Strategies of FMCG Products in Rural Markets with Special Reference to Rajasthan. Accessed from *Shodhganga* http://hdl.handle.net/10603/222000 on 10th October, 2020.

Upadhyaya, M. (2012). Marketing in Rural India: The Innovative Selling Mantra. *Abhinav: Journal of Research in Commerce and Management, Volume 1, No.* 10, 2012.

Vaswani, L.K., Aithal, R., Pradhan, D., & Sridhar, G. (2005). Rural Marketing in the Development Paradigm. *International Journal of Rural Management, Volume 1, No.* 2), 246–262.

Walmsley, B.A. (2012). Re-defining Rural Marketing: Insights from Touring Theatre. *International Journal of Rural Management, Volume 8, No.* 1–2, 49–62.

World Economic Forum (2019). Report on Future of Consumption in Fast-Growth Consumer Markets: INDIA. Accessed from https://www.weforum.org/reports/future-of-consumption-in-fast-growth-consumer-markets-india on 21st October, 2020.

12 Consumer Perception and Purchase Intention for Green Consumer Durable Products

An Analytical Study

Shweta and Md. Shahnawaz Abdin

Introduction

As far as environmental concern matters, so many changes occurred in the consumer market due to the same. In the starting of the 21st century, the social and environmental consequences of the unquestioning effect of economic growth have become so clear and green marketing field originated as the savior of the environmental balance. Green marketing has emerged as a new phenomenon in the marketing discipline and has become one of the promotional strategies to increase consumers' awareness and concern towards the environment that in what way consumers may try to show their interest to buy and consume green products.(Peattie & Charter, 2003) This change has brought the pattern of green consumerism among consumer sphere.(Moisander, 2007) Although consumers are slowly influenced and motivated to buy and consume green products, many reasons restrict consumers from doing it.(Prothero, 1990) Generally, consumers are environmentally conscious but due to their protecting or maintaining their sense of self and consumer attachment to the brand and some other attributes, they are showing non-green purchase behavior.(Johnstone & Tan, 2015) That creates a gap between consumers' perception and their intention to buy and consume green products. But these terms are used interchangeably. Consumers intend to buy the green products but vagueness in terms of quality, features, attributes and price makes them reluctant to buy the green products and because of these reasons they go to the conventional products that are harmful to the ecological sphere. Here one thing has been acknowledged that the consumer perception and intention are different values in understanding consumers' behavior.(Hussain et al., 2011) It is also noticed that India is the largest consumer durable product market in the world that got fourth rank worldwide. So, to understand the consumer perception and their intention towards green products, the consumer durable product market could be analyze for the current research because of India's rapidly changing economic environment with division of rural and urban segments and diversified population.(Ghose & Chandra, 2018) Because of this, the study about consumer's perception and their intention for buying green durable products is taken as a serious matter for investigation. This chapter

DOI: 10.4324/9781003354703-15

tries to seek the changing behavior of consumers towards green consumer durable products and understand how their perception and intention may differ at once. This chapter also discusses the factors that may change consumer perception and intention towards green consumer durable products.

Literature Review

Green marketing has become a boom for the new century because of its promotion of ideas of protecting the environment and producing eco-friendly products. According to Polonsky, this marketing field is not achieving its potential to improve the quality of life of the consumers; rather, it is improving the natural ecosystem.(Polonsky, 2011) Therefore, scholars are seeking relationships between environmental concerns and consumer choice behavior in purchasing green products. (Biswas & Roy, 2015)

With this pattern, lots of studies are being conducted to prove that consumer intention is improving to buy green products.(Codini et al., 2018) And some scholars are checking the consumer perception towards the green products or their choice-making behavior.(Boztepe, 2012) But it is also acknowledged that consumers' intentions have been taken as on priority instead of their perception. Rather, these terms were used interchangeably. (Ariffin et al., 2016; Wu & Chen, 2014; Zhu, 2012) Since the last decade, consumer perception is getting importance in the field of green marketing and it is drawing a line between consumers' perception and their intention to buy green products.(Kong et al., 2014a) It is considered that consumers' perception and feelings influence their purchase intention and behavior towards green products. (Ghose & Chandra, 2020)

Here there are several studies have discussed changing perception and the intention of consumers for green products.

S. No.	*Author name and year*	*Objectives*	*Findings*
1	Kumar et al. (2012) (Kumar et al., 2012)	Authors investigated in their study consumer perception and purchase intention towards green products among youngsters in India.	The findings of the study revealed that consumers perceived green products as environment-friendly products and male respondents are more aware about green products than female consumers. Study also focused that consumers have intention to buy green products, but due to high prices they are reluctant to buy them and in that case their perception might be different from their intention.

(*Continued*)

(Continued)

S. No.	*Author name and year*	*Objectives*	*Findings*
2	Sachdev and Mahana (2013) (Sachdev & Mahana, 2013)	Study emphasized that there was difference between consumer intention of green products and actual purchase behavior to buy green products.	Authors found that consumers were reluctant to buy green products due to lack of information, benefits, authenticity, and high price of the green products. Consumers' confusion would remain the same for ethical issues, fair trade, and organic as compared with other products. In that case, consumers could not make their intention to buy green products and their perception would remain the same for green products.
3	Tseng and Hung (2013) (Tseng & Hung, 2013)	Paper measures the gap between consumers' expectations and their perception for green products.	As per the author, a larger gap exists between consumers' expectation and their perception related to green product information and the attributes of the green products.
4	Kong et al. (2014) (Kong et al., 2014b)	Study aimed to examine the influence of consumer perception of green products on green purchase intention.	Consumer perception towards green products might be influenced by various variables like eco-label, green advertising, green packaging and green values of the products. All these variables could make consumer perception towards green products, and on the other hand, consumer purchase intention is mainly influenced by eco-label, green product values and green advertising. Green packaging did not significantly influence consumer purchase intention towards green products. Hence, there was difference seen in the factors influencing consumer perception and their purchase intention towards green products.

(*Continued*)

(Continued)

S. No.	*Author name and year*	*Objectives*	*Findings*
5	Yusuf and Fatima (2015) (Yusuf & Fatima, 2015)	The study explores the consumer attitude and perception towards green products.	The authors stated that consumer perception about environmental concerns influence positively consumer intention to buy green products. In this study, it is discussed that many people believed eco-friendly products are good for environment and have benefits for health. Green products are good in quality and performance as compared to conventional products. Authors also highlighted that highest brand memory, brand recall, pricing, promotion of green products are the major elements that influence the consumer perception.
6	Maichum et al. (2016) (Maichum et al., 2016)	This study aim to investigate consumer purchase intention for green products by using a Theory of Planned Behavior (TPB).	The authors indicated in their study that consumers' intention for green products might be formed by various factors like perceived behavior control, environmental concerns, environmental knowledge and consumer attitude towards green products. These factors altogether significantly influence consumer intention to buy green products, although environmental knowledge had no significant influence on the purchase intention for green products. The authors discussed the theory of planned behavior (TPB) that determined consumer purchase perception and intention to prefer green products.

(*Continued*)

(Continued)

S. No.	*Author name and year*	*Objectives*	*Findings*
7	Ariffin et al. (2016) (Ariffin et al., 2016)	The purpose of this study is to investigate the relationship between green value, emotional value, environmental conscious, consumers' perceived quality and repurchase intention towards green products.	Authors invested in their study that green value has a significant relationship with both perceived quality and repurchase intention. The perceived quality of the green products has a significant relationship with the emotional value of the consumers. It is also observed in this paper that however aware and concerned people are for the environmental issues, they are not in the habit of using green products. Many factors are involved in the changing consumers' intention, including personal experience, price of the product, services quality, green values, emotional values, environmental values, etc.
8	Maichum et al. (2017) (Maichum et al., 2017)	The study aims to investigate the factors that influence consumer purchase intention towards green products among young consumers.	The authors indicated that environmental consciousness, environmental knowledge and environmental attitude have a significant influence on consumer purchase intention for green products. The study revealed environmental attitude as one of the important determinants to form consumer purchase intention for green products and it conciliates the relationship between environmental consciousness, environmental knowledge and consumer purchase intention towards green products.

(Continued)

(Continued)

S. No.	*Author name and year*	*Objectives*	*Findings*
9	Choshaly (2017) (Choshaly, 2017)	The study examined the consumer's perception towards green products and also discussed the factors influencing consumers' intention to buy green products. The factors are social factors, concern for self-image, social influence and perceived environmental responsibilities.	The study result found that there was positive impact of social influence, environmental concern and concern for self-image on purchase intention of consumers for green products. Perceived environmental responsibility and affective commitment also have a positive impact on consumer purchase intention for green products and all these factors also played a role in forming consumer perception towards green products.
10	Lavanya and Kumar (2019) (Lavanya & Madhan, 2019)	The author analyzed the theory of reasoned action to understand the consumer perception regarding green products.	Environment-friendly products were found to be more effective to form consumer perception with regard to green products and the price, availability, quality and consumers green values were also considered as important factors to change consumer perception for green products.
11	Liau et al. (2020)(Liau et al., 2020)	The study examined the effect of green customer values and attitude towards green products on green purchase intention.	The result revealed that both green customer values and attitudes have significant influence on customer purchase intention.

Objectives of the Study

1 To study the consumer perception and purchase intention for green consumer durable products in Delhi.
2 To identify the difference between consumer perception and purchase intention for green consumer durable products.
3 To identify the factors that differentiate between consumer perception and purchase intention for green consumer durable products.

Research Methodology of the Study

The present study is descriptive cum exploratory in nature and is based on both primary and secondary data. For this study, non-probability random sampling was employed to select Delhi-based respondents. The data has been collected from 126 respondents with the help of a well-structure questionnaire (see Table 12.1 for demographics).

Table 12.1 shows the demographic profile of the respondents, including gender, age, educational qualification, occupation and monthly income. The total number of respondents is 126, in which 64 (50.8%) are male respondents and 61 (48.4%) are female respondents. The study depicts that male are more inclined towards green products purchasing.

Table 12.1 Demographic Profile of the Respondents

Variable			*Frequency*	*Percentage %*
Gender	Valid	Male	64	50.8
		Female	61	48.4
		Total	125	99.2
	Missing	System	1	0.8
	Total		126	100.0
Age	Valid	18–24	70	55.6
		25–30	28	22.2
		31–45	26	20.6
		46 and above	1	0.8
		Total	125	99.2
	Missing	System	1	0.8
	Total		126	100.0
Educational Qualification	Valid	Undergraduate	66	52.4
		Graduate	19	15.1
		Post-graduate	37	29.4
		M-Phil	1	0.8
		Ph.D.	2	1.6
		Total	125	99.2
	Missing	System	1	0.8
	Total		126	100.0
Occupation	Valid	Student	67	53.2
		Government employed	22	17.5
		Self-employed	32	25.4
		Unemployed	4	3.2
		Total	125	99.2
	Missing	System	1	0.8
	Total		126	100.0
Monthly Income	Valid	Less than 10,000	55	43.7
		11,000–30,000	22	17.5
		31,000–50,000	40	31.7
		More than 50,000	8	6.3
		Total	125	99.2
	Missing	System	1	0.8
	Total		126	100.0

Source: Created by Author.

As far as the age of the respondents is concerned, from the given table it is clear that out of 126 respondents, 70 (55.6%) respondents are in the age group of 18–25 years, 28 (22.2%) respondents are 25–30 years, 26 (20.6%) respondents are 31–45 years and only 1 (0.79%) respondent is above 45 years of age.

As per the survey, it is clear that under-graduate respondents are more in number, 66 (52.4%) out of 126; the rest of the respondents are from graduate (19, 15.1%), post-graduate (37, 29.4%), M-Phil (1) and Ph.D. (2).

As far as the occupation and income are concerned, out of 126, students = 67 (53.2%), govt. employed = 22 (17.5%), self-employed = 32 (25.4%) and unemployed = 4 (3.2%). The monthly income groups of the respondents are as follows: less than 10,000 = 55 (43.7%), 11,000–30,000 = 22 (17.5%), 31000–50,000=40 (31.7%) and more than 50,000 = 8 (6.3%), respectively.

Measures

The online questionnaire contained two sections: the demographic aspects and questions related to variables which were included in this study. In the first part, the demographic profile of the respondents, including age, gender, educational qualification, occupation and monthly income (see Table 12.1), was collected. The second section consisted of questions related to the perception of consumers (calculated by SPSS) with an internal reliability of Cronbach's Alpha ($\alpha = .789$). This section consisted of five items (quality, environmental protection responsibility, future concern for climate change, potential increase of product quality and satisfaction) on a 5-point Likert scale (Strongly agree = 1, Agree = 2, Neither agree nor disagree = 3, Disagree = 4, Strongly disagree = 5).

Statistical Analysis/Procedure

Keeping in mind the physical constraints of this pandemic period, the primary data was collected by the respondents through an online survey. The survey was designed and carried out with Google Forms. The descriptive statistics was used to analyze the data to test the hypothesis with the help of Statistical Package for Social Sciences (SPSS) version 26.0. Chi-square test was used to test the demographic profile of the respondents with the purchase intention. With the help of flow chart diagram, different factors that influence the consumer perception and intention for green consumer durable products has been discussed.

The secondary data has been studied to review the previous work such as research articles, books and reports to discuss the consumers' intention and perception for green consumer durable products.

Hypotheses of the Study

The main objectives of the research is to study the consumer perception and purchase intention, to identify the difference between the two and to identify the factors that create a difference between them for green consumer durable products. The following hypotheses are framed to attain the objectives of the study:

H01: Demographic factors cannot change the consumer intention to buy green consumer durable products.
H02: There is no relationship between consumer perception and purchase intention to buy green consumer durable products.

Result and Discussions

In the study, the descriptive statistics is used to explain the main features of the collected data in quantitative terms. Statistical analyzing method such as frequency distribution is used to measure the data. We found Cronbach's alpha between 7 and 8, which shows that our data is reliable. Chi-square test was employed to explore the relationship between the demographic variables (see Table 12.2) and factors influencing consumer perception and intention that is shown in percentage with the help of pie-diagram (see Figure 12.1).

Descriptive Statistics

H01: Demographic Factors Cannot Change the Consumer Intention to Buy Green Products

Table 12.2 shows the comparison between purchase intention and the demographic profile of the respondents. The chi-square table shows the comparison between gender, age, educational qualifications, occupation and monthly income with the consumer purchase intention of green products. In the matter of gender and purchase intention for green products, Table 12.2 shows that the significance of chi-square is 0.107, which is greater than 0.05 (5%), So null hypothesis cannot be rejected at 5%

Table 12.2 Result of Chi-square

	Pearson chi-square value	*Degree of freedom*	*Asymptotic significance (2-sided)*
Gender X purchase intention	2.605[a]	1	0.107
Age X purchase intention	2.355[a]	3	0.502
Educational Qualifications X purchase intention	12.929[a]	4	0.012
Occupation X purchase intention	2.858[a]	3	0.414
Monthly Income X purchase intention	6.380[a]	3	0.095

Source: Created by Author.

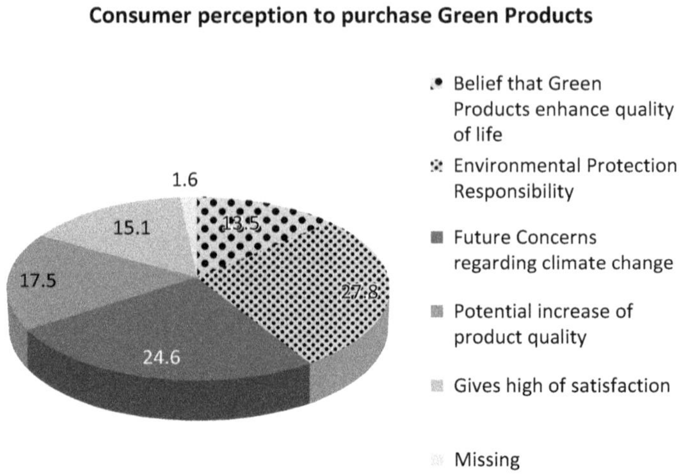

Figure 12.1 Consumer perception to purchase green products.

Source: Created by Author.

significance level, concluding that there is no significant relationship between the consumers' intention to buy green products and the gender of the consumers. The consumers intend to buy green products irrespective of their gender.

In case of the age of the respondents and purchase intention for green products, Table 12.2 shows that significance of chi-square is 0.502, which is greater than 0.05 (5%), So null hypothesis cannot be rejected at 5% significance level, concluding that there is no significant relationship between the consumer intention to buy green products and the age of consumers. As far as the occupation of the respondents is concerned the null hypothesis cannot be rejected because significance value of chi-square is 0.414, which is greater than 0.05 (5%), So null hypothesis cannot be rejected at 5% significance level, concluding that there is no significant relationship between the consumers' intention to buy green products and the occupation of the consumers.

In case of educational qualification and monthly income of the respondents, Table 12.2 shows that in educational qualification, the significance of chi-square is 0.012, which is less than 0.05 (5%). So the null hypothesis can be rejected at 5% significance level, concluding that there is a significant relationship between the intention to buy green products and the educational qualification of consumers. Significance of chi-square is 0.095 in case of monthly income of respondents, which is greater than 0.05 (5%), so null hypothesis cannot be rejected at 5% significance level, concluding that there is no significant relationship between the consumers' intention to buy green products and the monthly income of respondents.

H02: There Is No Relationship between Consumer Perception and Purchase Intention to Buy Green Consumer Durable Products

Consumer perception is mainly considered as customers' awareness, perceived experience, opinion about the product and brand, quality, education and other motivating factors. (Bilgihan et al., 2016) Perception, on the other hand, can be considered as the psychological process and it takes a long time for consumers to make up their minds to buy particular goods and services. Sometimes it is very tedious and challenging for the companies to change the perception of consumers. It is very difficult to make the consumer aware of the green consumer durable products so that they can have a clear perception of these products. Academic data reveals that a lack was found in this way due to non-campaigning efforts for making consumers' perception regarding the same.

Consumer intention refers to consumer's willingness to buy particular goods and services. As per the study, the perception and intention may be affected by factors like environmental knowledge, environmental concerns, perceived knowledge, organizational green image, social influence, price, and instant opportunities.

Here the discussion shows that consumers' perception and their intention are partially unrelated with each other because some of the factors are used interchangeably in both, e.g. perceived experience and knowledge, price, quality, brand image, etc., of the products create an ambiguity in the conceptual framework.

Conclusion

This study indicated that consumer intention and perception are used interchangeably in many of the previous studies, but in this study, it is clearly stated that these two terms are not interchangeable. The consumer perception and intention are different from each other or partially related with each other. This study also reveals that perceived quality of green consumer durable products had a positive influence on consumers' purchase intention, which can change the consumers' perception for green consumer durable products at the demographic level. Only educational qualification showed a significant relationship with the purchase intention of the consumers and the rest of the factors, like age, income and occupation, did not show a positive relationship with the purchase intention of the consumers. This means that educated consumers are already aware about the environmental concerns; therefore, their planned behavior makes their perception strong. Therefore, the study reveals that planned behavior and ultimate intention have some differences.

Although this study has provided new insights into green products marketing, in terms of consumer perception and purchase intention, it still has some limitations; for instance, the findings can be applied only to green consumer durable products markets and the residents of Delhi.

References

Ariffin, S., Yusof, J. M., Putit, L., & Shah, M. I. A. (2016). Factors influencing perceived quality and repurchase intention towards green products. *Procedia Economics and Finance*, *37*(16), 391–396.

Bilgihan, A., Barreda, A., Okumus, F., & Nusair, K. (2016).Consumer perception of knowledge-sharing in travel-related online social networks. *Tourism Management*, *52*, 287–296.

Biswas, A., & Roy, M. (2015). Green products: An exploratory study on the consumer behaviour in emerging economies of the East. *Journal of Cleaner Production*, *87*, 463–468.

Boztepe, A. (2012). Green marketing and its impact on consumer buying behavior. *European Journal of Economic & Political Studies*, *5*(1), 5–21.

Choshaly, S. H. (2017). Consumer perception of green issues and intention to purchase green products. *International Journal of Management, Accounting and Economics*, *4*(1), 66–79.

Codini, A. P., Miniero, G., & Bonera, M. (2018). Why not promote promotion for green consumption? *European Business Review*, 30(5), 554–570.

Ghose, A., & Chandra, B. (2018). Consumption behaviour towards green durable products: The moderating role of demographics. *Indian Journal of Marketing*, *48*(6), 22–41.

Ghose, A., & Chandra, B. (2020). Models for predicting sustainable durable products consumption behaviour: A review article. *Vision*, *24*(1), 81–89.

Hussain, S., Ali, S., Ibrahim, M., Noreen, A., & Ahmad, S. F. (2011). Impact of product packaging on consumer perception and purchase intention. *Journal of Marketing and Consumer Research*, *10*, 1–10.

Johnstone, M. L., & Tan, L. P. (2015). An exploration of environmentally-conscious consumers and the reasons why they do not buy green products. *Marketing Intelligence & Planning*. Vol. 33 No. 5, pp. 804–825.

Kong, W., Harun, A., Sulong, R. S., & Lily, J. (2014a).The influence of consumers' perception of green products on green purchase intention. *International Journal of Asian Social Science*, *4*(8), 924–939.

Kong, W., Harun, A., Sulong, R. S., & Lily, J. (2014b). The influence of consumers' perception of green products on green purchase intention. *International Journal of Asian Social Science*, *4*(8), 924–939.

Kumar, S., Garg, R., & Makkar, A. (2012). Consumer awareness and perception towards green products: A study of youngsters in India. *International Journal of Marketing & Business Communication*, *1*(4), 35.

Lavanya, K. & Madhan, K (2019). Consumer perception towards green products and strategies that impact the consumers perception. *International Journal of Scientific & Technology Research*, *8*(11), 3543–3548.

Liau, Y. K., Wu, W. Y., & Pham, T. T. (2020). Examining the moderating effects of green marketing and green psychological benefits on customers' green attitude, value and purchase intention. *Sustainability*, *12*(18), 7461.

Maichum, K., Parichatnon, S., & Peng, K. C. (2016). Application of the extended theory of planned behavior model to investigate purchase intention of green products among Thai consumers. *Sustainability*, *8*(10), 1077.

Maichum, K., Parichatnon, S., & Peng, K. C. (2017). Factors affecting on purchase intention towards green products: A case study of young consumers in Thailand. *Young*, *16*, 17.

Moisander, J. (2007). Motivational complexity of green consumerism. *International Journal of Consumer Studies*, *31*(4), 404–409.
Peattie, K., & Charter, M. (2003). Green marketing. *The Marketing Book*, *5*, 726–755.
Polonsky, M. J. (2011). Transformative green marketing: Impediments and opportunities. *Journal of Business Research*, *64*(12), 1311–1319.
Prothero, A. (1990). Green consumerism and the societal marketing concept: Marketing strategies for the 1990's. *Journal of Marketing Management*, *6*(2), 87–103.
Sachdev, S., & Mahana, Vinod. (2013). Green purchase behavior: An Indian perception. *Indian Journal of Commerce & Management Studies*, 2(1), 85–90.
Tseng, S. C., & Hung, S. W. (2013). A framework identifying the gaps between customers' expectations and their perceptions in green products. *Journal of Cleaner Production*, *59*, 174–184.
Wu, S. I., & Chen, Y. J. (2014).The impact of green marketing and perceived innovation on purchase intention for green products. *International Journal of Marketing Studies*, *6*(5), 81.
Yusuf, S., & Fatima, Z. (2015).Consumer attitude and perception towards green products. *The International Journal of Indian Psychology*, 2(3), 140–146.
Zhu, B. (2012, October). The impact of green advertising on consumer purchase intention of green products. In *Proceedings of World Business and Economics Research Conference.*

13 Determinants of Quality Perception of Students in Online Learning in Higher Education

Hediye Gamze Türkmen

Introduction

Covid-19-related life conditions have had a solemn impact on all educational institutions in the world (Mailizar et al., 2020). Due to the Covid-19 outbreak, online learning has become a crucial field for educators to continue instruction and training. Every level of teaching has distinctive challenges due to various readiness levels and ways of learning in different age groups. Since the student awareness and perception of quality are more developed in higher education, educators and education training leaders and managers are required to focus on specific issues to achieve the best results both in terms of education outcome and education quality. Most research focuses on the determinants of effectiveness and categorizes the effectiveness of online learning into three groups: (a) students' outcomes as a result of test scores and grades; (b) student attitudes about learning; and (c) overall student satisfaction with online learning (Robinson and Hullinger, 2008).

Nardali and Tanyeri (2011) analyze the way private higher education institutions act as service enterprises and tend to interact with their students as customers in fortifying their corporate reputation and branding. The key aim is to provide a competitive advantage. Whereas private universities aim to gain an advantage over competitors to attract students as customers based on divergent criteria such as student amount, qualified human capital or quality, quality perception, among other factors, has become an important aspect in determining generally intended outcomes in terms of customer satisfaction (Mang'unyi and Govender, 2014). Regarding the fact that private universities as private enterprises have a market to provide for, how well they can adapt themselves to emerging conditions is a value to their future entity and achievement (Abouchedid and Nasser, 2002). Every service organization, including private universities, is under vast pressure to provide a higher level of service quality and ensure that it is well perceived by its stakeholders (Shekarchizadeh et al., 2011). Higher education institutions must ensure a standard quality of service to sustain in the market they function in since they operate as service firms that can segment and target markets depending on the dimensions of higher education quality (Akareem and Hossain, 2016). Since the sudden Covid-19 outbreak forced education

DOI: 10.4324/9781003354703-16

institutions to utilize the means of online learning worldwide, private universities have been inclined to reassess quality perception as one of the significant elements to evaluate customer service quality.

Students' quality perception regarding online learning has been analyzed based on various factors such as technical specifications, instructor quality, and learning environment. Therefore, students' satisfaction is frequently analyzed based on the quality of education that they obtain from an educational institution. Perceived quality is the primary criteria that increases satisfaction and leads students to determine a higher education institution of their choice (Naidu and Derani, 2016).

However, it should be noted that quality is cognitive judgment (Oliver, 1993) whereas quality perception is what is generated within the perspective of the customer (Morgan, 1985). The studies on the "perceived quality" approach emphasize the term "perceived quality" instead of "quality" to highlight that quality judgments depend on the perceptions, needs, and goals of the consumer (Steenkamp, 1990). "Perceived quality" does not mean that the service or product is perfect or of the highest quality (Garvin, 1984). Thus, the determinants of quality perception are not always equal with the determinants of customer satisfaction and could be varied according to service categories. This fact underlines the significance of a delicate analysis of the determinants of quality perception of students in online learning.

While evaluating quality and quality perception, it is a seminal approach to observe emerging cases from various fields such as education. As it is widely accepted in contemporary marketing that successful results are achieved through a customer-based approach (Shepherd, 2005), it has become an underlying process to analyze the determinants of quality perception from the student perspective.

Research Objectives and Research Questions

Based on the issues resulting in customer satisfaction, the main objective of this study is to reveal and analyze students' quality of perception on online learning in private higher education institutions.
There are three research hypotheses:

H1: Service satisfaction regarding online learning has a significant effect on the quality perception of the students who are enrolled in online higher education classes.

H2: Corporate reputation of the higher education institution has a significant effect on the quality perception of the students who are enrolled in online higher education classes.

H3: Service satisfaction regarding online learning has a significant effect on the overall customer satisfaction of the students who are enrolled in online higher education classes.

Literature Review

Students' quality perception in online learning has been a widely discussed subject in recent years. Most of the literature was led by the studies in the field of education due to the fact that it is a requirement for the field of education to determine the predictors and rationales of the construct to achieve ultimate efficiency in online learning. For education leaders, putting forward perception of quality in a central position in education as a means of stakeholder satisfaction enhances the motives that lead to development and innovation and educational institutions are required to focus on the perspective of its stakeholders (Abidin, 2015). Nonetheless, as a narrowed and specified issue, students' role as customers in private education institutions has not been overpassed by marketing literature and has been studied in the scope of service quality and quality perception.

In education literature, student satisfaction in online learning has been generally associated with parties and facilities which are actively involved in the education activity. Akareem and Hossain (2016) analyzed the determinants of education quality in general and revealed how quality perception of students was differentiated and stated that the commercialization of education became more apparent and requirement to utilize marketing tools is more important than ever. According to a study conducted in university-level online learning, it was reported that the e-learners were satisfied with the knowledge level of the instructors and course materials, which in total led to a general satisfaction with the process (Elango et al., 2008). Rockwell, Schauer, Fritz, and Marx (1999) pointed out the important role of qualified human resources, mainly faculty as the key element of efficiency in online learning environment. Nevertheless, more recent studies indicate that integrated marketing communications dimensions defined in the marketing communications mix – advertising, online marketing, promotions, personal selling, and public relations, all of which build a strong corporate reputation – play a significant role on customer satisfaction in higher education institutions (Abimbola et al., 2020).

Student perceptions of quality and satisfaction in regionally accredited online courses were the focus of a depth analysis where the current literature was reviewed to determine which factors were significant in regard to student-perceived quality and satisfaction in online learning (Simpson, 2012). The study indicated that there was not a significant relationship between four demographic variables (age, gender, comfort with distance learning, and the number of previous online courses taken) and overall student satisfaction in online learning.

Aman (2009) revealed that course overview and introductions, learning outcomes, student assessment, course materials, interactions, technology, and support were in the forefront as the standards of quality in the student perspective. In a three-year study of graduate and undergraduate students' level of satisfaction with online instruction at one university, it was found out that "convenience" was the most important factor of satisfaction whereas "lack of interaction" was the most cited reason for dissatisfaction (Cole et al., 2014).

In a study conducted by Yener and Taşçıoğlu (2018), it was pointed out that one of the most significant measures of online learning effectiveness was technical and functional quality. The data collected and analyzed indicated that the image of the higher education institution also had a positive effect on students' perceived service quality.

Service Quality

"Service" has several definitions in marketing literature. It is generally defined as "any intangible act or performance that one party offers to another that does not result in the ownership of anything" (Kotler, 2009). Utilization of service is observed in a distinctive range of sectors of business from retailing to education and this is the reason why it is not easy to define it without conceiving issues and debates based on the different elements of each sector. Applying service marketing literature in the scope of private high education institutions has provided a framework to help universities to develop an insight on marketing orientation and in what ways students value offered services. This approach aims to reveal the challenges and idiosyncrasies of education as a service and expands services marketing literature (Ng and Forbes, 2009).

There has been a critical debate around defining students as customers in higher education even when private universities are considered. The objection has rooted from the fact that if the student was considered as a customer, they would have to be presented what they wanted, which could cause a conflict when the institution and faculty focused on providing a quality education (Guibault, 2016). However, private higher education is a service organization (Mazzarol, 1998). Analyzing private education in the discipline of services marketing does not cause a conflict with pedagogical objectives; on the contrary, conceptualizing the student as a customer highlights the significance of developing "a two-way interactive, dialogue-based relationship between the institution and its student body" in an approach that views both the university and the student "subsequently inherently and inseparably involved in service production and value extraction" (Bowden, 2011). This approach is far from creating conflicts with pedagogical interests because the theoretical construct intends to define higher education provided by private institutions as a service and students as the leading actors of a part of customer co-production process.

Broadly, services are products which involve a high range of customer involvement and customer experience is an essential element of analyzing service quality. As a consequence, perceived quality is "an outcome of an evaluation process" (Gronroos, 1993). To achieve a perspective of a customer orientation to quality, it is necessary to understand customer behavior and to focus on predicting product or service performance (Shewfelt, 1999).

How to measure perceived quality requires a delicate examination of the field of operation and outcomes. It is also crucial to follow the recent research on the subject since there are new data to expand the studies and occasionally challenge primary findings. Once, Parasuraman, Zeithaml, and Berry (1988) claimed high perceived service quality led to an increase in customer satisfaction; however, subsequent studies demonstrated that customer satisfaction was an antecedent of service quality (Cronin and Taylor, 1992). The fundamental study developed a conceptual model of service quality which revealed how customer's perceptions of service quality were formed (Parasuraman, Zeithaml, & Berry, 1985).

Methodology

The primary objective of this research study was to identify the relations among the determinants of quality perception of higher education students towards obligatory online learning higher education courses in line with the current marketing literature. The sample of the study included 148 undergraduate higher education students: 81 female and 67 male participants. Convenience sampling was used in the selection of participants who were obliged to complete two semesters, spring and summer semesters, online due to the Covid-19 pandemic. The participants were graduate students who were in their first year.

An online validated structured questionnaire was shared to collect data. A modified version of the SERVQUAL model developed by Parasuraman et al. (1988) was utilized to achieve a model which indicated the determinants of quality in online learning. The questionnaire was divided into three parts on Likert scale with five items. The participants were required to rate their responses to several statements based on the Likert-type scale of 1 to 5, with 1 (completely disagree), 2 (disagree), 3(neutral), 4 (agree), and 5 (completely agree). The first part consisted of questions on the dimensions of higher education quality, which are dependent variables, whereas the second part of the questionnaire contained questions regarding students' view on the reputation of the institution and the third part on overall customer satisfaction.

Data Analysis and Results

All data were analyzed using the SPSS (version 17.0) statistical program. The initial Cronbach α (alpha) coefficient was 0.96.8 for the 21-item questionnaire responded to by 148 participants and it ensures the reliability and internal consistency of the scales which were used. The value is sufficient to ensure both internal consistency and reliability of the scales since reliabilities of 0.70 or higher are considered "acceptable" (Nunnally, 1978). SPSS Kolmogorov-Smirnov test for normality was used to determine whether the scores were likely to follow some distribution in the population and the result is $p < 0.05$. The results revealed that the data follow a normal distribution in the specific population.

The data were analyzed based on the parametric test results. When each response was analyzed the results achieved are given in Table 13.1.

As observed in Table 13.2, the majority of participants answered as "Neutral" for questions 6, 7, 9, 10, 11 and 14 and it is significant that this response is the most frequent for the service satisfaction regarding the online learning process. The responses to the items regarding the corporate reputation demonstrate that the most frequent answer is "Agree" except the 14th question. In the 14th question, it was asked whether the participants concluded that the institution was successful and the most frequent answer was "Neutral". It revealed that both the perceived quality and the customer satisfaction are high based on the analysis of the results of the relevant analysis.

Table 13.3 reveals the correlation coefficients as indicators of the strength of the relationship. To determine if the correlation between variables is significant, the p-value was compared. A p-value lower than 0.05 results in concluding that the H_0 hypothesis is rejected whereas H_1 hypothesis is accepted. The highest correlation is between quality perception and customer satisfaction.

Table 13.4 indicated the multiple regression analysis results for all dimensions. The model reveals that service satisfaction regarding online learning, corporate reputation, and perceived quality have a positive and significant effect on customer satisfaction. The regression analysis was significant at the 0.05 level and since $p = 0.000 < 0.05$; it has been revealed that all dimensions are positively related. According to the analysis, the highest correlation among dimensions is the ones with customer satisfaction. The relations between variables are positive and high. The values are between 0.562, the lowest, and 0.750, the highest, thus indicating the relations between the variables researched are positively related. When the data (F value) was analyzed, it was revealed that customer satisfaction was positively related to online learning efficiency, corporate reputation, and perceived value. The findings supported all hypotheses for this study.

Table 13.1 Reliability and Validity

Dimensions	*Cronbach's alpha*	*Range*
All items in questionnaire	0.968	1–21
Service satisfaction regarding online education	0.941	1–11
Corporate reputation	0.843	12–15
Perceived quality	0.858	16–18
Customer satisfaction	0.946	19–21

Table 13.2 Average Scores on Each Scale

Items	*SD*	*Mean*	*Evaluation*
S1	1.090	3.62	Agree
S2	1.090	3.76	Agree
S3	1.283	3.64	Agree
S4	1.178	3.72	Agree
S5	1.064	3.71	Agree
S6	1.262	3.32	*Neutral*
S7	1.113	3.36	*Neutral*
S8	1.193	3.73	Agree
S9	1.119	3.32	*Neutral*
S10	1.176	3.39	*Neutral*
S11	1.103	3.49	*Neutral*
S12	0.948	3.86	Agree
S13	1.029	3.72	Agree
S14	1.237	3.49	*Neutral*
S15	1.053	3.66	Agree
S16	0.957	3.76	Agree
S17	1.051	3.64	Agree
S18	1.142	3.75	Agree
S19	1.064	3.68	Agree
S20	1.125	3.80	Agree
S21	1.258	3.83	Agree

Table 13.3 Correlations between Factors

		Service quality regarding online education	*Corporate reputation*	*Perceived quality*	*Customer satisfaction*
Service satisfaction regarding online learning	Pearson Correlation	1			
	Sig. (2-tailed)				
	N	148			
Corporate reputation	Pearson Correlation	.826**	1		
	Sig. (2-tailed)	.000			
	N	148	148		
Perceived value	Pearson Correlation	.750**	.787**	1	
	Sig. (2-tailed)	,000	.000		
	N	148	148	148	
Satisfaction	Pearson Correlation	.825**	.847**	**.861****	1
	Sig. (2-tailed)	.000	.000	.000	
	N	148	148	148	148

Table 13.4 Multiple Regression of Three Predictors of Student Satisfaction

MODEL	F	R^2 (%)	β	t	p
Online learning – corporate reputation	312,508	68.2	826	17,678	.000
Online learning – perceived quality	187,546	75.0	562	13,695	.000
Online learning – satisfaction	311,699	68.1	825	17,655	.000
Corporate reputation – perceived quality	237,585	61.9	787	15,414	.000
Corporate reputation – perceived quality	370,201	71.7	847	19,241	**.000**
Perceived value – satisfaction	419,652	74.2	**861**	20,485	.000

Limitations

The limitations of the research can be identified to guide future studies in this subject. First of all, given the small sample size of the research, it is recommended to work on larger groups for further studies to validate and generalize the results among a diverse range of students. Secondly, new factors and variables can be included to further investigate the potential relationships among other constructs. Other variables, such as customer loyalty and trust, may also be added to expand the questionnaires and apply different measurement scales to present additional evidence. Thirdly, the study was conducted under Covid-19 conditions. To generalize the results and clarify the issue, future studies should be held far from the difficult conditions of a pandemic.

Managerial Implications

The study offers managerial implications for improving the quality of online learning in higher education. The main results, subject to the limitations of the study, can provide an insight into the significant relations among service satisfaction, corporate reputation and overall customer satisfaction regarding online learning in the higher education context. The proposed framework can be used to prioritize the components of quality and enhance the quality improvement efforts as a part of marketing. The results can be reassessed to interpret customer behavior within institution-specific or culture-specific conditions. Given the fact that the quality determinants in online learning have been mostly researched in education studies perspective so far, it is essential to apply the marketing approach for further consideration. It is also important to identify the role of perceived quality so that higher education institutions can apply a substantial quality policy by analyzing what makes a higher education enterprise a service organization. Considering the rapid changes in education technologies and market demands, relevant aspects of the marketing approach should be applied in higher education to find solutions to the problems of stakeholders in a way to obtain a competitive advantage. Marketing approach of higher educational services should include a careful review of customer behavior and perceptions to readjust the constantly changing conditions. It is vital to create a strong corporate reputation as a means of sustainability in a competitive market.

Conclusion

This study is one of the first steps to question the wide topic regarding the determinants of quality perceptions of higher education students in online learning. The findings did not contradict the current marketing literature (Sivadas, and Baker-Prewitt, 2000; Bou-Llusar et al., 2001; Olorunniwo, et al., 2006; Calvo-Porral, et al., 2013). The evidence indicated service satisfaction regarding online learning and corporate reputation of the higher education has a significant effect on the quality perception reveal that it is required to selectively examine higher education institutions as enterprises since high-quality perception could not be an outcome of solely service satisfaction. It has been pointed out that service satisfaction regarding the online learning process plays an important role in the overall customer satisfaction of those who are enrolled in online higher classes. However, it is worth further consideration that in the study, service satisfaction was less determined by the quality of the instructors or course materials. It was revealed that the participants were likely to evaluate the online learning process as a whole. The roles of mediator and predictor were not researched within the scope of this study; however, it is implied that corporate value, combined with service quality, could completely mediate the effect of perceptions on customer satisfaction. The determinants of quality perception regarding online learning should not be limited to the education stakeholders and technical specifications, or design. As the study refers, quality perception is a consequence of a holistic approach rather than a mere outcome of a process. It is essential to analyze the determinants of quality perception regarding online learning in integration with previously revealed impacts and correlations within the frame of corporate reputation, perceived value, and overall satisfaction. The significance of this study lies in supporting online learning and quality perception contextualization based on its impact on customer satisfaction beyond education sciences. Nonetheless, the analysis in this chapter provides an empirical framework to guide further studies of online learning in the means of perceived quality within marketing literature.

References

Abidin, M. (2015). Higher education quality: Perception differences among internal and external stakeholders. *International Education Studies*, 8(12), 185–192.

Abimbola, A. E., Oluwole, B. A., & Kolawole, A. G. (2020). Effect of integrated marketing communications on customer satisfaction of selected private universities in South–West Nigeria. *International Journal of Marketing Studies*, 12(2), 78–84.

Abouchedid, K., & Nasser, R. (2002). Assuring quality service in higher education: Registration and advising attitudes in a private university in Lebanon. *Quality Assurance in Education*, 10 (4), 198–207.

Akareem, H. S., & Hossain, S. S. (2016). Determinants of education quality: What makes students' perception different? *Open Review of Educational Research*, 3(1), 52–67.

Aman, R. R. (2009). Improving student satisfaction and retention with online instruction through systematic faculty peer review of courses. Dissertation. Oregon State University.

Bou-Llusar, J. C., Camisón-Zornoza, C., & Escrig-Tena, A. B. (2001). Measuring the relationship between firm perceived quality and customer satisfaction and its influence on purchase intentions. *Total quality management*, 12(6), 719–734.

Bowden, J. L. H. (2011). Engaging the student as a customer: A relationship marketing approach. *Marketing Education Review*, 21(3), 211–228.

Calvo-Porral, C., Lévy-Mangin, J. P., & Novo-Corti, I. (2013). Perceived quality in higher education: An empirical study. *Marketing Intelligence & Planning*, 31(6), 601–619.

Cole, M. T., Shelley, D. J., & Swartz, L. B. (2014). Online instruction, e-learning, and student satisfaction: A three year study. *The International Review of Research in Open and Distributed Learning*, 15(6), 112–131.

Cronin Jr, J. J., & Taylor, S. A. (1992). Measuring service quality: A reexamination and extension. *Journal of Marketing*, 56(3), 55–68.

Elango, R., Gudep, V. K., & Selvam, M. (2008). Quality of e-learning: An analysis based on e-learners' perception of e-learning. *Electronic Journal of E-learning*, 6(1), 31–43.

Garvin, David A. (1984). What does "product quality" really mean? *Sloan Management Review*, (Fall 1984), 25–43.

Gronroos, C. (1993). A service quality model and its marketing implications. *European Journal of Marketing*, 18 (4), 36–44.

Guilbault, M. (2016). Students as customers in higher education: Reframing the debate. *Journal of Marketing for Higher Education*, 26(2), 132–142.

Kotler, P. (2009). *Marketing Management*. London, UK: Pearson.

Mailizar Almanthari, A., Maulina, S., & Bruce, S. (2020). Secondary school mathematics teachers' views on e-learning implementation barriers during the Covid-19 pandemic: The case of Indonesia. *Eurasia Journal of Mathematics, Science and Technology, Education*, 16(7), em1860.

Mang'unyi, E. E., & Govender, K. K. (2014). Perceived service quality (sq) and customer satisfaction (cs): students' perceptions of Kenyan Private Universities. *Mediterranean Journal of Social Sciences*, 5(23), 2739–2739.

Mazzarol, T. (1998). Critical success factors for international education marketing. *International Journal of Educational Management*, 12(4), 163–175.

Morgan, Leonard A. (1985). *The Importance of Quality, in Perceived Quality*, Jacob Jacoby and Jerry C. Olson, eds. Lexington, US: Lexington Books.

Naidu, P., & Derani, N. E. S. (2016). A comparative study on quality of education received by students of private universities versus public universities. *Procedia Economics and Finance*, 35(2016), 659–666.

Nardalı, S., & Tanyeri, M. (2011). Yükseköğretimde markalaşma. *Dokuz Eylül Üniversitesi Işletme Fakültesi Dergisi*, 12(2), 309–319.

Ng, I. C., & Forbes, J. (2009). Education as service: The understanding of university experience through the service logic. *Journal of Marketing for Higher Education*, 19(1), 38–64.

Nunnally, J. C. (1978). *Psychometric Theory*. New York, US: McGraw-Hill Book Company.

Oliver, R. L. (1993). A conceptual model of service quality and service satisfaction. *Advances in Services Marketing and Management*, 2, 65–86.

Olorunniwo, F., Hsu, M. K., & Udo, G. J. (2006). Service quality, customer satisfaction, and behavioral intentions in the service factory. *Journal of services marketing*, 20 (1), 59–72.

Parasuraman, A., Zeithaml, V., & Berry, L. (1988). A multiple item scale for measuring consumer perceptions of service quality. *Journal of Retailing*, 64(1), 12–37.

Parasuraman, A., Zeithaml, V. A., & Berry, L. L. (1985). A conceptual model of service quality and its implications for future research. *Journal of Marketing*, 49(4), 41–50.

Robinson, C. C., & Hullinger, H. (2008). New benchmarks in higher education: Student engagement in online learning. *Journal of Education for Business*, 84 (2), 101–109.

Rockwell, S. K., Schauer, J., Fritz, S., & Marx, D. B. (1999). Incentives and obstacles influencing higher education faculty and administrators to teach via distance. *Faculty Publications: Agricultural Leadership, Education & Communication Department*, 2 (3), 43–53.

Shekarchizadeh, A., Rasli, A., & Hon-Tat, H. (2011). SERVQUAL in Malaysian universities: Perspectives of international students. *Business Process Management Journal*, 17 (1), 67–81.

Shepherd, I. D. H. (2005). From cattle and coke to Charlie: Meeting the challenge of self-marketing and personal branding. *Journal of Marketing Management*, 21, 589–606.

Shewfelt, R. L. (1999). What is quality? *Postharvest Biology and Technology*, 15(3), 197–200.

Simpson, J. M. (2012). Student perceptions of quality and satisfaction in online learning. Dissertation, University of Alabama.

Sivadas, E., & Baker-Prewitt, J. L. (2000). An examination of the relationship between service quality, customer satisfaction, and store loyalty. *International Journal of Retail & Distribution Management*, 28(2), 73–82.

Steenkamp, J. B. E. (1990). Conceptual model of the quality perception process. *Journal of Business Research*, 21(4), 309–333.

Yener, D., & Taşçıoğlu, M. (2018). Gender role on service quality perception about online education. *The Online Journal of Quality in Higher Education*, 5(3), 26–33.

14 Examining the Role of Prices in Readership Trends of Newspaper Industry

Vikas Singla and Rajiv Sood

Introduction

Newspaper is one of the credible sources that work to inform the reader about current events happening all around – locally and globally. All around the world, due to the change in the preferences of today's reader from print to digital the newspaper industry is undergoing a transition from the traditional print approach of disseminating news to digital technology. The digital world has developed new ways to communicate, so there is a change in the way people engage with and consume media content (Thornton 2016). With the penetration of low-cost mobile devices enabled with 4G high-speed internet, a user can access news content anytime, anywhere and quickly. Most importantly, digital media provides content in abridged format free of cost fulfilling the need of young consumer to stay abreast of happenings rather than consuming elaborate information. Thus in lieu of the alternate sources of free news availability, the traditional business models are facing tremendous pressure to generate revenue (Casero-Ripollés & Izquierdo-Castillo 2013).

Furthermore, due to digitization of the newspaper, the industry is losing revenues from both sources of subscription due to lack of circulation and advertisement as advertisers shift their ads to the online medium. In addition, over the years the increased cost of print newspaper production and its distribution has forced the newspapers to increase the cover price (Lundén 2009). Print media market being price sensitive, these increased prices negatively influence newspapers' circulation. Such a scenario makes the sustainability of newspaper challenging.

Price, Circulation and Revenue Relationship

To signify the relationship between price and circulation of print newspaper, it is important to understand the interplay of digitization, circulation, growth and revenues. This has been revealed by extracting and understanding the study of the data from PwC's (PricewaterhouseCoopers) Entertainment & Media Outlook report, 2015–2020. The study illustrates that with an increase in digitization, the growth rate has declined. This was

DOI: 10.4324/9781003354703-17

more exemplified in the case of developed economies like the US, UK, Australia and Canada with a cut-throat competitive newspaper industry. On the other hand, developing economies where the rate of digitization is slow showed that projected revenues are on the positive side. Data persuades to infer that a higher degree of digitization results in incurring negative influence on overall growth. This further emphasizes that consumer intends to consume news in cheap, easily accessible and fast manner which is provided by digital mode. However, the adoption of digitization has a detrimental effect on the circulation of print newspaper, thus reducing total revenues. The major reason for such assertion emanates from freely available online content.

It would be interesting to note the contribution of two sources of revenue, namely, advertisements and circulation, in order to understand the reduction in total revenues due to reasons such as digitization and price of content. This was illustrated by PwC's data of global revenues from newspaper circulation and advertising during the period 2012–2020 (Figure 14.1). It shows that the revenue of print newspaper has shown a drastic reduction from advertisements, whereas it has remained almost consistent from circulation. This fall in ad earnings could be attributed primarily to increased digitization that discourages advertisers to place ads in print editions of newspaper. However, the enhanced level of adoption of online medium does not have a significant impact on circulation revenues. This consistency of revenues from circulation could be attributed to willingness to pay despite higher prices of print newspaper.

Thus, revenues of advertisements and circulation with regard to both print and online editions, price trend of print paper and willingness to pay are some of the attributes that should be examined in understanding the impact on circulation.

Indian Trends

Due to exponential growth of broadband and digital media in India, the examination of above-mentioned scenario of the interaction between various aspects influencing print newspaper circulation becomes noteworthy. According the Ficci-EY Media and Entertainment Industry report, digital media grew by 31% in 2019 as compared to the year 2018. The report also recorded that internet penetration grew by 20% in the year 2019. By the same year, broadband subscription reached 661 million in number. This growth potentially makes the newspaper industry essentially shift to or provide alternate to print medium by adopting the digital platform. The shift has been justified by the report indicating an increase in total revenues from sources of advertising and subscription with regard to the online medium. The report explicitly showed the growth of revenues from both advertising and subscription for digital news that is way above the growth in revenues for print newspaper. It also emphasized that the increase in advertising revenue for digital news is very high as compared to the increase in

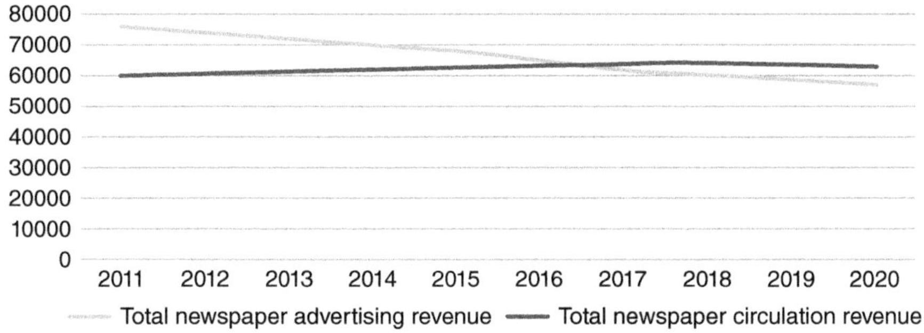

Figure 14.1 Total newspaper circulation and advertising revenue (US$mn), 2011–2020.

Source: Global entertainment and media outlook 2016-2020, PWC, Ovum.

corresponding revenue with regard to print newspaper. For instance, data showed 24.02% increase in revenues from advertisement in year 2019 from 2018. Correspondingly, for print newspaper there was a decline of 5.02% in the same period. This comparison with revenues of print newspaper clearly revealed increasing adoption of digital over print.

In addition, intriguingly report showed that advertising revenue of print newspaper in 2019 has declined from previous year whereas that of digital news has grown positively. However, in the same time period, revenues from subscription have increased. In addition, in year 2022 predominant growth of estimated 6% in total revenue of print newspaper comes from subscription. This clearly provides an inference that though there is heavy adoption of digital medium for news consumption resulting in advertisers to shift their loyalties from print to digital, print newspaper are increasing their revenues from subscription route.

Thus, the report amply demonstrated the impact on revenues due to adoption of online medium; however, it also shows consistent increase in circulation revenue of print newspaper, implying that either the number of people buying and reading print medium has increased or the increase in revenues is accrued from an increase in price per paper even though consumer base has not shown an increasing trend.

To investigate these two causes this study intended to explore the relationship between circulation, i.e. the number of print newspaper sold, and its price over a period. To understand this relationship better, respective data of both English and Hindi national dailies was examined. These two language dailies were selected as they were having highest circulation.

The article followed a structure of, firstly, reviewing past studies in order to provide a background of constructs of digitization, revenues, price and circulation in newspaper industry; secondly, methodology to extract relevant information from secondary data would be discussed; and lastly a conclusion would be presented.

Review of Literature

In today's digital world, where social media environment is highly prevalent, people across the world access free news content online via mobile devices especially smart phones, tablets, laptop, etc. (Burggraaff & Trilling 2020). Millions of users navigate in user-friendly ways through services like search, social networking, messaging, video sharing and many more. The increased use of social media and online websites has changed the behavior of individuals finding the current news in larger domain. Therefore, in the present scenario, the distribution of news is comparatively easier and the trend of digital advertising has increased because companies can reach to a much larger audience by spending comparatively lesser (Ardyan & Aryanto 2020). Hence, advertisers shift their ad offerings on online news media.

No doubt, print newspaper would always remain very important producers of news, but as digital news media increases its reach, the importance of print newspaper is becoming less demanding among the young generation. To be able to remain in the race of generating profits, print newspaper companies are also under growing pressure to develop new digital business model. Sridhar and Sriram (2015) examined whether advertisers perceived the two media options as substitutes or complements. If advertisers perceived these two media options as complements, the online newspaper ad growth contributed on positive side and may not have much impact on print ad revenue. However, if the advertisers perceived these options as substitutes, then because of comparatively lower ad rates, advertisers would shift to alternative platforms to online, provoking further decline in print.

The penetration of internet at low cost and the availability of bandwidth at a subsidized price accounted for 20% loss of paid subscribers in the US print newspaper industry (Pattabhiramaiah et al. 2018). Data of top-50 US print newspaper showed that despite the decrease in circulation, the price of newspaper has increased. Examining the impact of such consistent increase in price on advertisers and readers led to segregating market into customers with high willingness-to-pay (WTP) and those with low WTP. In case of significant increase in price, customers with low WTP are more inclined to shift to online alternative for news consumption. The focus on high WTP was justified as a strategic decision as they would drive generation of optimal profit (O'Brien et al. 2020). This focus on smaller segment of market also made newspapers reduce incentive to subsidize readers at the expense of advertisers (Chyi & Ng 2020). The decline in WTP among readers in the presence of heterogeneous preferences explains only the small fractions of the increase in subscription prices, but the decline in the ability of the newspaper to subsidize readers by extracting surplus from advertisers explains most of (over 90%) the increase in subscription prices (Rahman 2019).

Amadu et al. (2018) stated that despite the increase in price, nearly two-third of the readers remain loyal to the print edition, proving that the print form is still the cash cow for newspaper industries. Despite the sharp declining trends found in print newspaper circulation and readership among newsreaders, the study also concluded that the traditional print newspaper media is still being trusted and maintains the image of reliable and credible source of news. Van der Burg and Van den Bulck (2017) in the same vein observed that newspaper publishers retain their profits despite the falling demand of print newspaper as loss in readership is reimbursed by increasing the price of the newspaper. Similarly, emphasizing on relation between price and circulation, Chyi and Tenenboim (2019) expressed that even during the financial crisis of 2008, the prices of both daily and weekend editions of major newspaper increased. They found that despite the increase in price, nearly two-third of the readers remained loyal to the print edition, proving the print form is still the major source of income for newspaper industries.

Therefore, studies highlight relationship between price and circulation in the wake of digitization. This is further examined in this study by studying three major English and Hindi language dailies.

Methodology

To examine the role of price in influencing circulation, this study has analyzed circulation and price data of three top English and Hindi national newspapers. As indicated in the literature, studies have revealed a conundrum, i.e. price increase of print medium can result in as expected decrease in circulation; however, despite this, circulation has increased. To understand this issue study has observed both English and Hindi language dailies as their circulation and readership was significantly higher than other language newspapers. In addition, the concentration of readership pertaining to English papers is more urban- centric; therefore, focusing only on English dailies would be subject to bias. Pitting them against the more widespread readership of Hindi papers would provide a more accurate and wholesome role of price. Lastly, only top three were selected because data extracted from certified authority of Audit Bureau of Circulations showed a significant gap in circulation indicating their low readership.

The three English dailies selected were *Times of India* (TOI), *The Hindu* and *Hindustan Times* (HT), whereas the three Hindi national dailies were *Dainik Bhaskar* (DB), *Dainik Jagran* (DJ) and *Amar Ujala* (AU). Data pertaining to six monthly circulations and prices was collected over past ten years, i.e. from 2010 to 2019 from website http://www.auditbureau.org.

The purpose of the study was to examine by bifurcating it into two specific aims: firstly, to analyze the trend in circulation of selected newspapers. This was evaluated simply by applying trend analysis and representing it through line charts. It would indicate that over a period of time how readership or adoption of print newspaper has fared. The second aim was to correspond this trend with price data over the same time period. This was analyzed by applying Pearson correlation. A positive relation would entail that despite increase in price customers are still willing to pay for print newspaper. However, a negative relation would entail that higher price has influenced circulation negatively. It is imperative to specify that as the purpose was only to find association between two variables and not the degree of impact of more than one variable on circulation, regression analysis was not considered appropriate.

Results

Aim 1: Trend Analysis

The line graph in Figure 14.2 clearly shows a decrease in circulation of all three English newspapers over the past ten years. Undoubtedly, *Times of India* has maintained its leadership position in terms of circulation, but its circulation has still been decreasing.

One-way ANOVA results indicate a significant association ($F = 11.154$; $p = 0.002 < 0.05$) between the type of newspaper and the circulation, implying that readers' pattern of consumption of news varies with the type of newspaper. The inference from mean values indicate that TOI (3.173 million) circulation is highest as compared to that of *The Hindu* (1.426 million) and HT (1.168 million). More importantly, data represented in Figure 14.2 shows that a fall in circulation of TOI is more significant than other two dailies.

A similar analysis for the selected Hindi national newspapers again showed a significant association ($F = 15.631$; $p = 0.004 < 0.05$) between the circulation and the type of newspaper, implying a variation in readership with regard to the type of newspaper. Mean values indicate DJ (3.246 million) being the highest circulated paper as compared to DB (3.231 million) and AU (2.058 million). These values also infer significant difference of AU with the other two papers, concluding that AU has noteworthy less circulation than DJ and DB. However, the line graph in Figure 14.2 shows that over the last ten years circulation of all three Hindi newspapers has increased.

These findings are interesting, as Hindi and English newspapers have shown opposite trends over the same time period. Such opposite conclusions make investigating causes for such trends imperative. As discussed in addition to digitization, increase in production and distribution costs, shift in advertisements price has an important role to play. This study has focused on examining only the role of price, thus limiting its scope in pursuit of exploring the cause of contradictory trends.

Aim 2: Relationship between Price and Circulation

Circulation data over a ten- year period and price per paper of TOI had a negative though significant correlation ($r = -0.581$; $p = 0.031 < 0.05$), implying that the decrease in circulation of TOI, as shown in Figure14.2, could be attributed to price, though it cannot be the only singular factor. A similar result of negative and significant ($r = -0.423$; $p = 0.041 < 0.05$) correlation was calculated for HT, indicating the importance of price

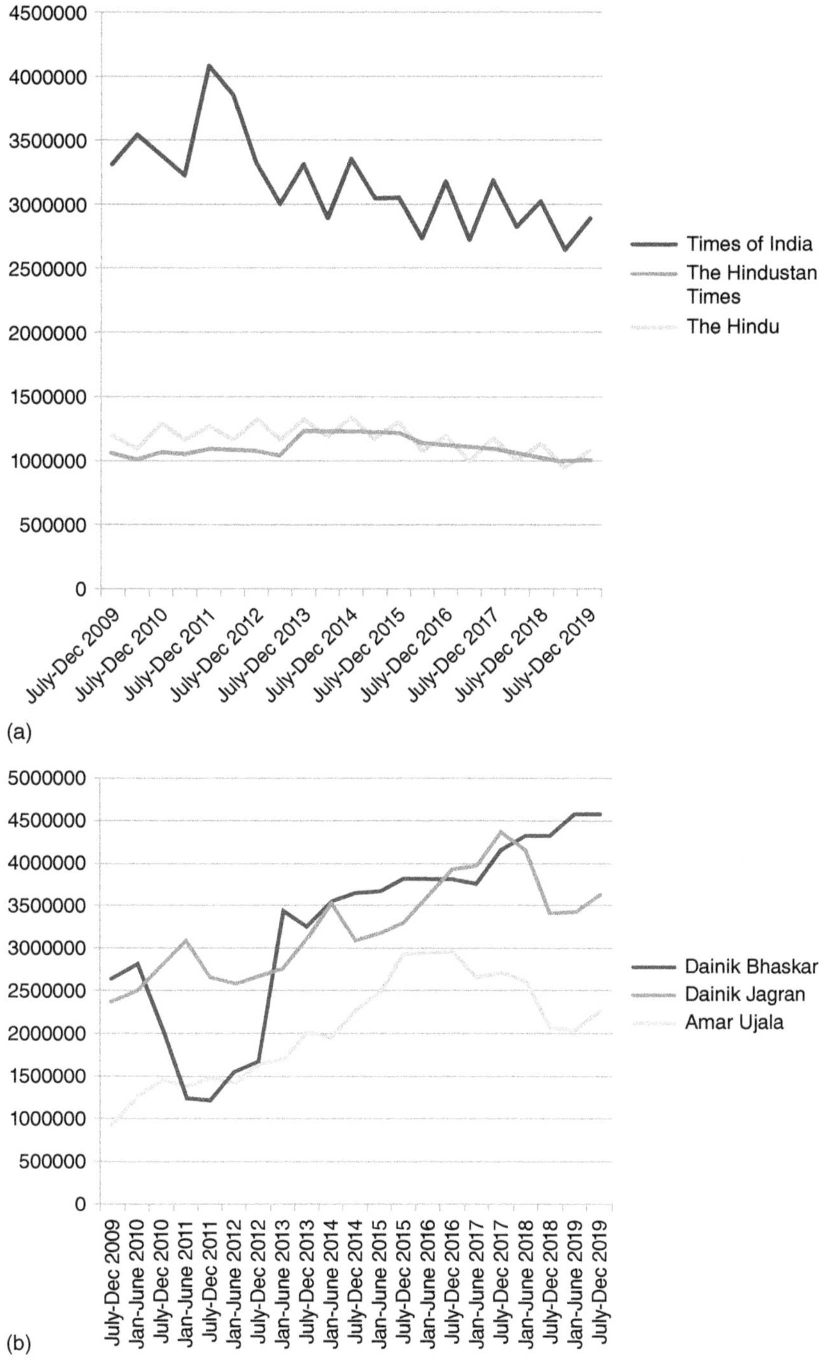

Figure 14.2 (a) Trend of circulation of English newspapers (b) Trend of weekday circulation of Hindi newspapers.

Source: Audit Bureau of Circulation (http://www.auditbureau.org).

augmentation influencing reduction in circulation. Lastly, correlation results, though negative, were insignificant ($r = -0.138$; $p = 0.114 > 0.05$) for *The Hindu*. Even Figure14.2 showed circulation variation to be much more consistent for *The Hindu* as compared to TOI and HT.

Interestingly, the results with regard to Hindi dailies showed opposite results as compared to the English newspapers. For all three papers, DB, DJ and AU, high and positive correlation coefficients were found. The results showed coefficients to be 0.781 ($p = 0.003 < 0.05$), 0.471 ($p = 0.027 < 0.05$) and 0.645 ($p = 0.012 < 0.05$), respectively. Thus, in case of Hindi dailies circulation increases with increase in price, though it cannot be the sole factor. However, it suffices to emphasize that price has significant association with circulation.

Conclusion

This study intended to examine the trends in print edition of top three English and Hindi national dailies. The study extracts its importance from the fact that with firm establishment of online medium of news consumption, it is being hypothesized that print medium should show decreasing circulation. Results of the study throw an interesting picture. English dailies showed a decreasing trend. However, Hindi dailies showed an opposite trend. In the first step of our project in this study, we examined the reason for such a trend by correlating the circulation data with the price of newspapers. Again, the results were quite contradictory. A decrease in circulation of English papers was found to be negatively correlated with price, whereas an increase in circulation of Hindi papers was found to be positively correlated with price. This indicates that circulation of English papers decreases due to increase in price; however, that of Hindi papers increases due to a similar increase. Results are interesting, as it has been assumed that vernacular papers are concentrated in rural segment that are more price sensitive than urban readers. However, the study shows conflicting results. This could be attributed to the level of digitization that is prevalent in urban geographies, making urban readers more price sensitive than rural consumers who rely only on print medium. Further studies would attempt to understand this phenomenon by examining other reasons such as costing, advertisement, online editions and other factors by developing an empirical model.

References

Amadu, M. F., Mohammed, A. M., Alhassan, A., & Mohammed, F. (2018). Assessment of newspaper circulation and readership in Northern Ghana. *UDS International Journal of Development*, 5(2), 108–120.

Ardyan, E., & Aryanto, V. D. W. (2020). The Importance of Electronics News Brand Trust: The Case of Online Newspapers in Indonesia. In Elia Ardyan & Vincent Didiek Wiet Aryanto (Eds.), *Global Branding: Breakthroughs in Research and Practice* (pp. 537–556). IGI Global.

Burggraaff, C., & Trilling, D. (2020). Through a different gate: An automated content analysis of how online news and print news differ. *Journalism*, 21(1), 112–129.

Casero-Ripollés, A., & Izquierdo-Castillo, J. (2013). Between decline and a new online business model: The case of the Spanish newspaper industry. *Journal of Media Business Studies*,10(1), 63–78.

Chyi, H. I., & Ng, Y. M. M. (2020). Still unwilling to pay: An empirical analysis of 50 US Newspapers' digital subscription results. *Digital Journalism*, *8*(4), 526–547.

Chyi & Tenenboim (2019). Charging More and Wondering Why Readership Declined? *A Longitudinal Study of U.S. Newspapers' Price Hikes, 2008–2016*. Routledge Taylor & Francis Group.

Lundén, K. (2009). The death of print? The challenges and opportunities facing the print media on the web. *Reuters Institute for the Study of Journalism. University of Oxford, Oxford.*

O'Brien, D., Wellbrock, C. M., & Kleer, N. (2020). Content for free? Drivers of past payment, paying intent and willingness to pay for digital journalism–A systematic literature review. *Digital Journalism*, 8, 1–30.

Pattabhiramaiah, A., Sriram, S., & Sridhar, S. (2018). Rising prices under declining preferences: The case of the US print newspaper industry. *Marketing Science*, 37(1), 97–122.

Rahman, M. T. (2019). Perception on advertising media: The case of newspaper advertising. *Perception*, 5(4), 22–25.

Sridhar, S., & Sriram, S. (2015). Is online newspaper advertising cannibalizing print advertising? *Quantitative Marketing and Economics*, 13(4), 283–318.

Thornton, L. J. (2016). The road to "reader-friendly": US newspapers and readership in the late twentieth century. *Cogent Social Sciences*, 2(1), 1189055.

van der Burg, M., & Van den Bulck, H. (2017). Why are traditional newspaper publishers still surviving in the digital era? The impact of long-term trends on the Flemish newspaper industry's financing, 1990–2014. *Journal of Media Business Studies*, *14*(2), 82–115.

Index

Pages in *Italics* refer figures and **bold** refer tables.

For Product Safety Concerns and Information please contact our EU
representative GPSR@taylorandfrancis.com
Taylor & Francis Verlag GmbH, Kaufingerstraße 24, 80331 München, Germany

www.ingramcontent.com/pod-product-compliance
Ingram Content Group UK Ltd.
Pitfield, Milton Keynes, MK11 3LW, UK
UKHW021307260926
475702UK00048B/842
9781032309026